IMAGES
of America

OTTAWA

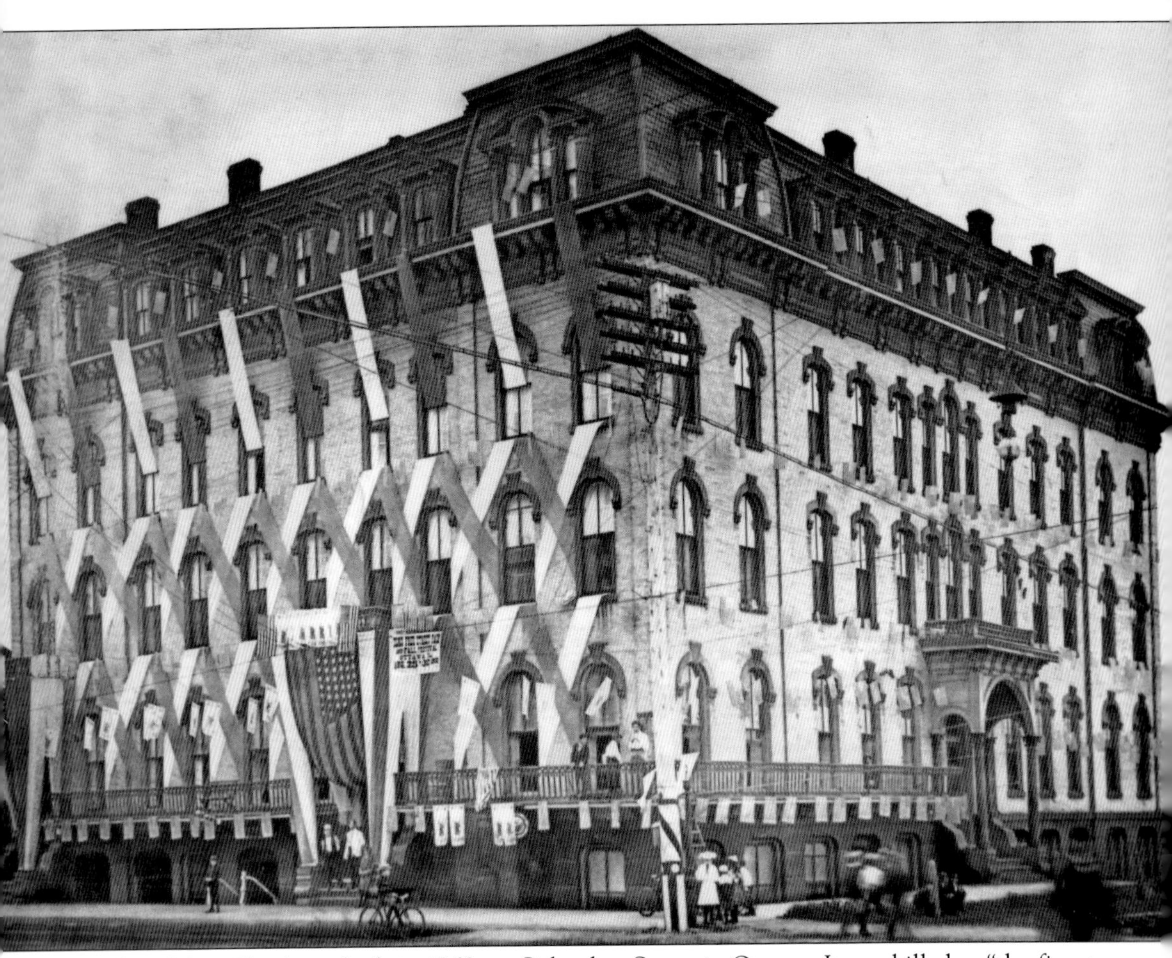

The Clifton Hotel was built in 1868 on Columbus Street in Ottawa. It was billed as "the finest hotel between Chicago and St. Louis." (Jim Ridings.)

On the Cover: Pictured is the Yellow Cab Company office on Jefferson Street. (Jim Ridings.)

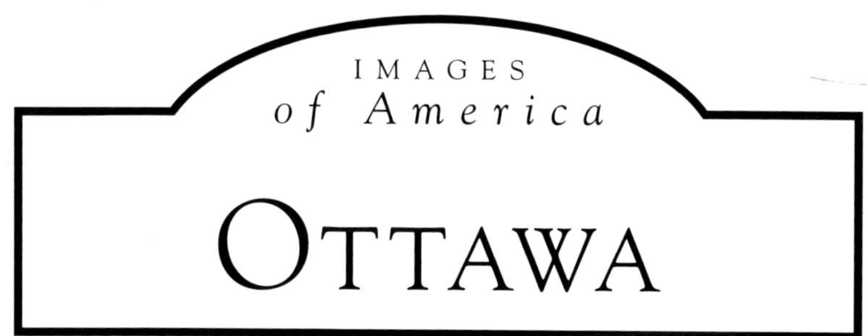

Jim Ridings

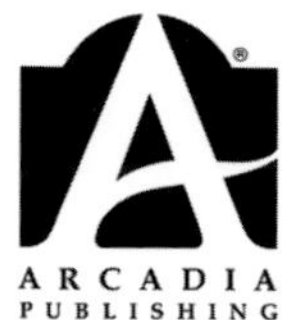

ISBN 978-0-7385-8857-5

Published by Arcadia Publishing
Charleston, South Carolina

Printed in the United States of America

Library of Congress Control Number: 2011938561

For all general information, please contact Arcadia Publishing:
Telephone 843-853-2070
Fax 843-853-0044
E-mail sales@arcadiapublishing.com
For customer service and orders:
Toll-Free 1-888-313-2665

Visit us on the Internet at www.arcadiapublishing.com

To my wife, Janet, and my daughters, Stephanie and Laura.

CONTENTS

ACKNOWLEDGMENTS

Ottawa is fortunate to have local historians Margaret Dorothy Clemens, Tom Jobst, Jenan Jobst, Bob Jordan, Walter Alsene, Mollie Perrot, Dave Mumper, Charles Stanley, Steve Stout, the LaSalle County Historical Society, the LaSalle County Genealogy Guild, the Ottawa Scouting Museum, and many others who help preserve local history.

Images are from the author's collection of photographs and books and from the collection of Dorothy Clemens of Ottawa, who has spent her 86 years collecting and preserving the history of Ottawa. Her efforts have resulted in a collection that rivals the local museums and will be a benefit to the citizens of Ottawa for generations to come.

Books cited include *Holland's Directory to Residences and Business Houses for Ottawa, Illinois* (1884); *Art Work: Ottawa and Vicinity* (1893); *Nattinger's Souvenir of Ottawa, Illinois, in Nineteen Hundred, Complete Review* (1900); *Life and Letters of General W.H.L. Wallace, by Isabel Wallace* (1909, reprinted 2000); *Ottawa Old & New* (1914); *Ottawa Sesquicentennial 1837–1987* (1987); *Old Ottawa Scenes*, by Bob Jordan and Jim Ridings (2006); *Greetings From Ottawa, A Picture Postcard View of Old Ottawa*, by Jim Ridings (2006). Newspaper files were used from the *Ottawa Daily Republican Times* and the *Daily Times.*

Jim Ridings was a reporter at the *Daily Times* in Ottawa and the *Beacon-News* in Aurora and won awards for investigative reporting at both newspapers. He was presented with a Studs Terkel Humanities Service Award from the Illinois Humanities Council in 2006. He is the author of 20 books on Illinois history. Three of his books won awards from the Illinois State Historical Society.

Books by Ridings with an Ottawa interest include *Greetings From Ottawa: A Picture Postcard View of Old Ottawa* (2006); *Old Ottawa Scenes* (2006); *Len Small: Governors and Gangsters* (2009); *Chicago To Springfield: Crime and Politics in the 1920s* (2010), which was published by Arcadia; and *Greetings From Starved Rock: A Picture Postcard View of Starved Rock State Park, Including Scenes From Matthiessen State Park* (2011).

Unless otherwise noted, the images in this volume appear courtesy of Dorothy Clemens (DC) or Jim Ridings (JR).

INTRODUCTION

Every town has a history of how it was founded and how it developed. Every town also has a history that is more interesting than the basic story.

Ottawa has always been a factory town. One of the more interesting industries was the Davis-Harrison Company, billed as "the world's largest cucumber greenhouse." It had 6,000 plants and five swarms of bees inside to spread pollen. Also famous was the Peltier glass factory, which produced glass "marbles" for a very popular game that few boys know about today. Horse racing once was an important industry in Ottawa, and who would think that Ottawa would have a half-dozen cigar manufacturers?

The Carson, Pirie, Scott & Company department store chain got its start in Ottawa, with the J.E. Scott store at 708–710 LaSalle Street, beginning in 1868.

Ottawa had a tuberculosis sanitarium, where the "cure" was to have patients sleep outside in tents, even through the winter snows!

Prohibition still is enforced in Ottawa—on the south side. Many years ago, voters approved banning the sale of alcohol south of the river in the city of Ottawa. It still is the law.

Ottawa was the site of two executions. The first was on June 28, 1853, when George Gates was hanged for murder. The second was on May 14, 1891, when Charles Ford was hanged outside the jail on Columbus Street, north of the Methodist Church, for murdering a man in Allen Park.

Ottawa once had a college. Pleasant View Luther College opened in 1896 on Ottawa's south side. It closed in 1936, during the Great Depression. The facility reopened in 1937 as Pleasant View Luther Home.

W.D. Boyce, founder of the Boy Scouts of America, lived in Ottawa. The Illinois Supreme Court was located in Ottawa from 1860 until 1897. Since then, the courthouse on Columbus Street has been the appellate court. The Illinois State Fair was held in Ottawa in 1872, 1875, and 1876.

Today, the Illinois & Michigan Canal is not much more than a walking path in some places, but it was a massive engineering project in the 1830s and 1840s. It had a major impact on Ottawa's development, and the stone aqueduct that carried the canal over the Fox River was a marvel of architectural engineering.

This book is not a comprehensive history of Ottawa, but we are sure you will like the pictures and the accompanying information.

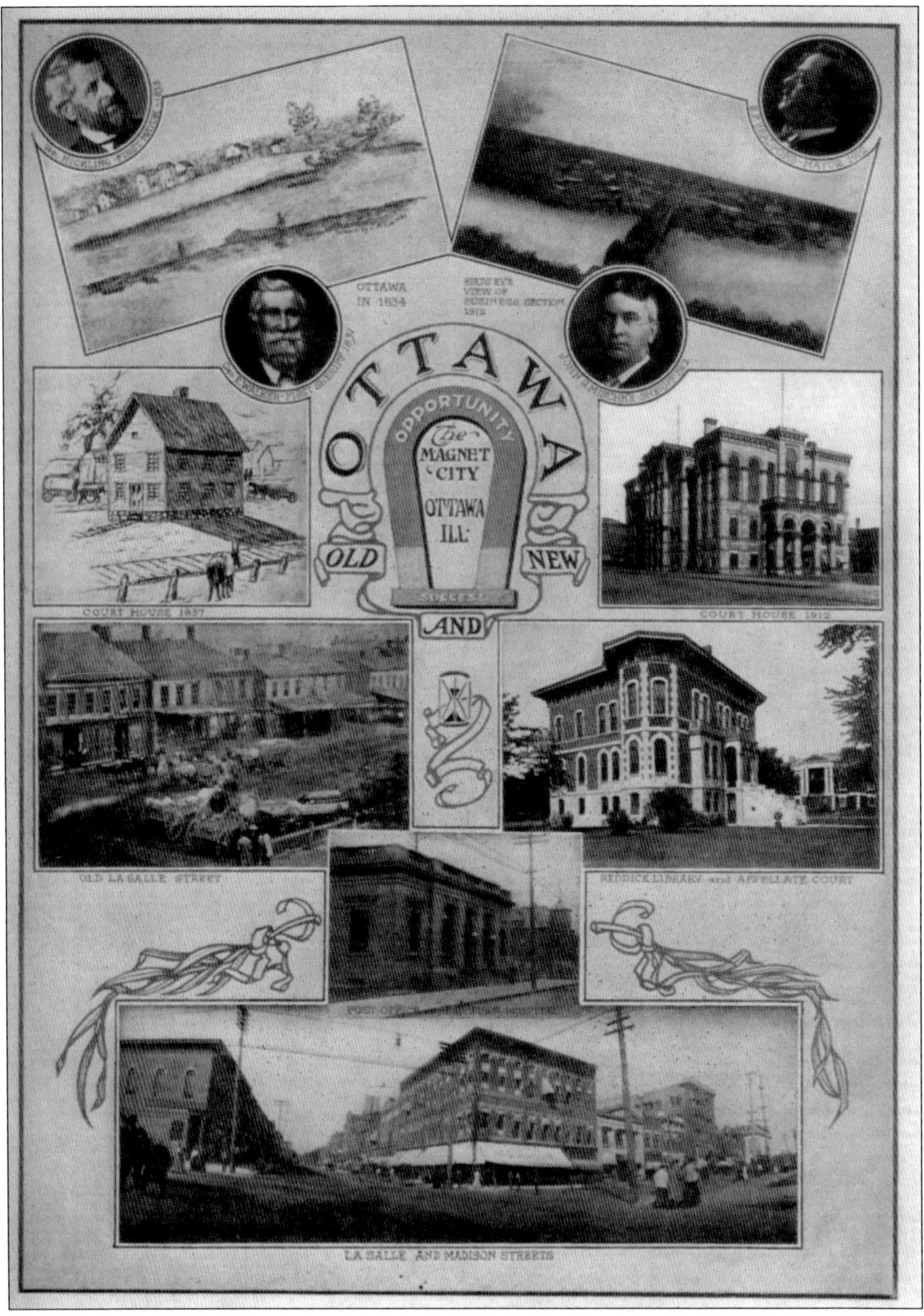

"Ottawa, the Magnet City" was a promotion from 1912. The top pictures show Ottawa's first mayor, William Hickling, in 1853, and the mayor in 1912, E.F. Bradford. Below them are George Walker, first sheriff in 1831, and John Mischke, sheriff in 1912. Scenes include views of Ottawa history. (JR.)

One

Early Ottawa

Settlers came to the Ottawa area as early as 1823, just five years after Illinois became a state. Ottawa was the name of an Indian tribe. Local accounts also say it was an Algonquin word meaning "to trade." Cree, Ottawa, Chippewa, Illiniwek, Nipissing, Algonquin, and Potawatomi all lived in the area over the centuries. The Indians were known as trader tribes, and they traded with the settlers.

The first settler was Dr. Davidson, who built a cabin on the Illinois River in 1823. A year later, Thomas Covel came from Alton and settled on a creek that would bear his name. Other early arrivals included a Methodist missionary, Rev. Jesse Walker.

The town was surveyed and platted in 1831, a charter was granted by the state in 1837, and the city was incorporated in 1853.

Ottawa is a river city, where the Fox and Illinois Rivers come together, and that played an important part in the founding and development of Ottawa.

The Illinois & Michigan Canal was an important part of Ottawa's early prosperity. The canal was the state's greatest public works project in the 19th century. It provided a waterway from Chicago to the Vermillion River. Work began in 1836 and was completed in 1848, mostly through the efforts of Irish immigrant laborers, many of whom settled in Ottawa. The canal was closed for commerce in 1915. Today, the canal land in Ottawa is a recreational path.

Ottawa gained nationwide fame on August 21, 1858, as the site of the first of seven debates between Abraham Lincoln and Stephen A. Douglas. Lincoln was challenging Douglas for his US Senate seat. Douglas won the election—but in a rematch two years later, with the presidency at stake, Lincoln was victorious.

It is interesting to note that there is a Lincoln-Douglas Park in Ottawa, north of East Norris Drive, even though the debate was not held there. Just north of that is Library Park, even though no library was ever located there.

Two of Ottawa's most famous early buildings are the LaSalle County Courthouse and Reddick Mansion. One hundred years ago, numerous beautiful mansions lined Ottawa's north bluff.

Ottawa once had a first-class opera house, several major hotels, a National Guard armory, and two busy train depots with passenger service. However, while many large factories and businesses have departed, new businesses and industries have taken the place of those of yesteryear.

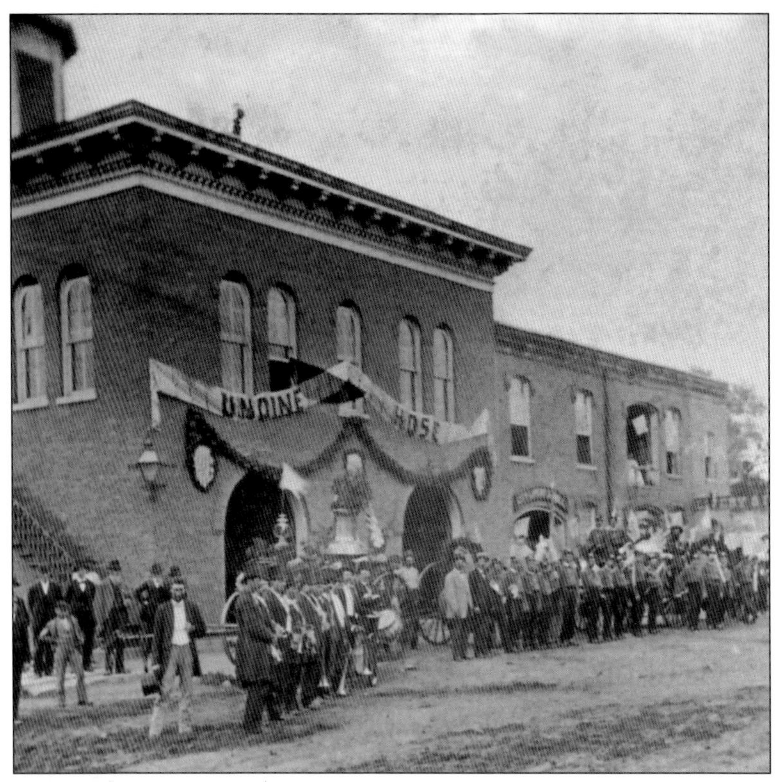

Undine Hose Company organized in 1859 as Ottawa's first volunteer fire department. Firemen pose with Niblo's Band in front of the engine house at the city hall building on Madison Street in this picture, taken on July 4, 1876. This building burned down in 1881. Pictured below is a view of Main Street in 1893. (Both, JR.)

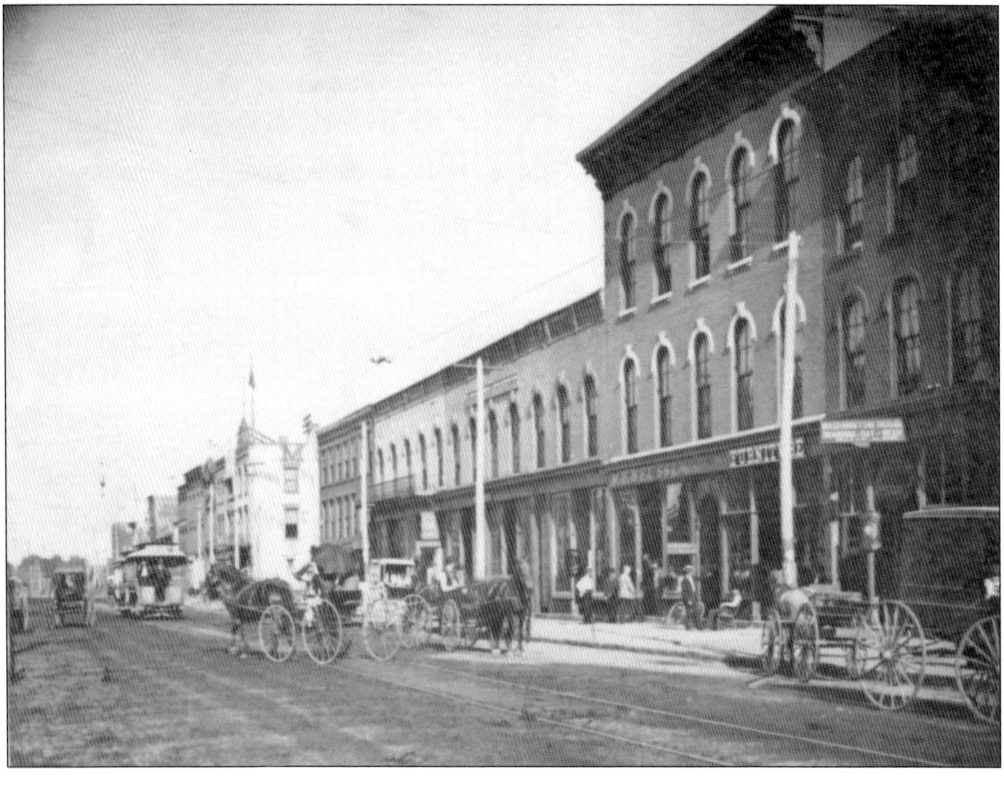

Holland's Ottawa Directory.

1865. 1885.

THIS ADVERTISEMENT IS INTENDED TO

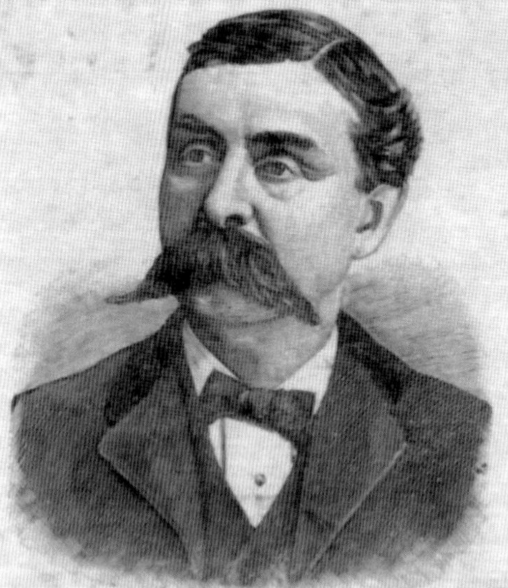

ARREST ON SIGHT!

Your special attention to Bowman's Popular Photograph Gallery at Ottowa, Illinois.

☞SUPERIOR PHOTOGRAPHY IS OUR SPECIALTY.

N. B.—Old Pictures reproduced to larger sizes and **Finished in First-class Manner.**

Our Crayon Portraits are **fine** in finish, **truthful** in likeness, **permanent** as to durability, **cheap** in price, hence are **very popular.**

We have an extensive variety of Photograph Frames, Mattings, Albums, Stereoscopes, Local and Miscellaneous Views. Having preserved the negatives taken for twenty years, we have hundreds and thousands of Valuable Negatives from which Duplicates can be secured if desired, at reduced prices.

☞**OPENING HOURS** { During the day, from 8 A.M. to 5 P.M.
Electric light from 7 to 9 P.M

Patronage solicited and Visitors always welcome.

W. E. BOWMAN, Proprietor.

William Emory Bowman was the preeminent Ottawa photographer from 1857 to 1910. His pictures of early Ottawa have become classic. This advertisement is from the 1884 Ottawa directory. (JR.)

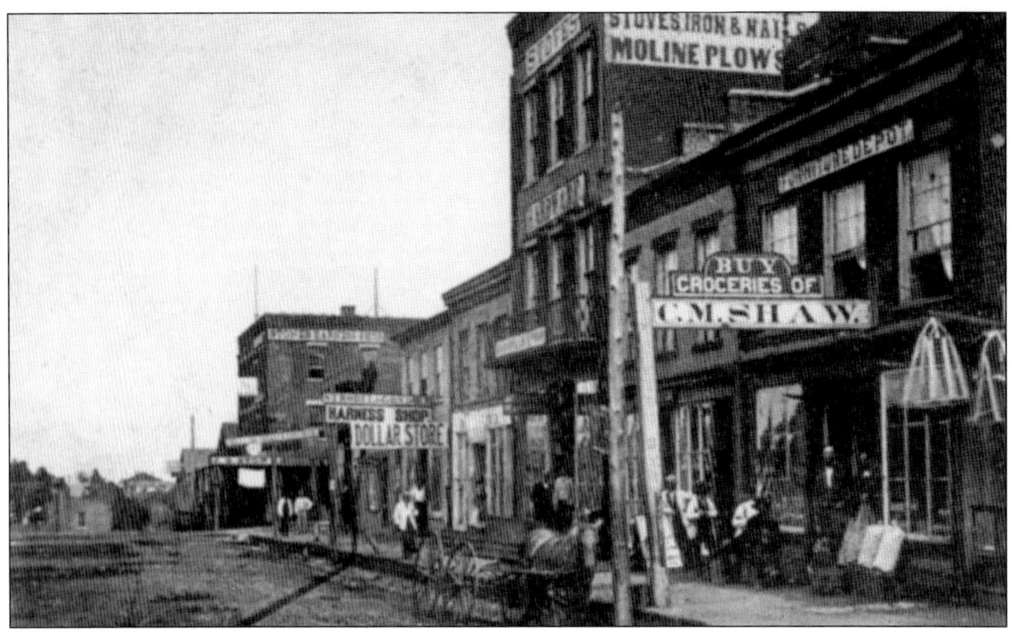

Pictured above is the 100 block of West Main Street in 1870. Below is Court Street, looking north from Main Street, in 1876. Bowman's Art Gallery was on Court Street. (Both, JR.)

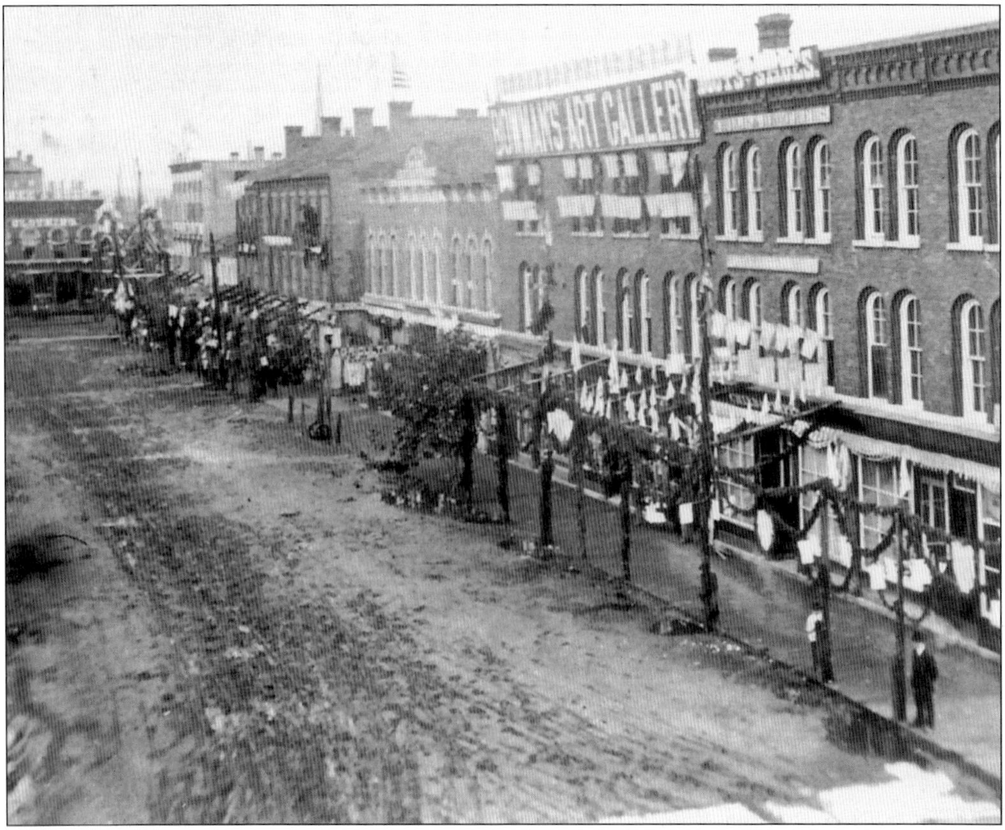

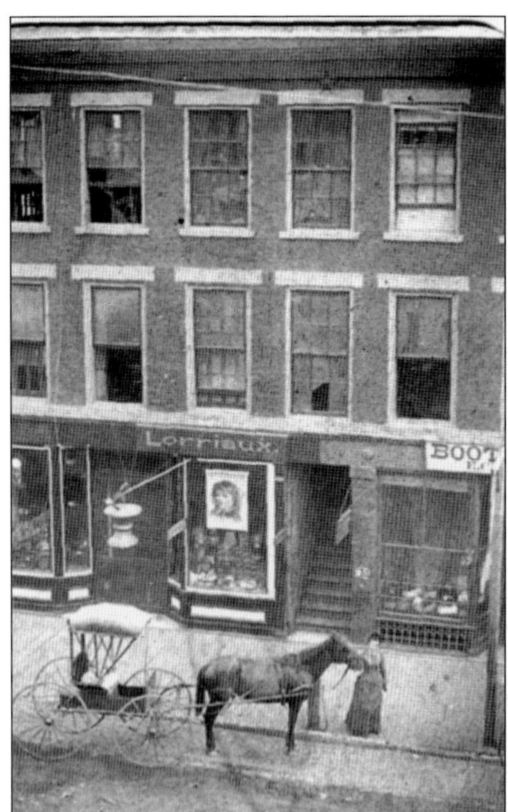

The shop of D. Lorriaux, at 617 LaSalle Street, is shown here in the 1870s. Lorriaux's place was a drugstore and stationery store. Lorriaux came to Ottawa in 1856, and he and his family lived at 310 North Clay Street. The picture below shows an unidentified public celebration from the 1870s or 1880s. (Both, JR.)

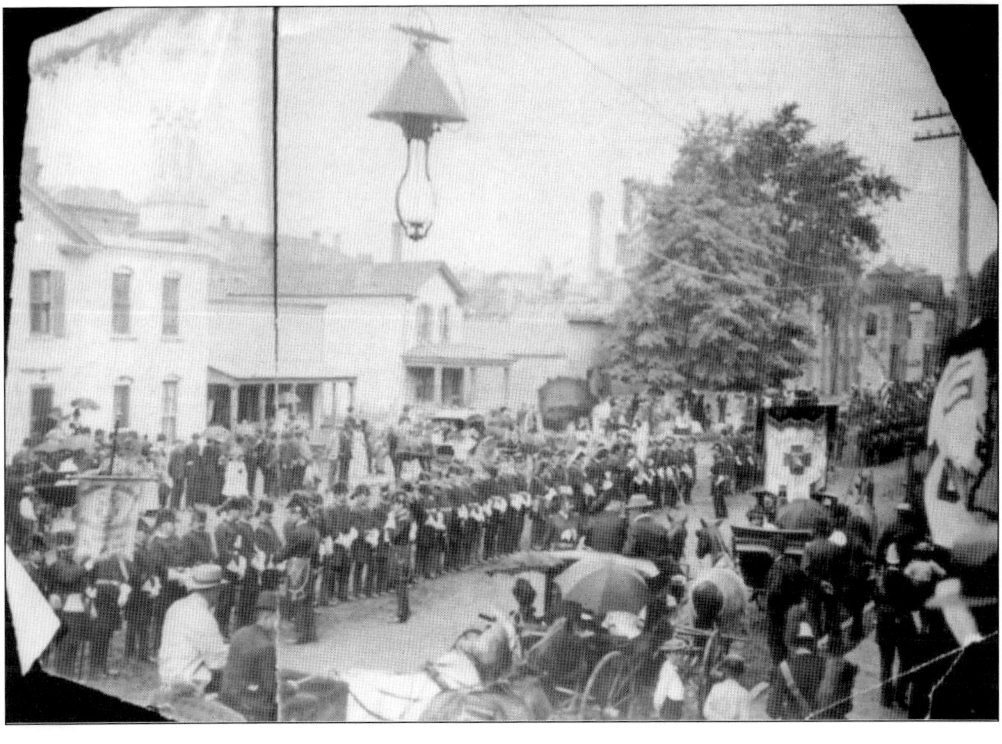

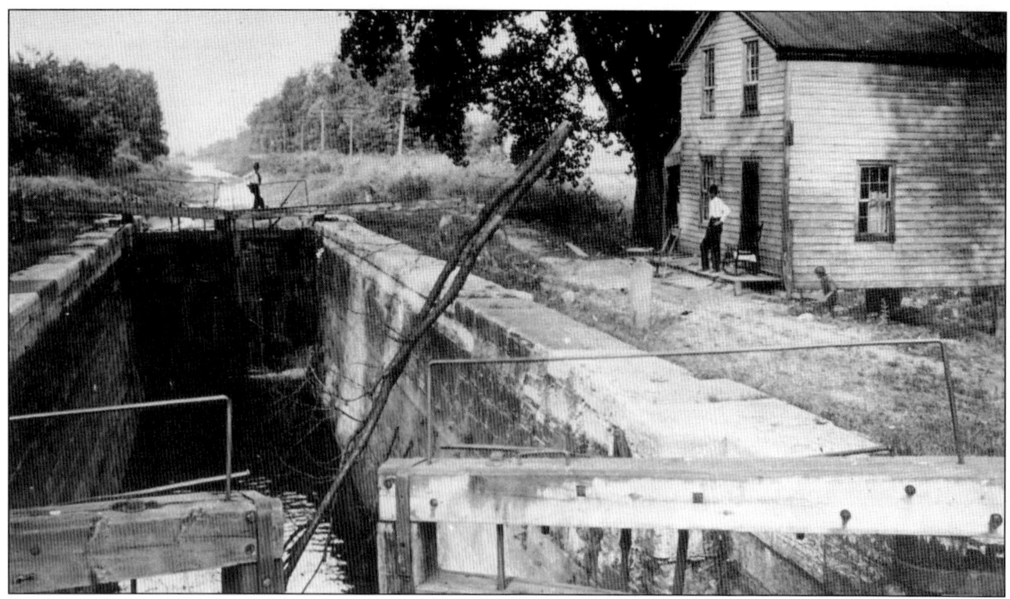

The 98-mile-long Illinois & Michigan (I&M) Canal was up to six feet deep and 60 feet wide. Canal boats were pulled by a horse or mule on a tow path along the canal. The canal included 15 locks along the way. A 464-foot limestone aqueduct (pictured below) carried the canal over the Fox River in Ottawa by East Superior Street, and it was an architectural marvel. Pictured above is a canal lock and canal tender's house. (Both, JR.)

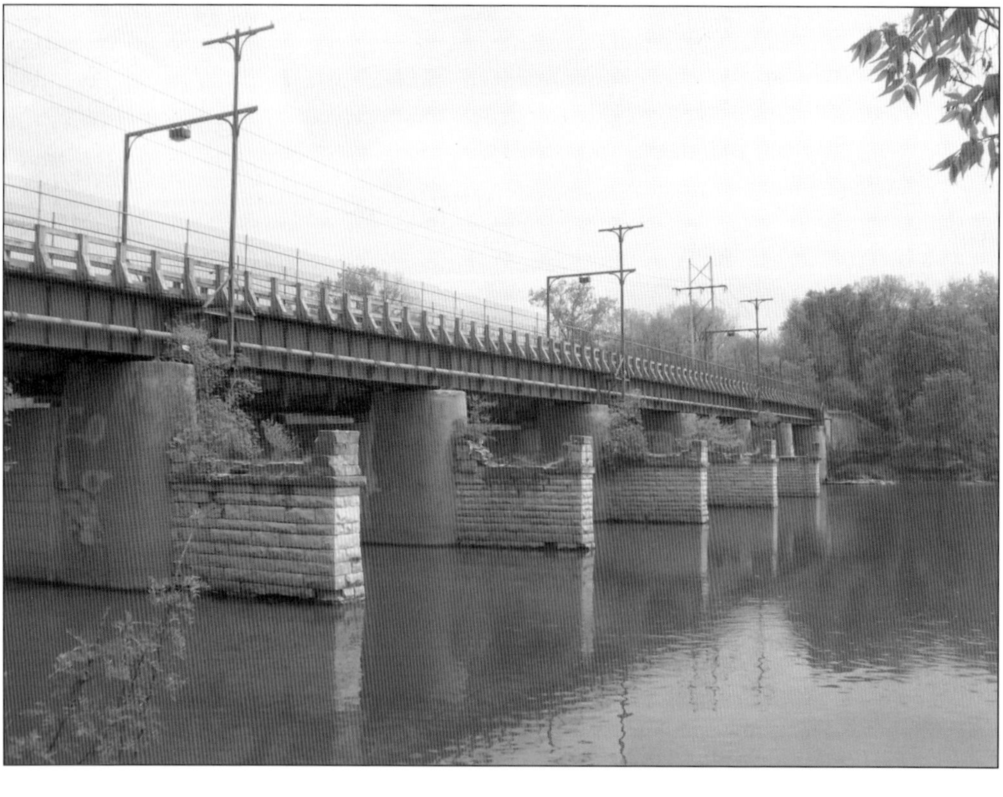

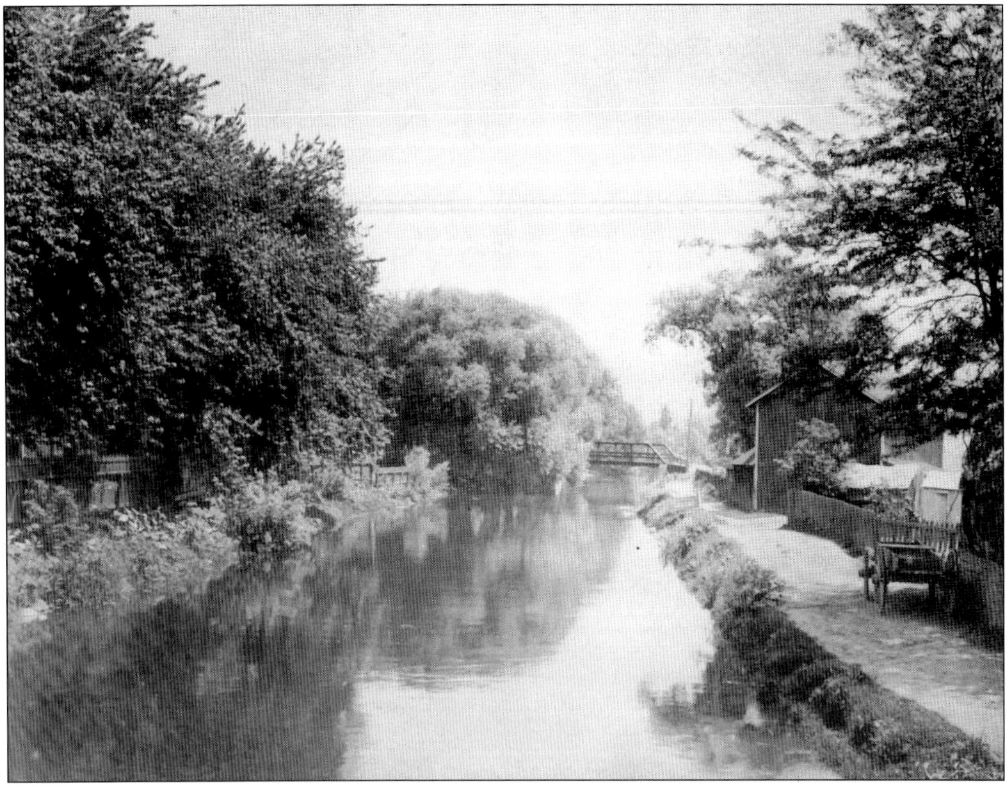

Pictured here is scenery along the I&M Canal in Ottawa in the 1890s. (Both, JR.)

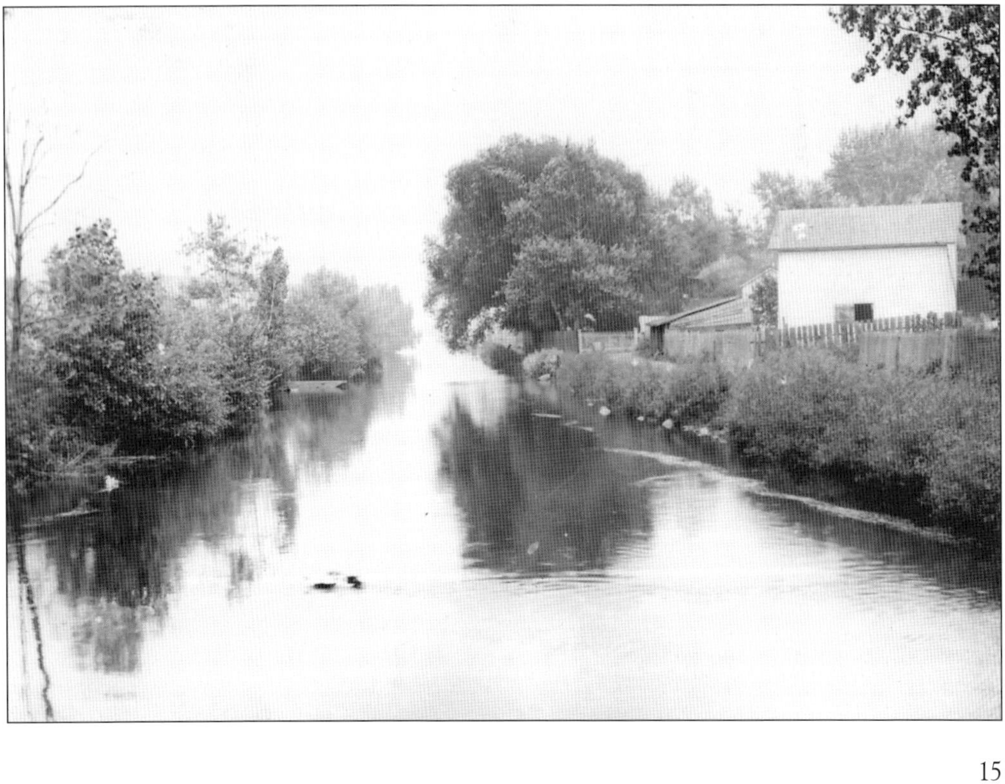

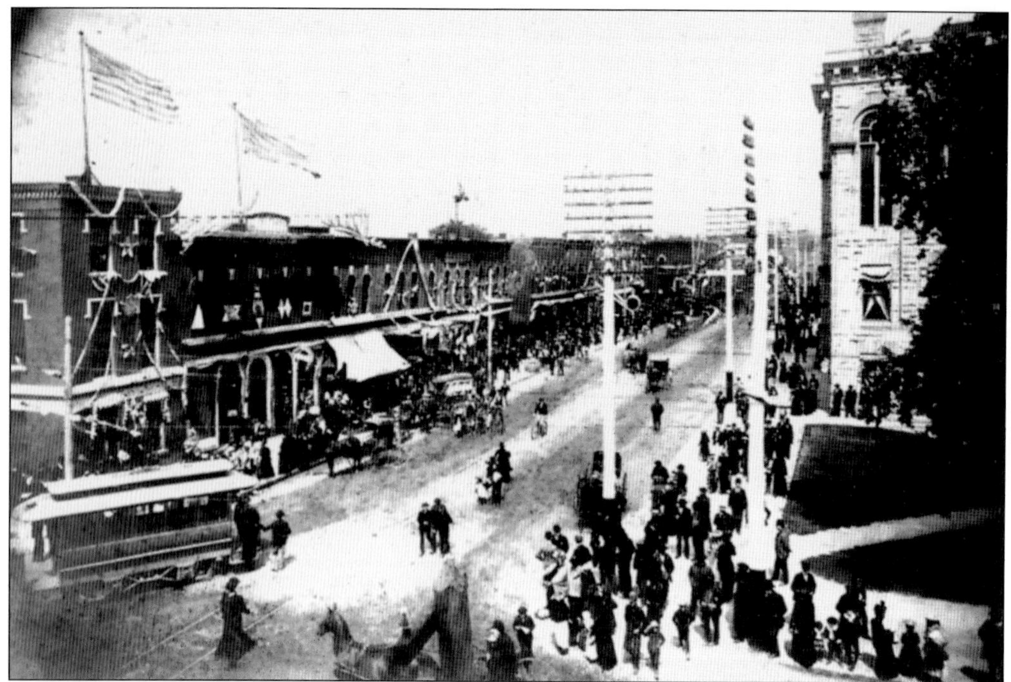

Ottawa appears decorated for a celebration, as a streetcar heads north on LaSalle Street from Main Street. The courthouse is on the right. Streetcar service began in Ottawa in August 1889. Interurban electric streetcars provided transportation between towns from 1901 to 1934. (JR.)

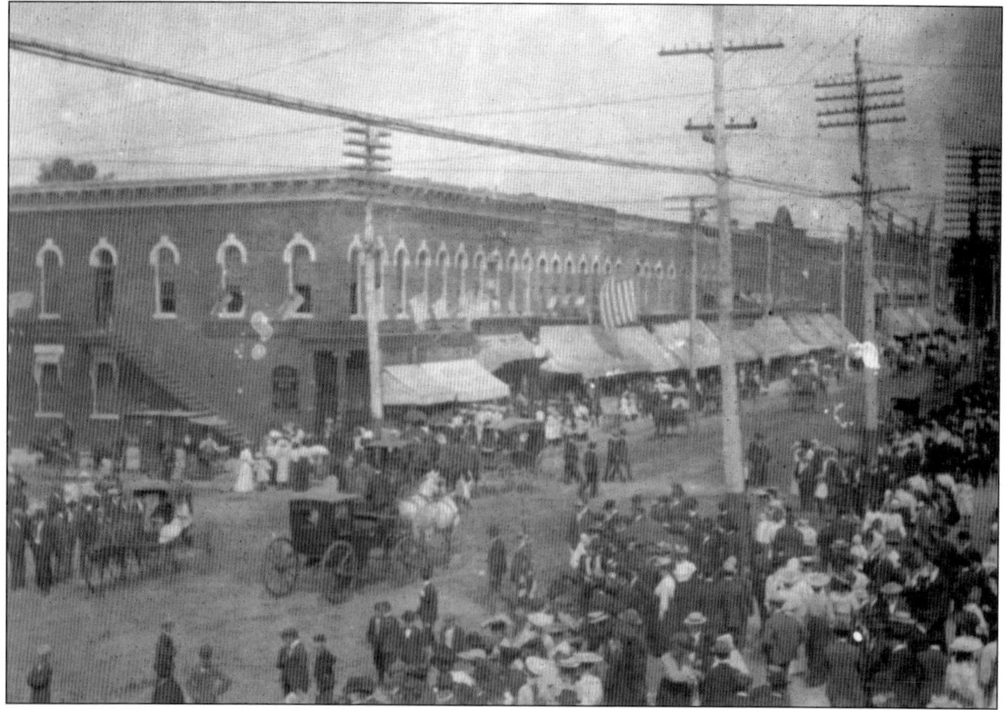

In this photograph, it appears to be quite a busy day on the 700 block of LaSalle Street in the 1890s. (JR.)

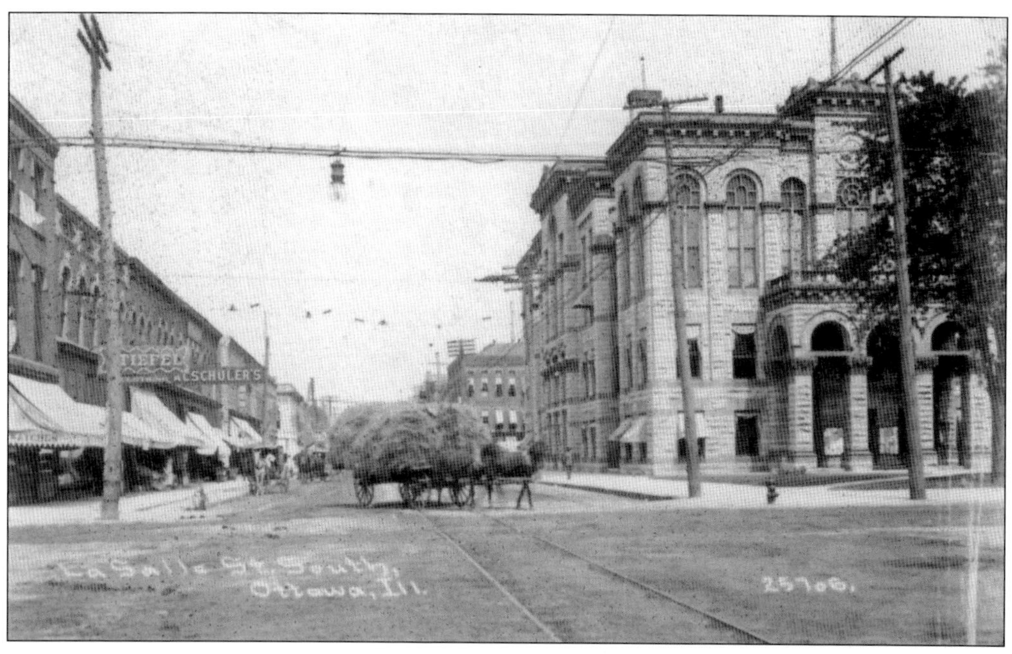

This is the fourth and present-day LaSalle County courthouse, built between 1881 and 1883. The Renaissance Revival–style structure is built of Joliet limestone with walls that are four feet thick. New county offices were built in 1975 on Etna Road, but the downtown courthouse still serves many of the county's needs. The picture below shows activity on the courthouse lawn in 1902. (Above, JR; below, DC.)

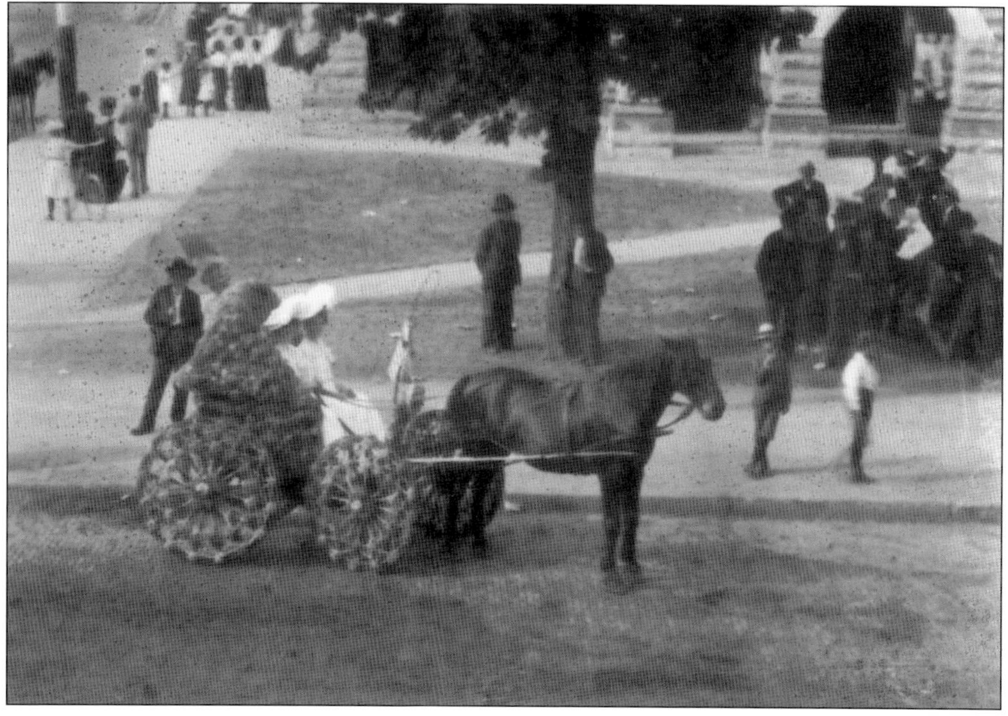

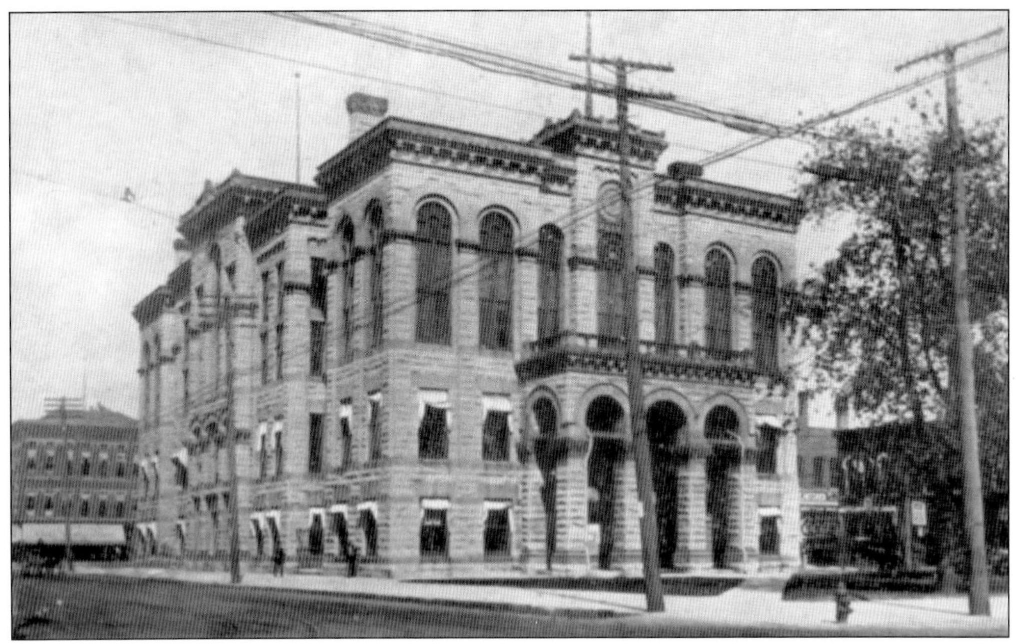

The courthouse cornerstone was laid on July 4, 1881, and work was completed in March 1883. The contractor was Thomas & Hugh Colwell of Ottawa, and the cost of the limestone structure was $127,127. A remodeling of the courthouse in 1962 cost $1,416,527. The above picture shows the courthouse in the 1890s, while the bottom picture is from the 1950s. (Both, JR.)

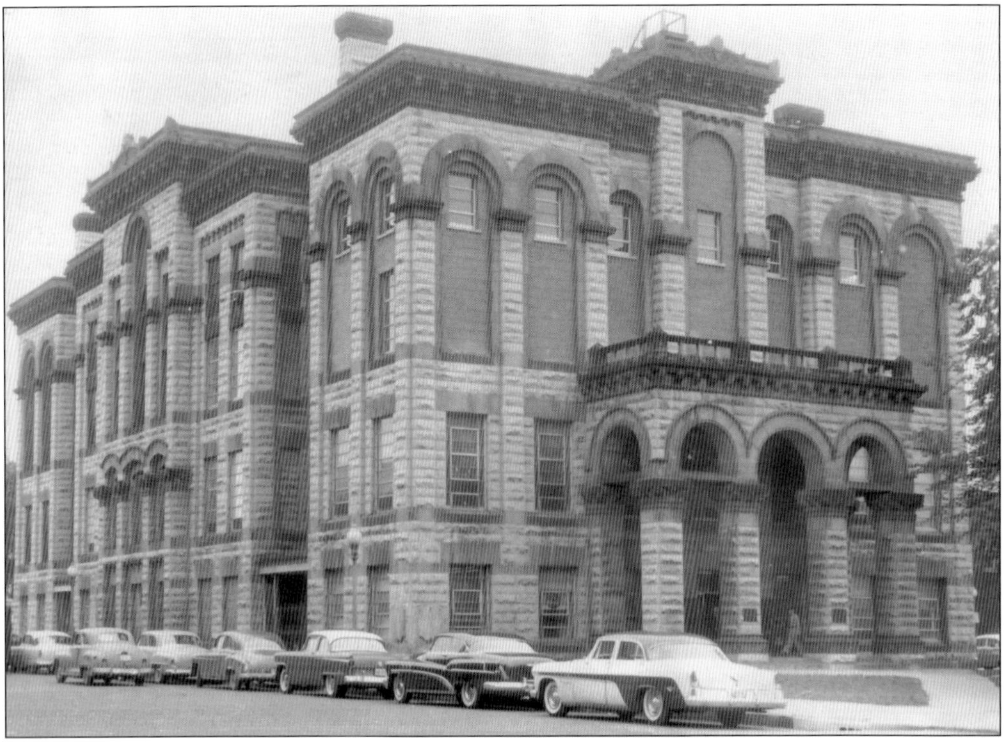

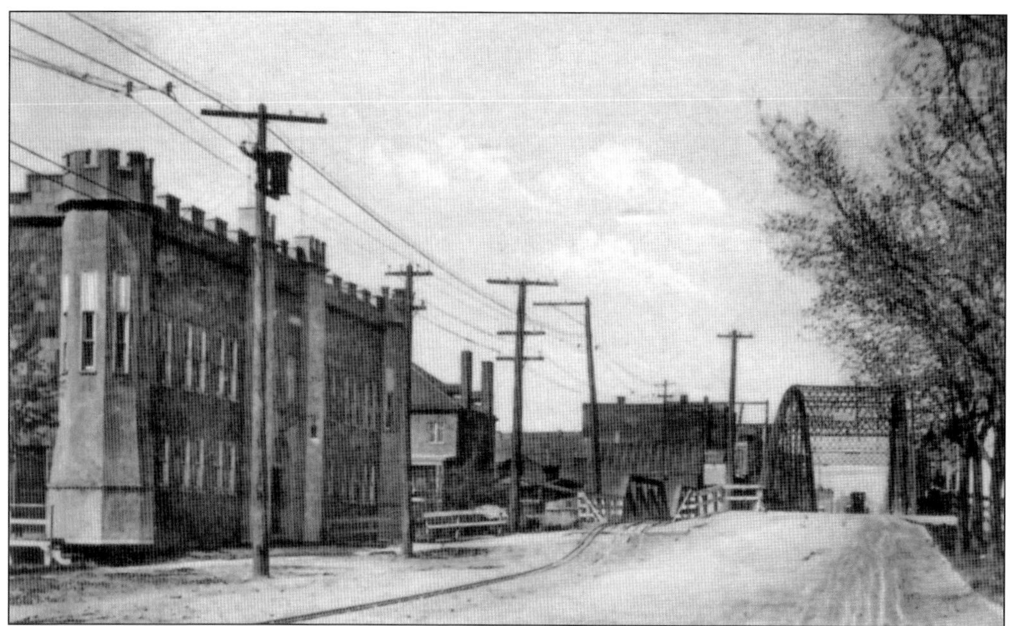

The first National Guard Armory, pictured above, was built on Main Street in 1904. It burned down in 1912. It was replaced by a second armory, built on the same spot, in 1914. The site is now a parking lot. (DC.)

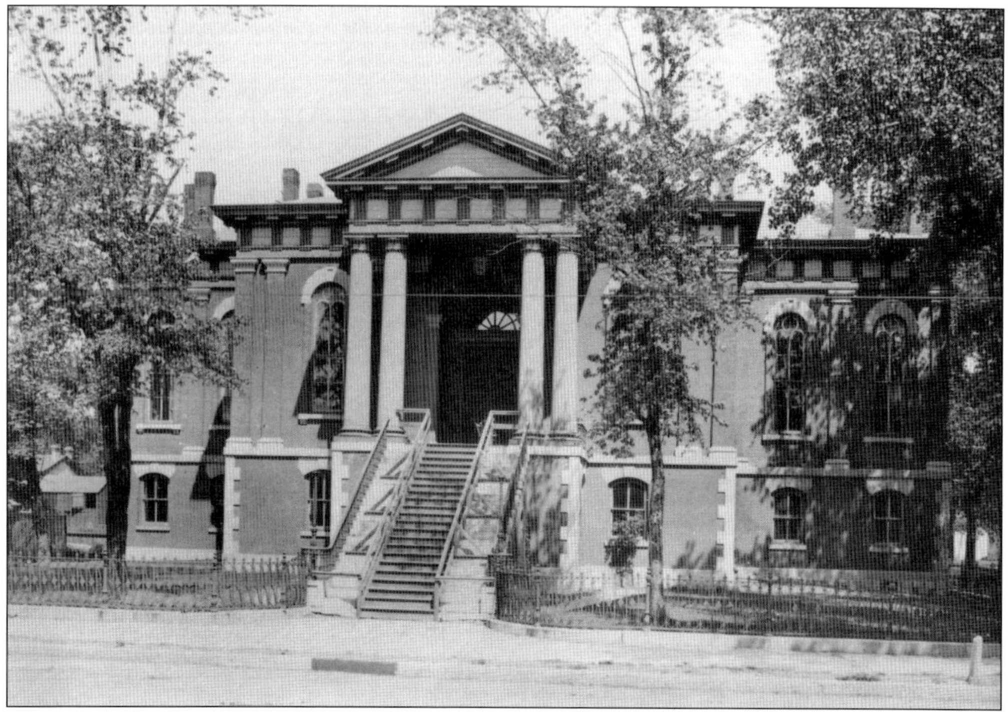

The Illinois Supreme Court was divided into three districts, with Ottawa being the seat of one district. This Supreme Court building was constructed on Columbus Street in 1860. When the districts were consolidated in Springfield in 1897, this building became an appellate court. This picture is from 1893, when this still was an Illinois Supreme Court building. (DC.)

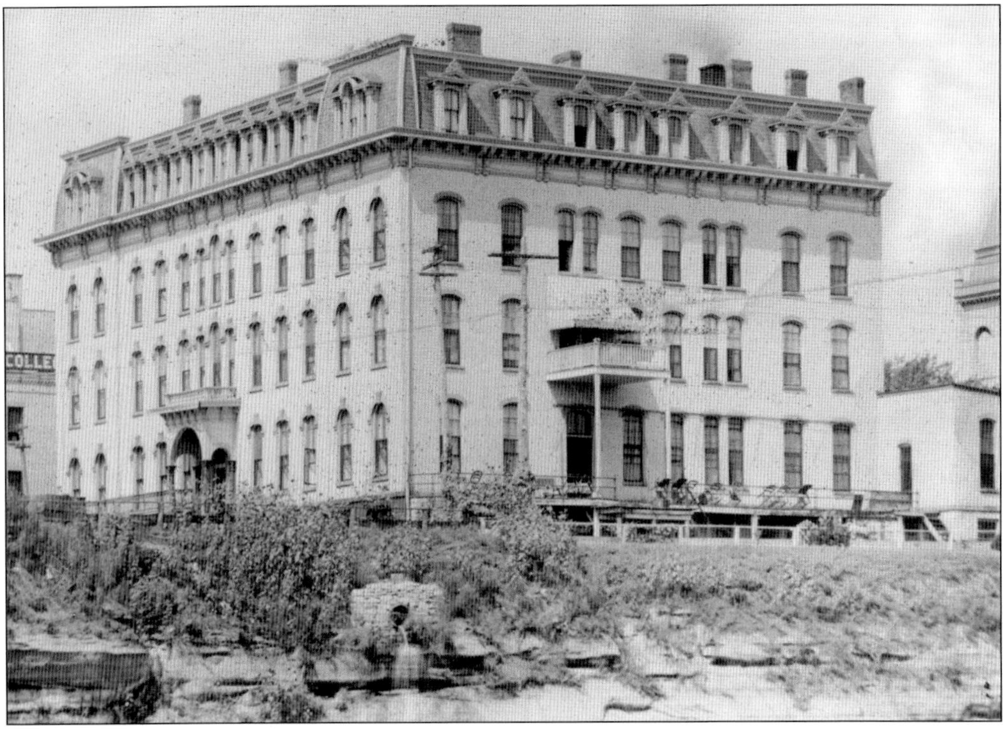

In an era when most cities had hotels, the Clifton Hotel on Columbus Street was considered first class. It was built in 1868. The back of the hotel is pictured above as it originally looked, complete with drainage pipe emptying into the Fox River. The picture below shows the front of the hotel after a renovation in 1910. The Clifton Hotel was torn down in 1929. A pizza place is now located on the site. (Both, JR.)

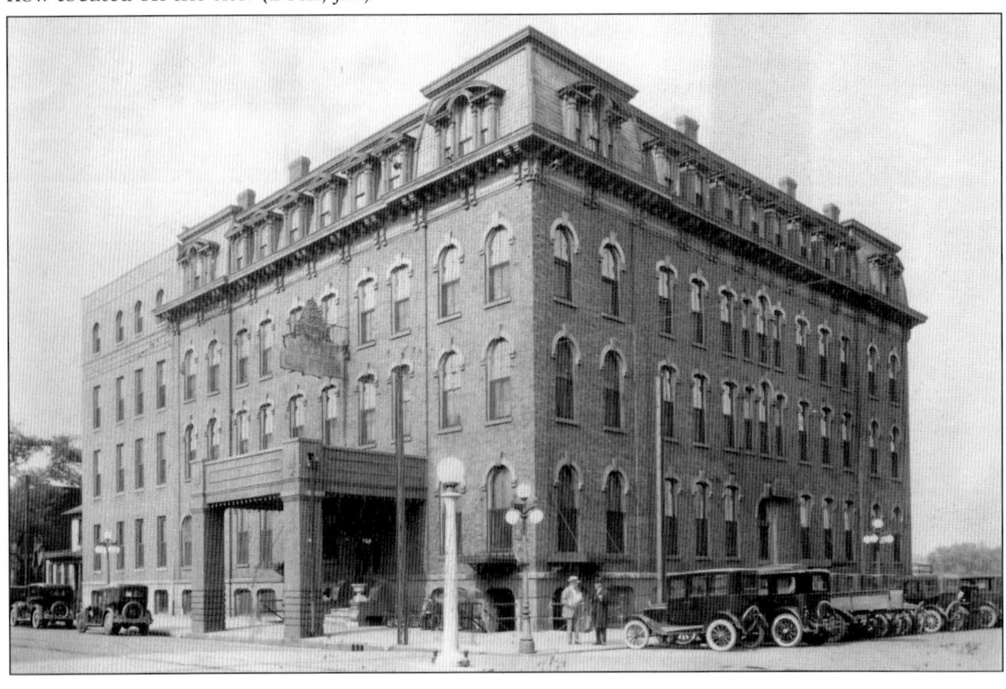

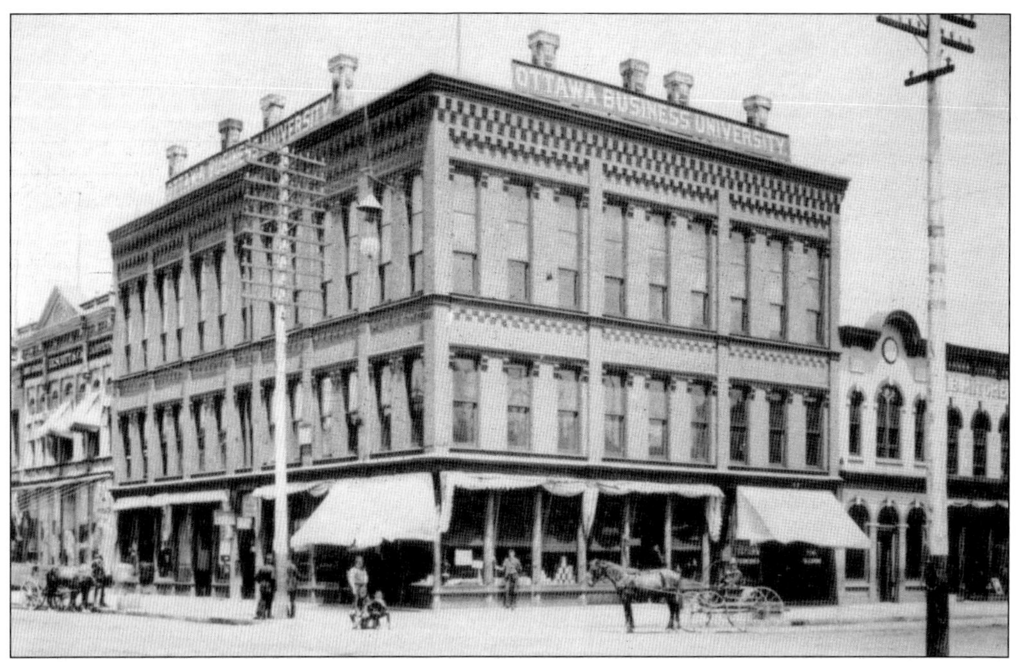

Ottawa Business University, at LaSalle and Madison Streets (above), started as Toland Business College in 1888 and became Brown's Business College in 1894. Below is the Ottawa Opera House, on the southeast corner of LaSalle and Jefferson Streets. It was owned by Frederick Sherwood, who was mayor of Ottawa from 1889 to 1891. The opera house was built in 1875 and seated 770 people. Both pictures were taken in 1893. (Both, JR.)

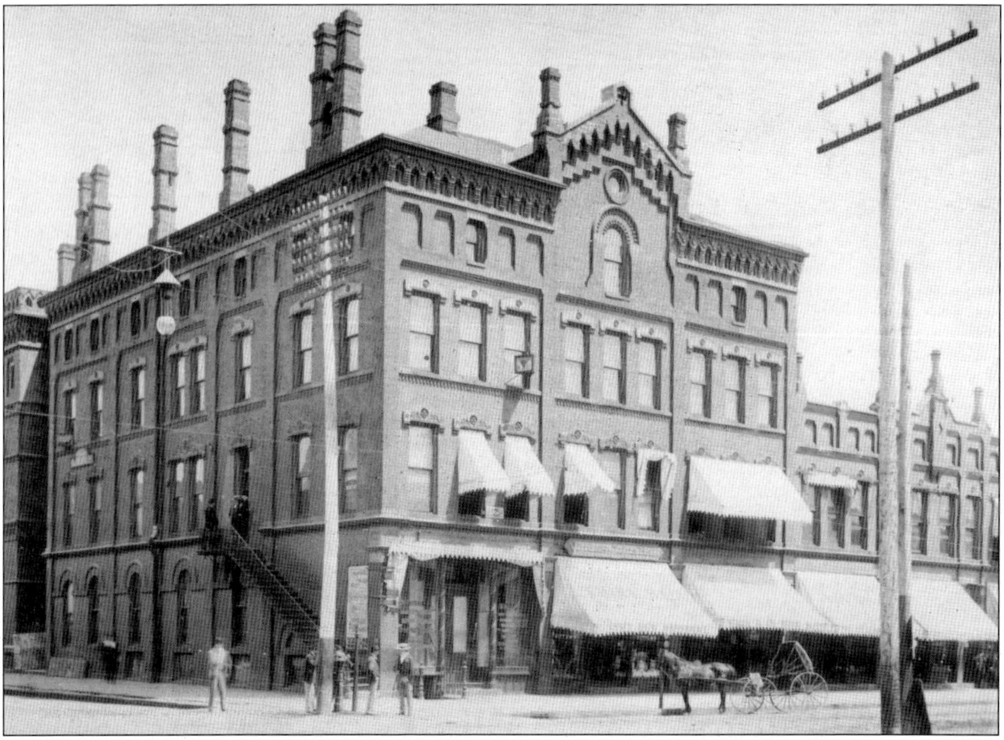

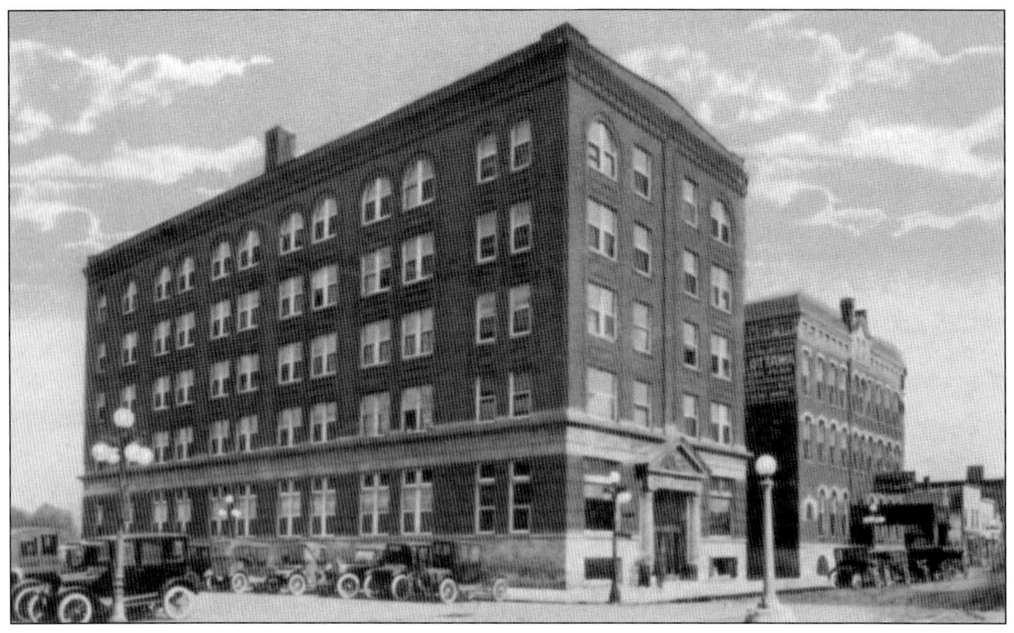

Jason F. Richardson Jr. designed the Central Life Building, which was constructed in 1915 on Columbus Street. The above picture shows the Hotel Ottawa to the right. A 1979 view is seen in the picture below. Richardson also designed the Masonic Temple, the Elks Club, and the Palmer Apartment House. (Both, JR.)

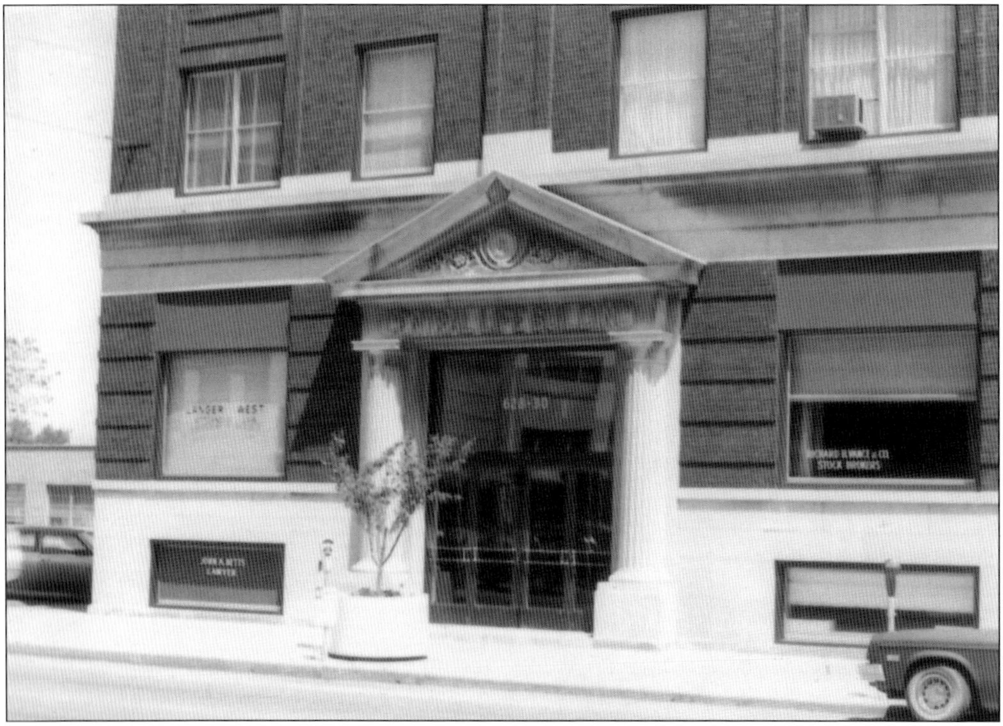

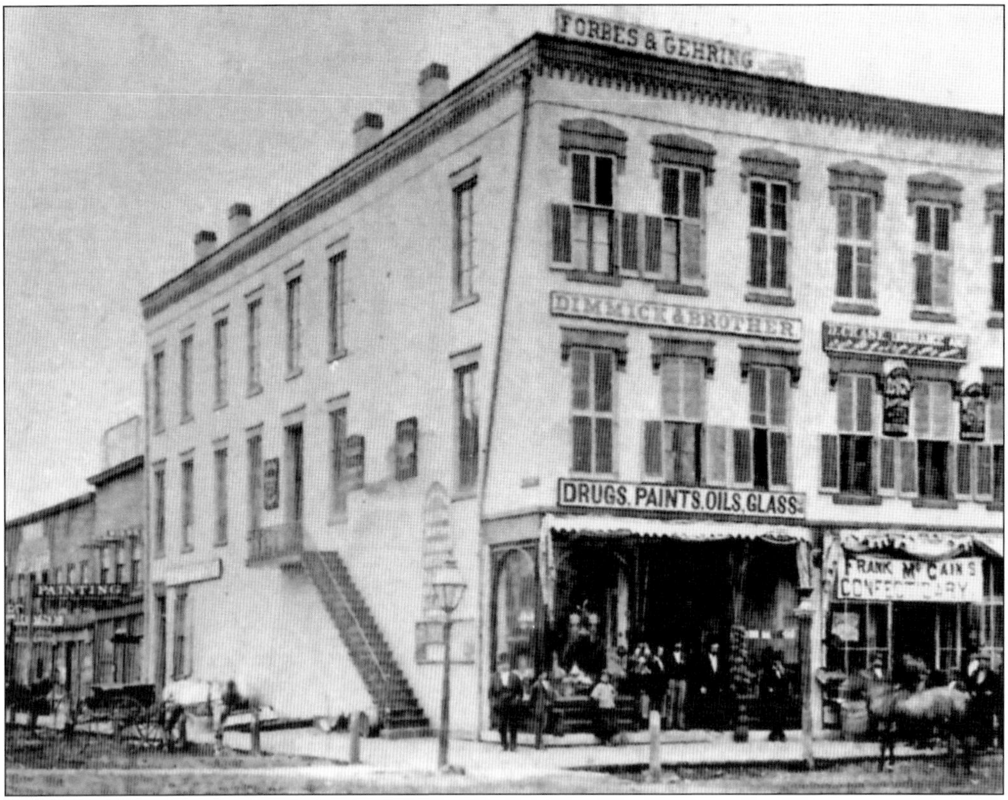

W.E. Bowman took this picture of the corner of LaSalle and Main Streets in the 1860s or 1870s. In the 1940s, the corner was the home of the Maple Leaf Sweet Shop. The picture below is from 1943, and it shows, from left to right, Rita Eichelkraut, unidentified, Dorothy Cook, Shirley Johnson, and Beverly Wilcox. (Both, DC.)

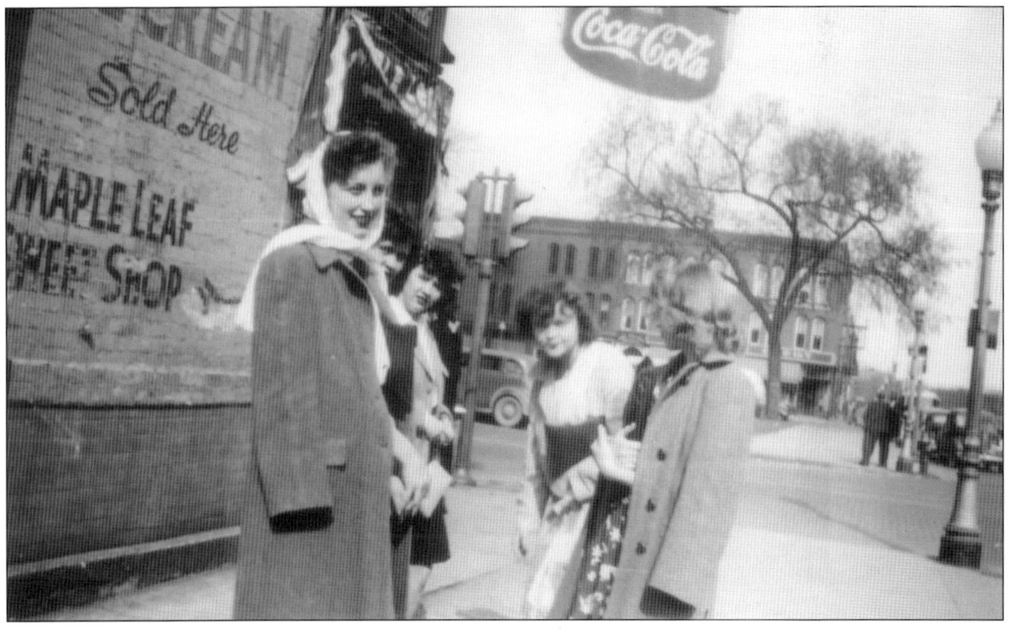

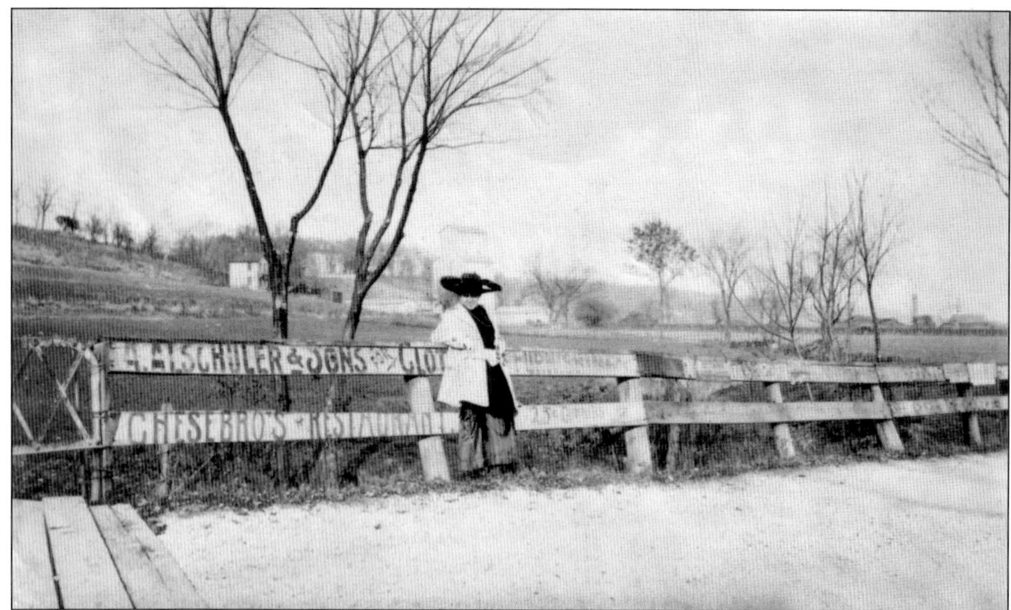

Advertisements for Alschuler & Sons and Cheesebros Restaurant in Ottawa are on the post; this view is looking east from Boyce Drive about 1920. Alschuler had a clothing store on LaSalle Street. Cheesebros had a café at 211 West Madison Street and a chop suey restaurant on Court Street. (DC.)

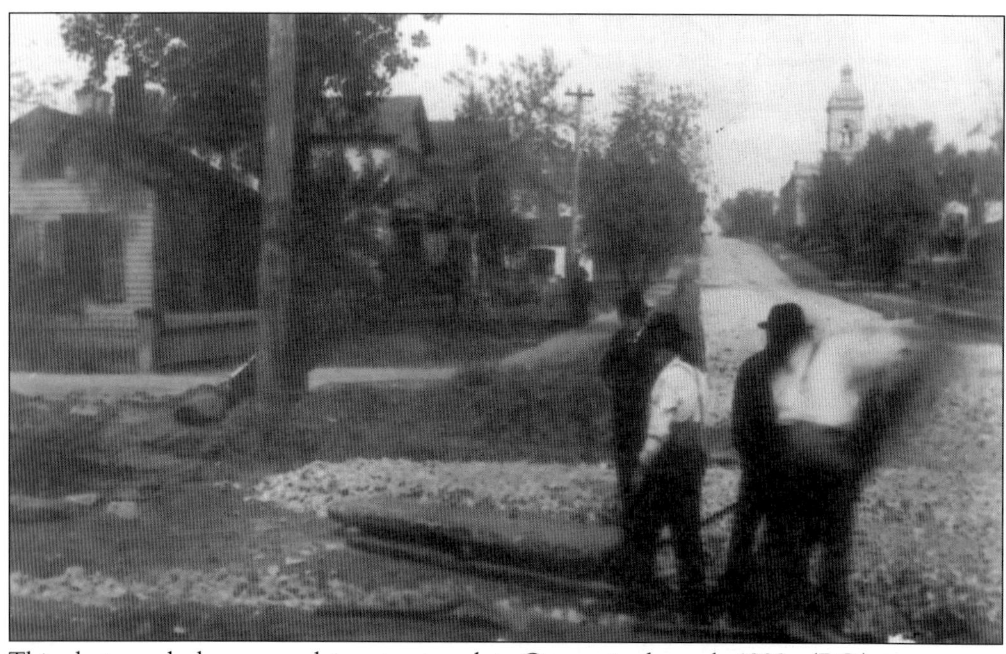

This photograph shows men doing street work in Ottawa in the early 1900s. (DC.)

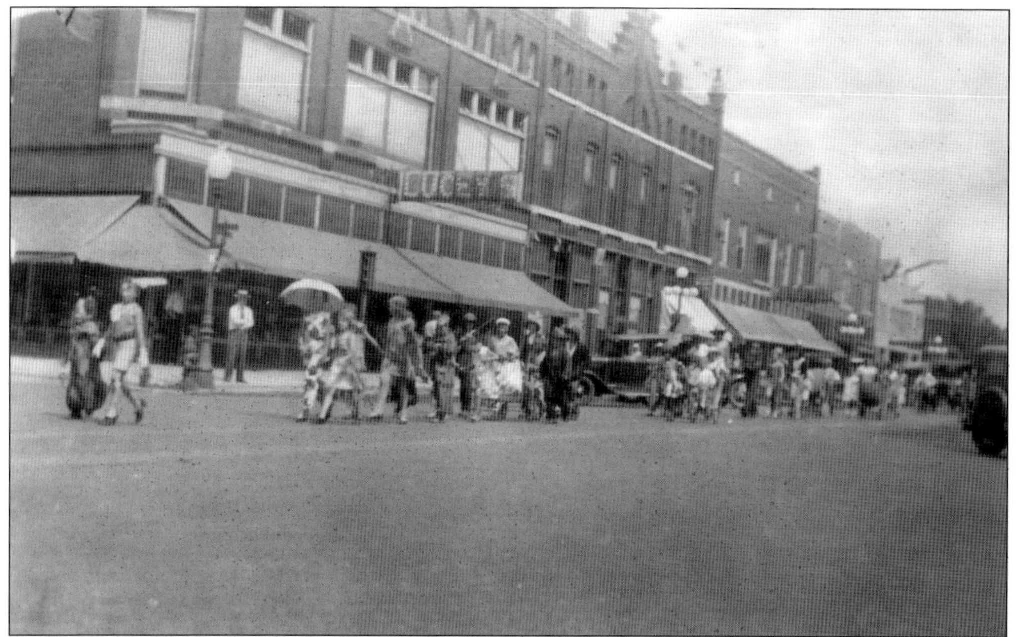

A parade makes its way south on LaSalle Street, at Jefferson Street, around 1920. On the corner is Lucey's department store, which opened at 707 LaSalle Street in 1898. It sold women's and children's clothing and a line of floor coverings. In 1908, Lucey's moved to a new building on LaSalle Street at Jefferson Street. (DC.)

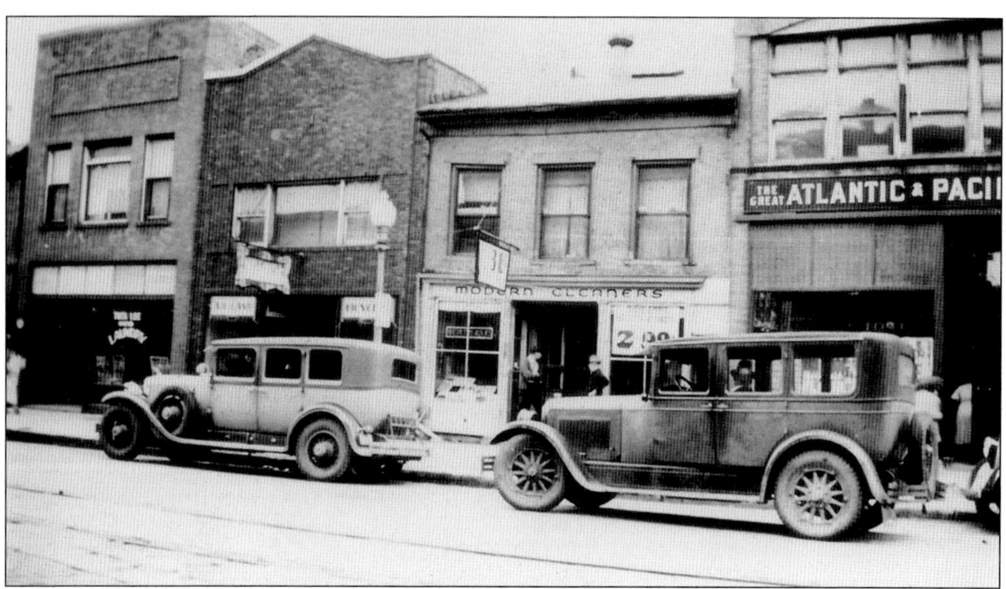

This 1920s view of the 200 block of West Main Street shows the Tuck Lee Laundry on the left, Modern Cleaners, and the A&P grocery. (JR.)

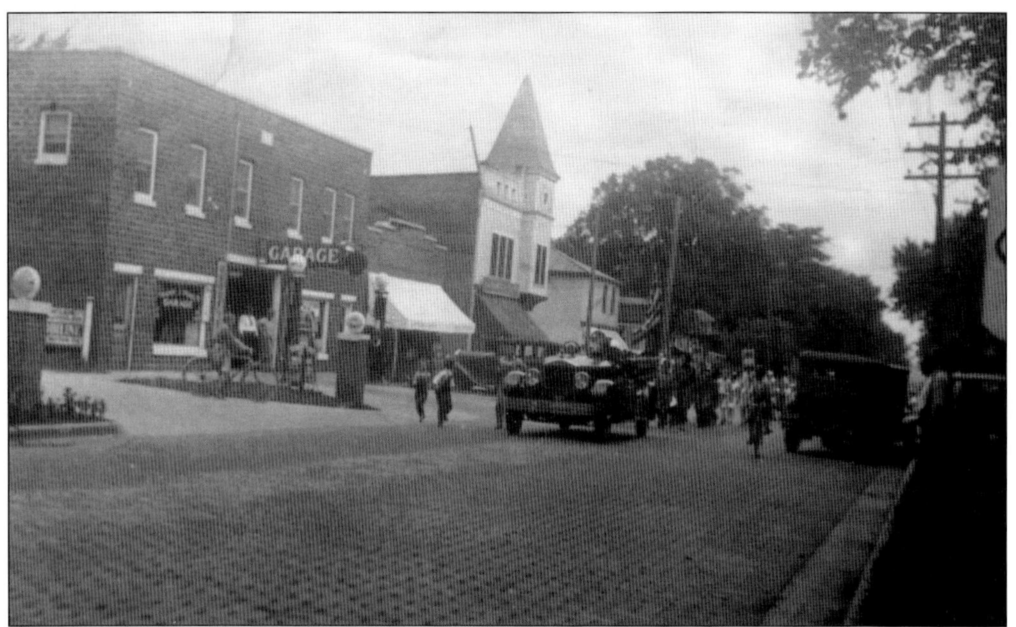

Above is a view of State Street, from Campbell Street, on Ottawa's south side, taken in the 1920s. (DC.)

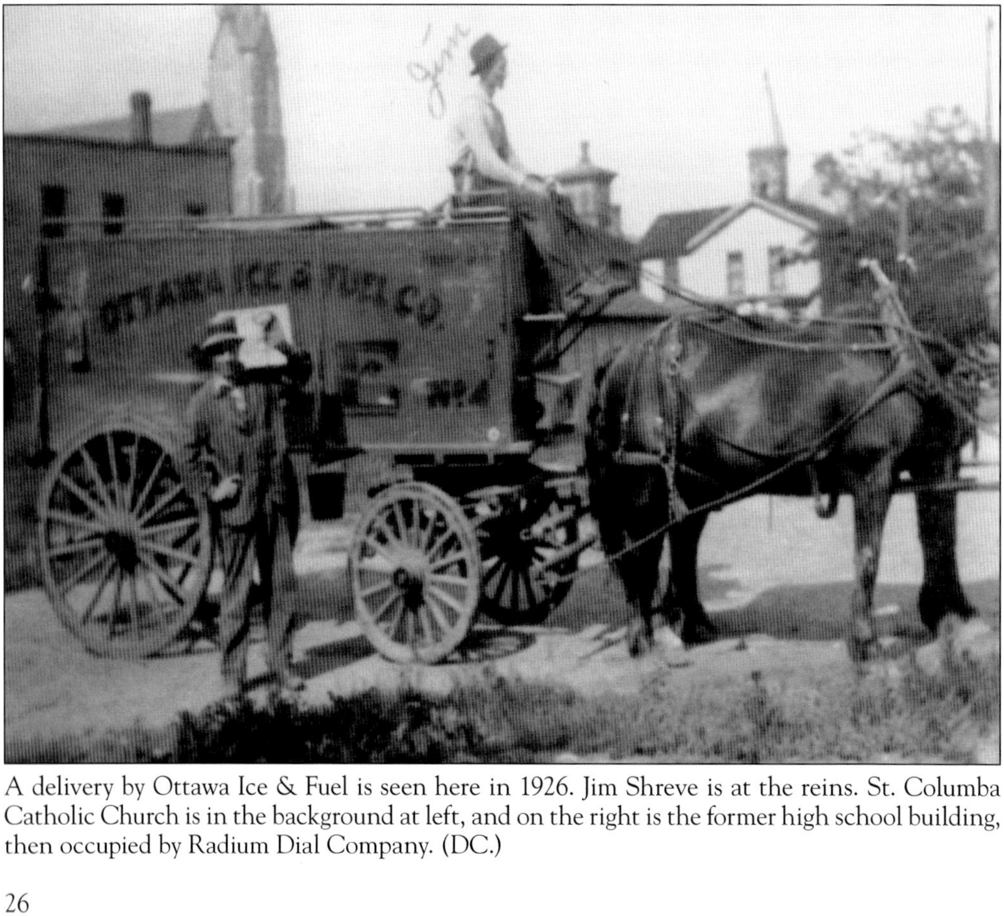

A delivery by Ottawa Ice & Fuel is seen here in 1926. Jim Shreve is at the reins. St. Columba Catholic Church is in the background at left, and on the right is the former high school building, then occupied by Radium Dial Company. (DC.)

This poster is from the 1906 election, in which O.E. Benson was the winning candidate for LaSalle County sheriff. (JR.)

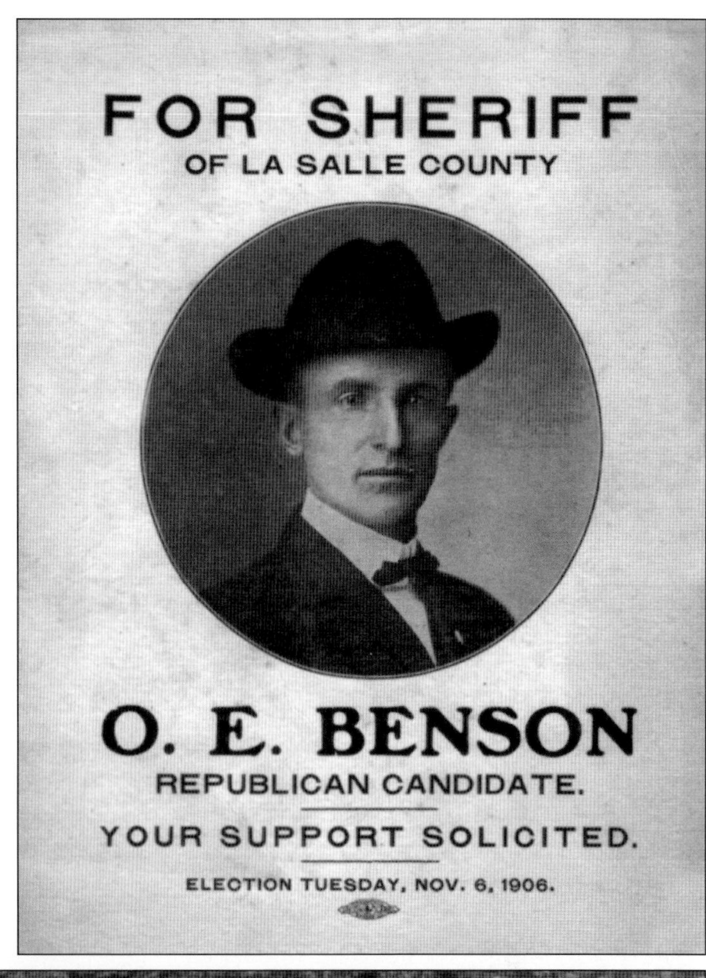

The Ottawa Police Department posed for this portrait in 1939. Pictured here are, from left to right, (first row) Sgt. Roy Barr, Chief Frank Frazier, Capt. Jerry Madigan, and Sgt. James Callison; (second row) Larry Weedig, Tom Bayer, Fred Johnson, Jack Jacobs, John McCormick, Jack Tersasant, Roscoe Milan, Mike Keim, and Charles Pennybaker. (DC.)

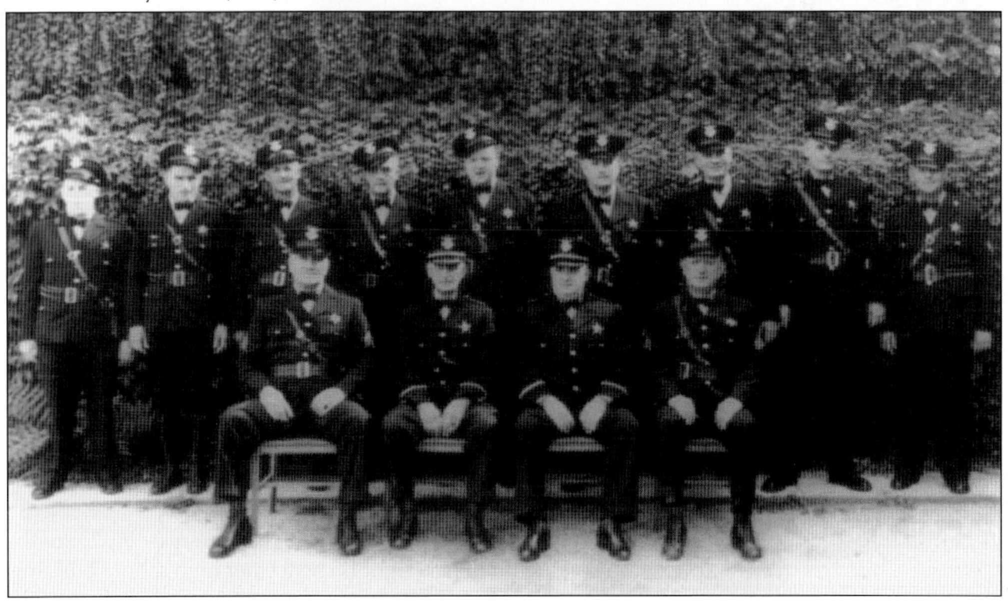

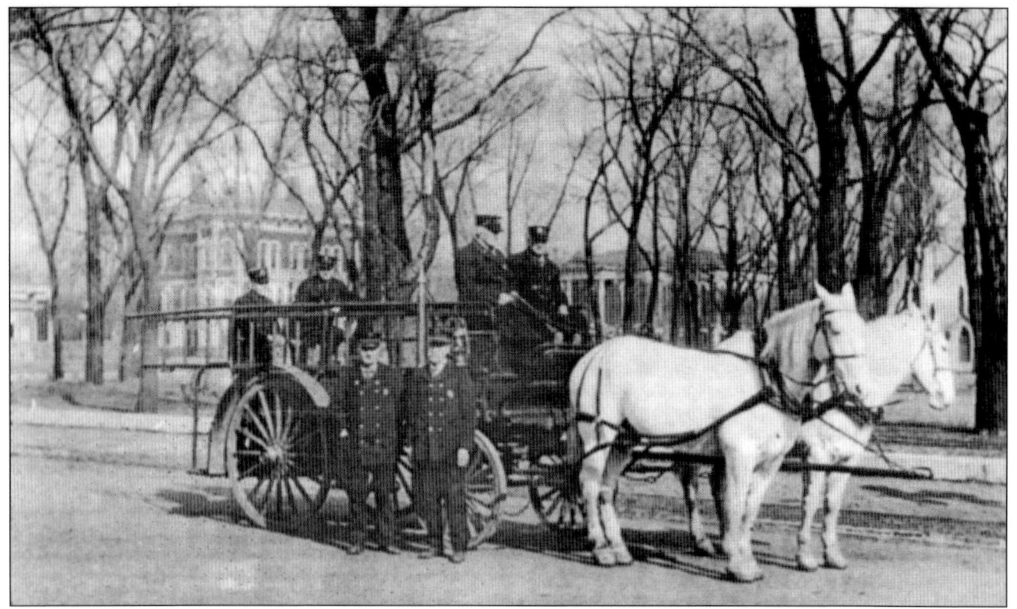

Ottawa firemen are pictured here with their new fire truck in the 1890s. Reddick Mansion and the Supreme Court are in the background. A huge blaze destroyed the fire station on Madison Street, and a good part of downtown Ottawa, on September 24, 1881. A new fire station, at LaSalle Street and Lincoln Place, served for 100 years, until a new station was built at 301 West Lafayette Street in 1981. (DC.)

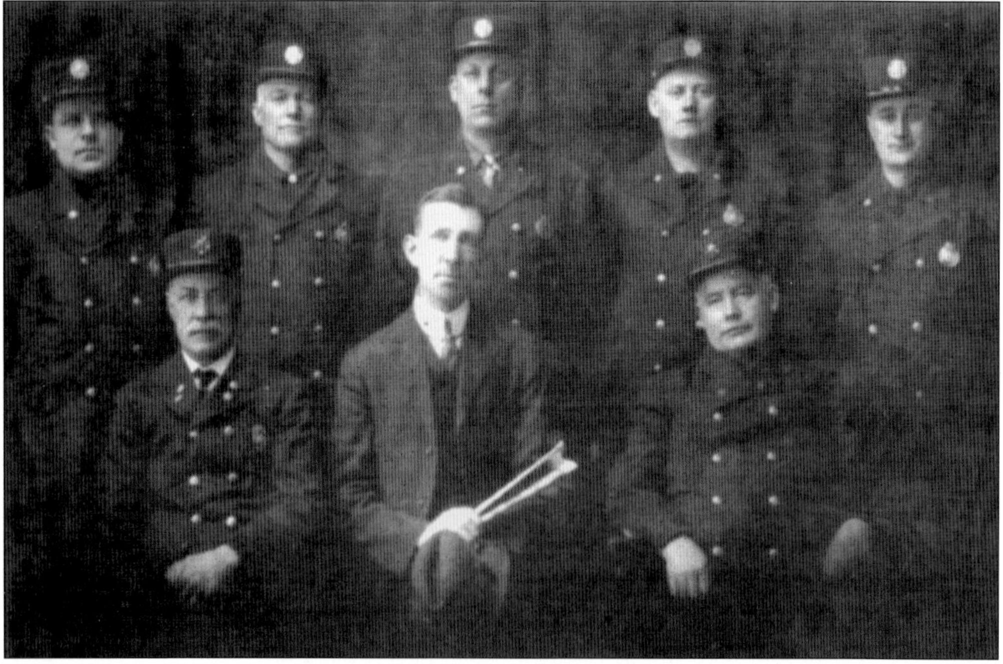

This picture shows Ottawa Fire Department personnel in the early 1900s. They are, from left to right, (first row) Chief Joseph Boissenin, Commissioner Walter Palmer, and Assistant Chief James Daughterty; (second row) Edgar Houston, Edward Haley, George Vey, Peter Creed, and George Stevenson. (DC.)

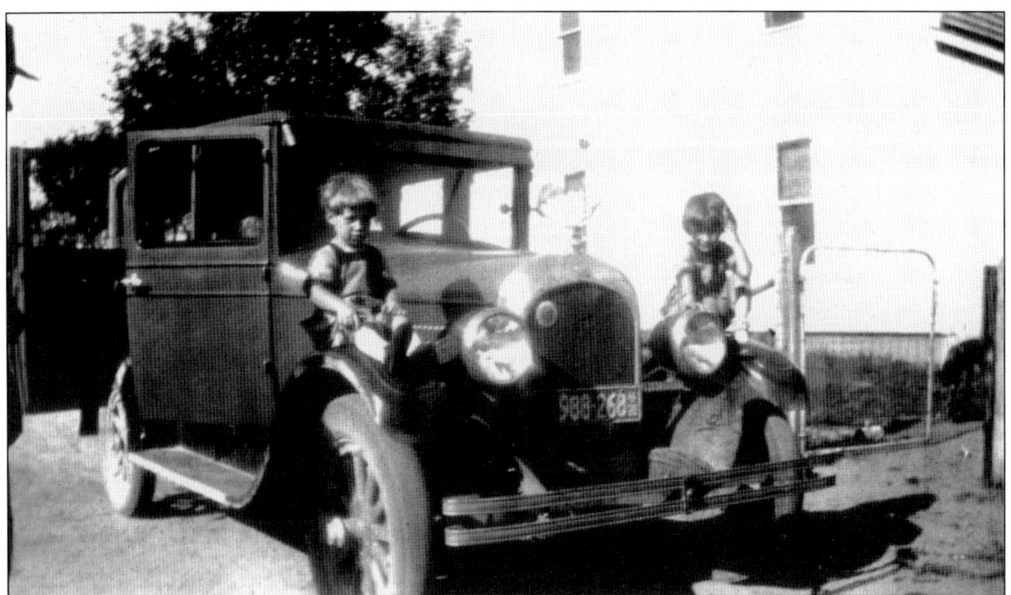

Beverly Wilcox and her sister Dorothy Wilcox (Clemens) pose for the camera in front of their Ottawa home at 1107 Poplar Street in 1928. (DC.)

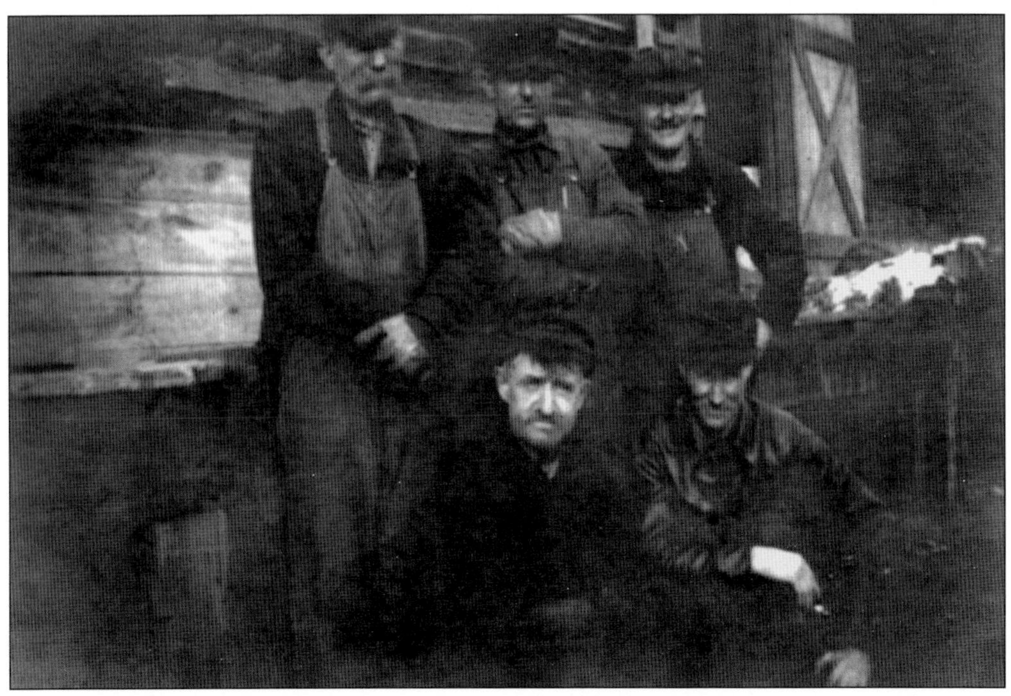

This candid photograph is a good, honest picture of hardworking Ottawa men in 1926. These men worked for Scherer's Ottawa Ice & Fuel Company. From left to right are (first row) John Barnhardt and Jim Shreve; (second row) Bill Saager, Archie Mattingly, and James Stalker. (DC.)

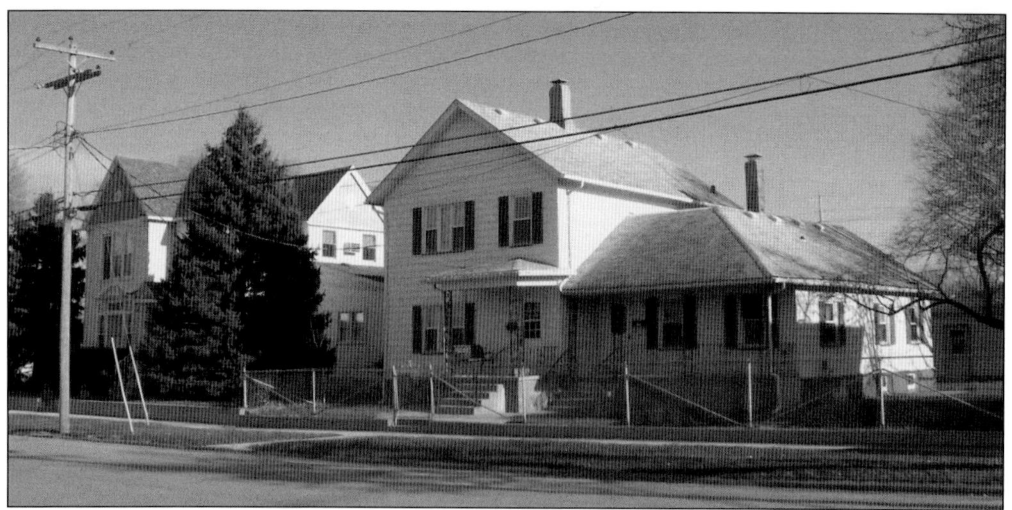

John Looney, a notorious gangster in the Roaring Twenties, was from Ottawa. Looney conducted his reign of terror in Rock Island. The 2001 movie *Road To Perdition*, starring Paul Newman and Tom Hanks, is loosely based on Looney's exploits in prostitution, bootlegging, gambling, auto theft, and extortion. Pictured above are the houses on Marquette Street in Ottawa where Looney lived as a child and the one he built for his wife. (JR.)

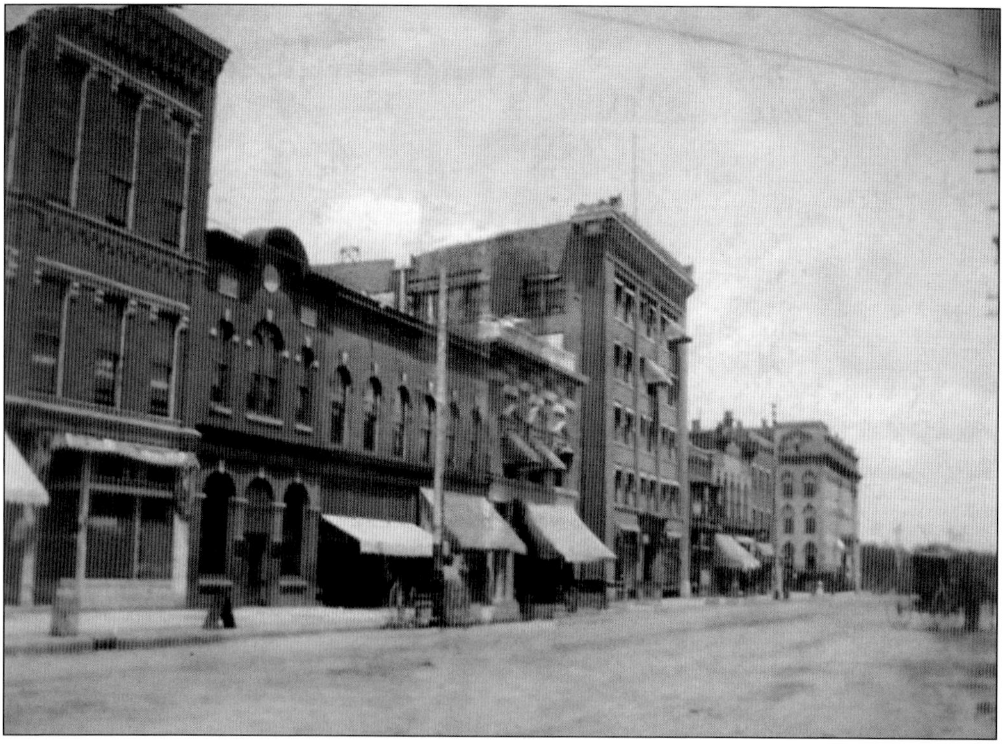

Looney continued his ties to Ottawa after moving to Rock Island. He was convicted of murder in 1926 and went to prison; he died in 1947. Looney's uncle was Maurice Maloney, an Irish immigrant who was elected Illinois attorney general in 1892 and mayor of Ottawa in 1899. He erected the Maloney Building (the tall structure in the middle) on Madison Street in 1900. In recent years, the building housed Little City Music. (JR.)

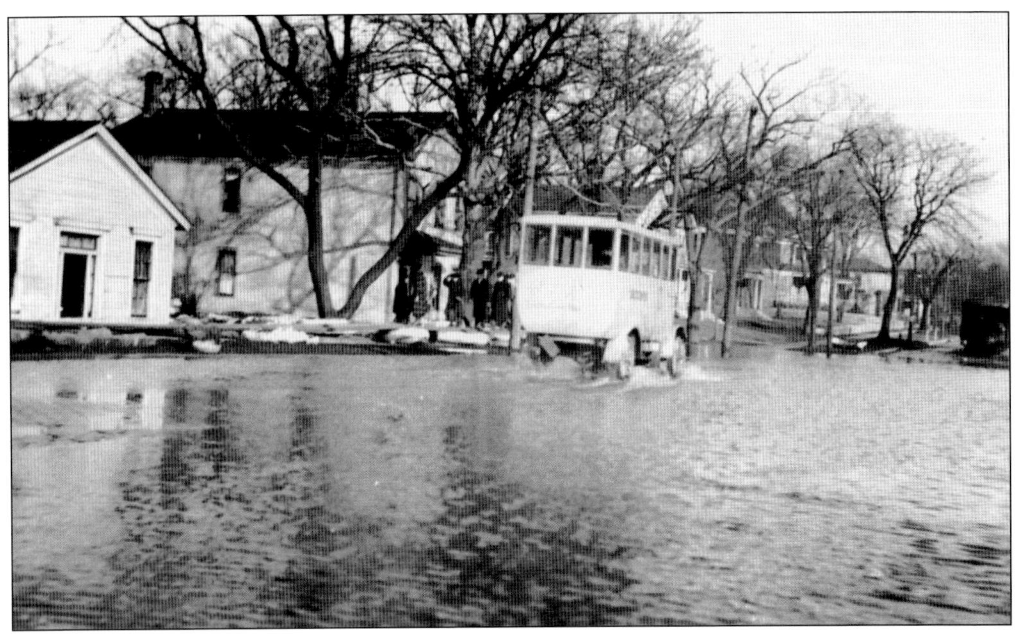

A river city always is prone to flooding, and Ottawa has seen its share of high waters. The photographs on this page are from a particularly bad flood on Ottawa's east side in January 1916. Pictured below is Ottawa Township High School, which had just been completed. The high school property has often been the victim of floodwaters. A flood in December 1982 caused more than $1 million in damage to the high school. (Both, JR.)

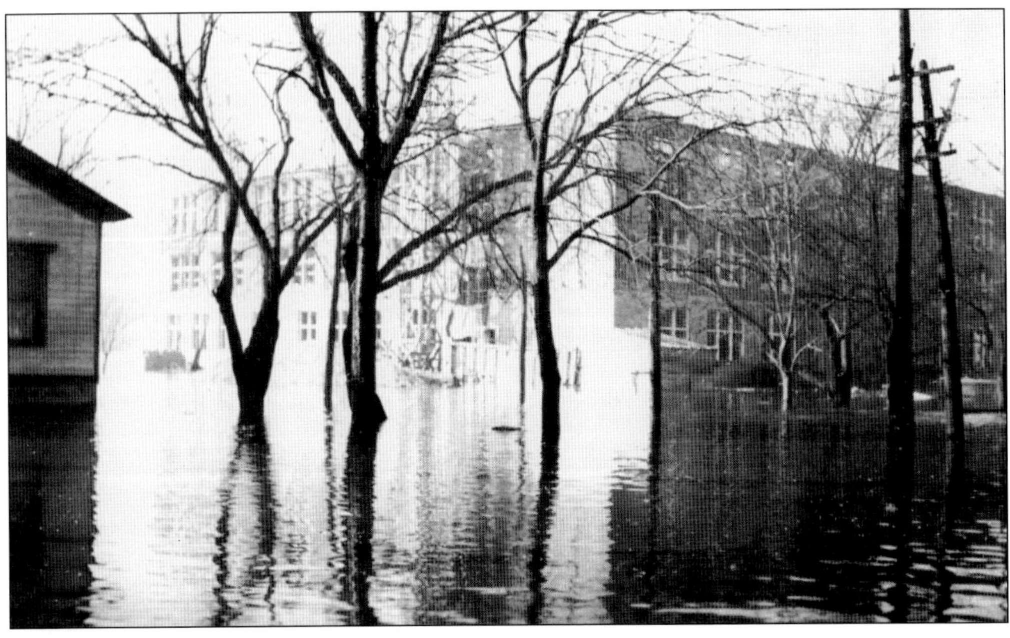

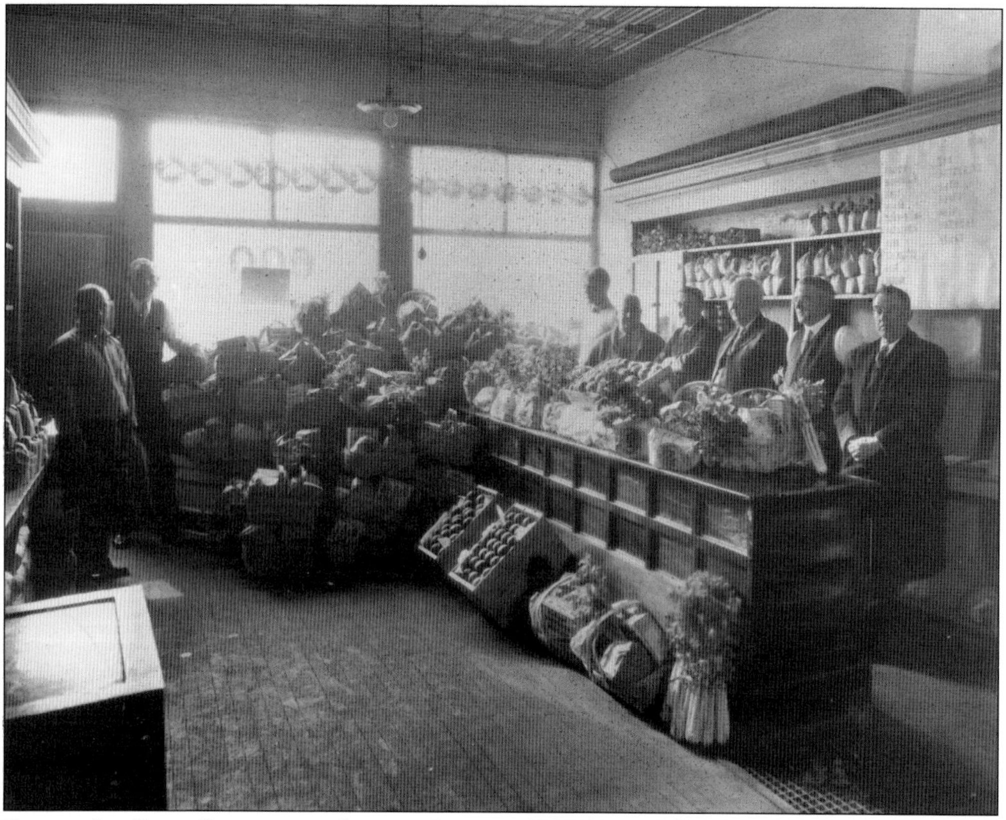

During the Great Depression, this storefront at 600 West Madison Street was known as the "commissary," where people on "relief" could get food and clothing. Below, unemployed men dig for coal in the I&M feeder canal. (Both, JR.)

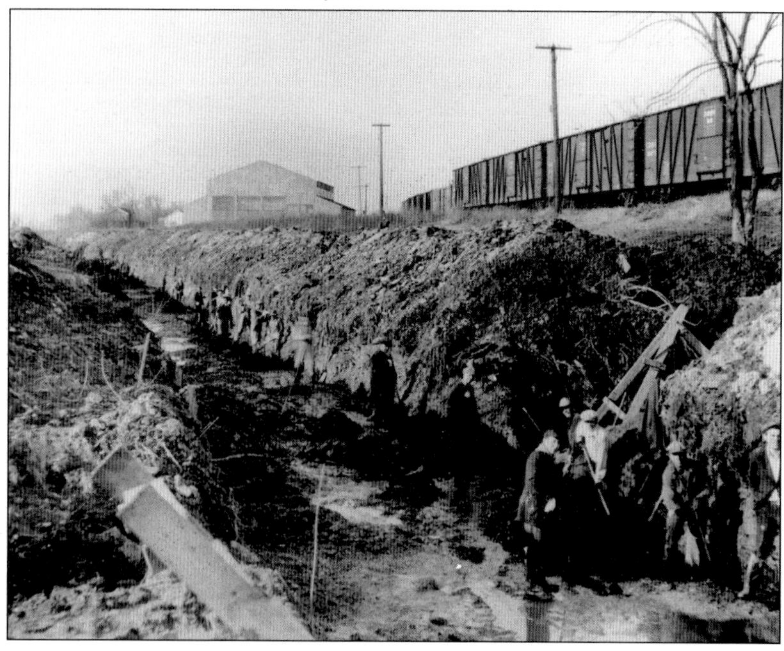

Two

People and Places

The men who built Ottawa were extraordinary individuals. Many of these men built magnificent mansions in Ottawa. The Ottawa Scouting Museum has presented programs on these "magnificent mansions" and is planning a book about these incredible houses. Many of the mansions are now gone.

One of Ottawa's extraordinary men was John Stuart Ryburn, who began practicing medicine in Ottawa in 1875. He died in 1892 before completing his work to establish the first hospital in Ottawa. His widow donated money in his name, and Ryburn Memorial Hospital opened in 1895. Industrialist Solomon King died in 1909 and left $50,000 for an annex to the hospital. It then became Ryburn-King Hospital, which served Ottawa until the present hospital replaced it in 1974.

William Reddick achieved wealth and political prominence. When he died in 1885, he left his mansion and a fortune to the city for a library, which served the community until a new library was built in 1974.

W.H.L. Wallace was a general in the Civil War. His father-in-law, T. Lyle Dickey, also fought in the war and was a prominent Ottawa lawyer. Both men were friends of Abraham Lincoln, and both men built beautiful mansions on Ottawa's north bluff.

Dickey was a justice on the Illinois Supreme Court from 1875 to 1885. Another Ottawan on the Supreme Court was John Dean Caton, who served from 1842 to 1864. Caton's mansion on the north bluff was magnificent.

Frederick Sherwood owned the Ottawa Opera House and was mayor of Ottawa from 1889 to 1891. He built a mansion that he later sold to W.D. Boyce, the man who founded the Boy Scouts of America.

Thomas D. Catlin was the president of both the United Glass Company and National City Bank, and he also served in numerous church and civic groups. His mansion and the mansions of Lorenzo Leland, John F. Nash, Solomon King, J.E. Porter, Lester Strawn, Jeremiah Strawn, Walter Strawn, Burton Cook, Maurice Moloney, Edward Swift, Vincent Duncan, John Anthony, Washington Bushnell, John Manley, M.H. Hollister, and Victor Peltier were among Ottawa's premier show places.

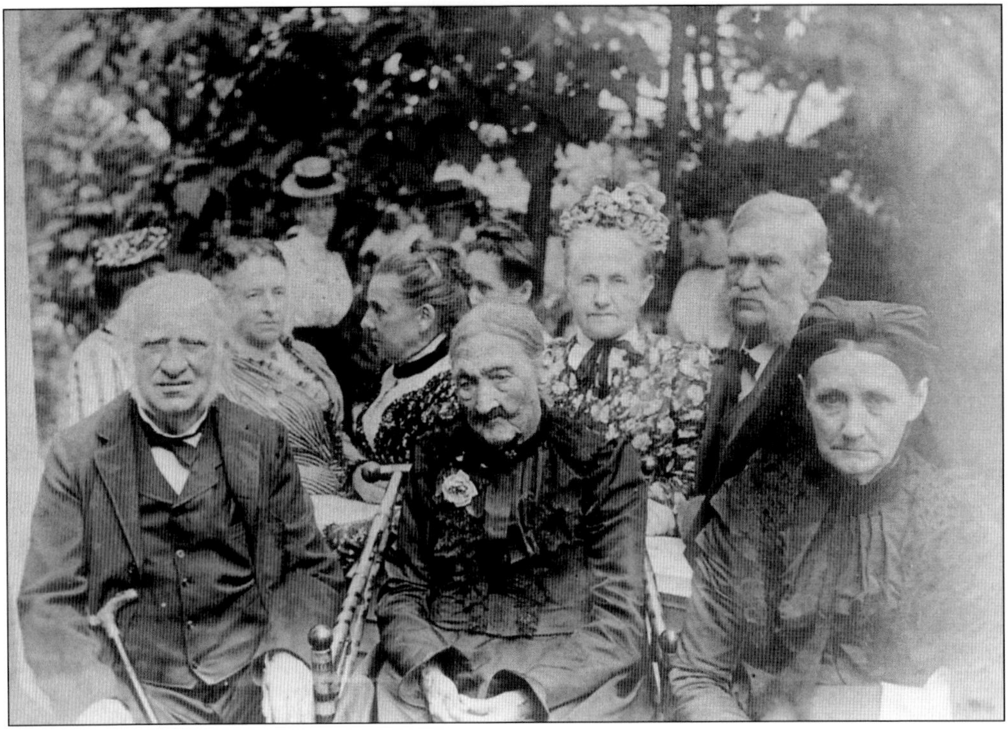

A family reunion was held at the J.E. Porter home at 222 West Prospect Avenue on April 23, 1900. The above picture shows a close-up of some of the old faces. (Both, JR.)

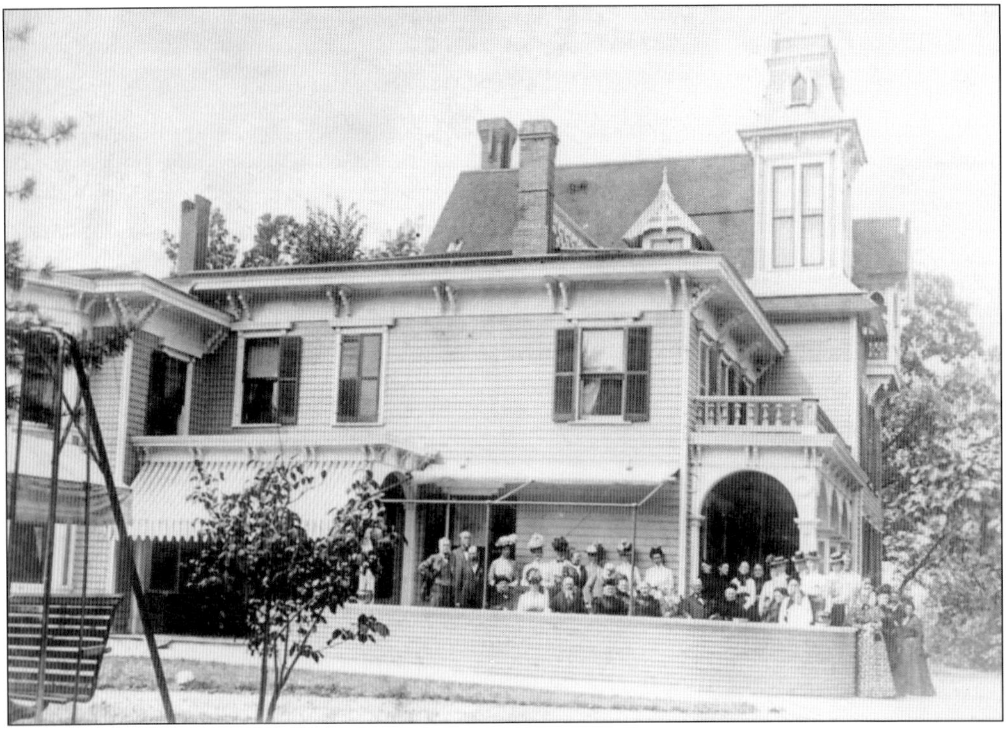

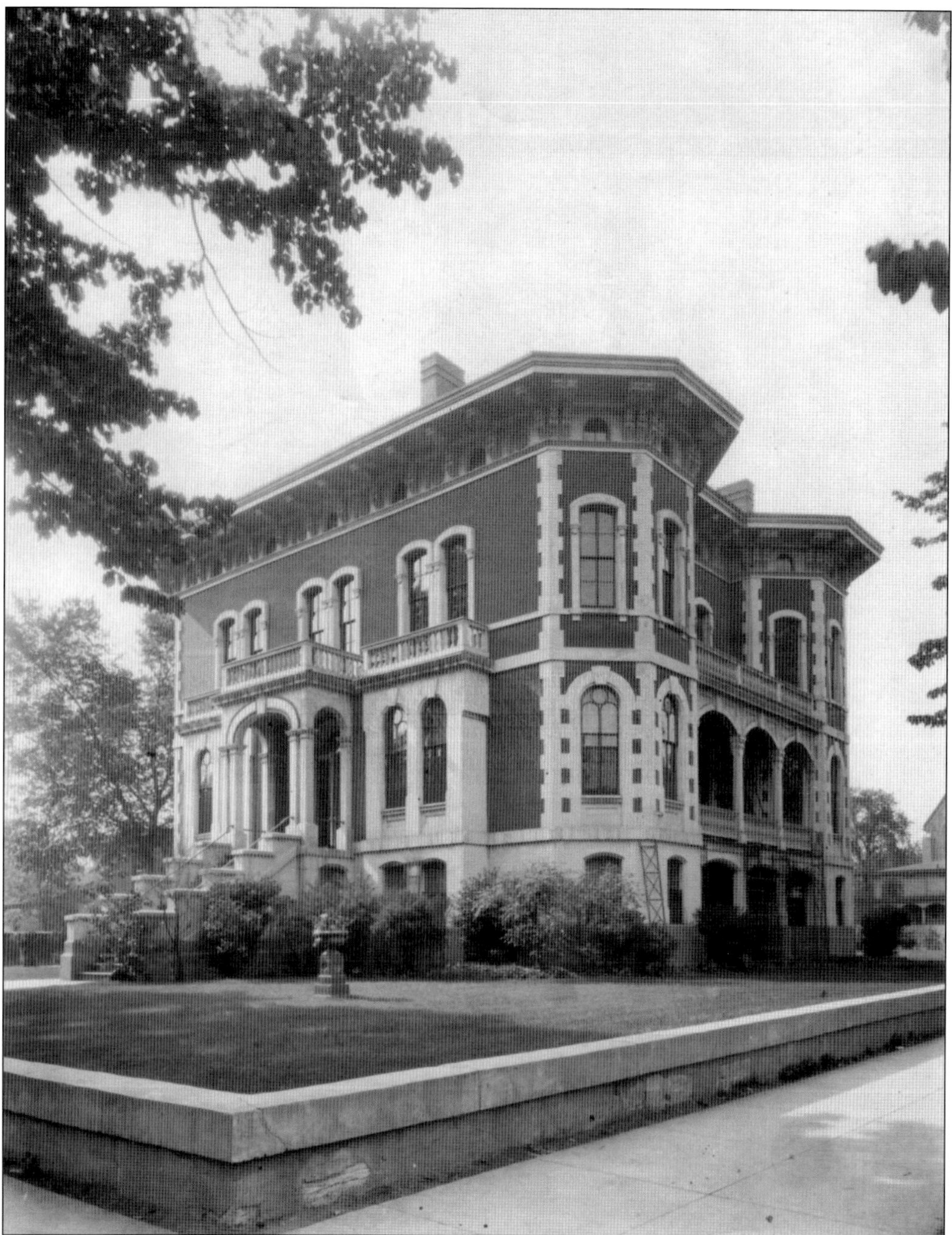

One of Ottawa's most magnificent buildings is Reddick Mansion, on Lafayette Street at Columbus Street (pictured above in the 1930s). It was built between 1856 and 1859 by William Reddick, an Irish immigrant who became sheriff and a state senator. Reddick died in 1885 and left his home, his large book collection, and money to the city to establish a library. This building served as Ottawa's library until 1974, when a new library was constructed on Canal Street. Today, Reddick Mansion is home to the Ottawa Visitors Center. (JR.)

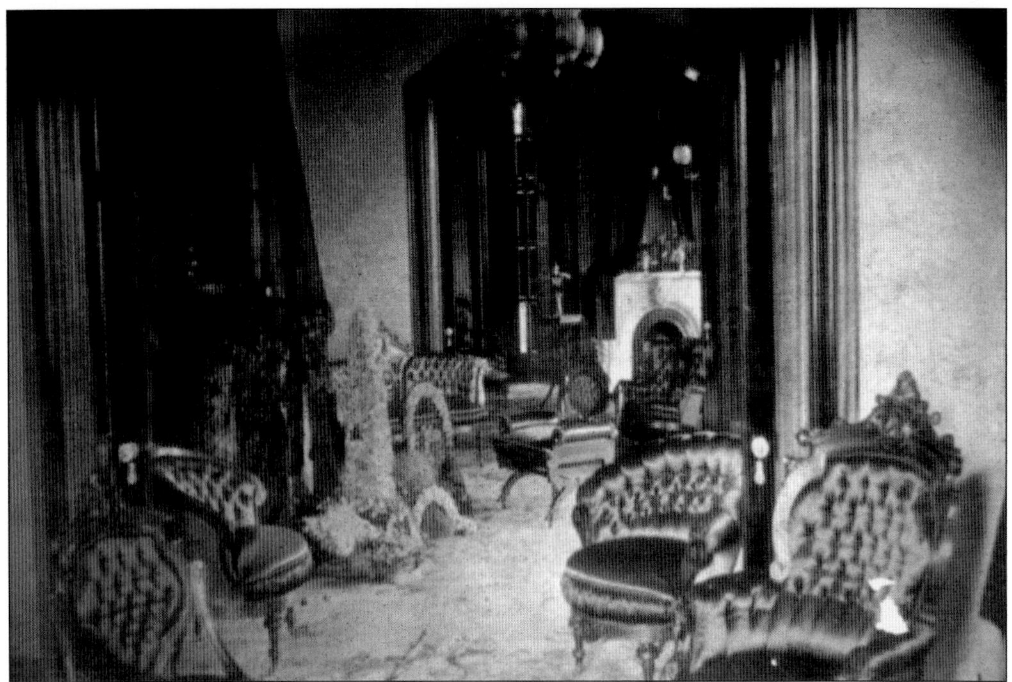

The view above shows a room in Reddick's 22-room mansion in the late 1880s, not long after his death. The photograph below is from the 1960s. Southeast of Ottawa, in Kankakee County, the village of Reddick was named for William Reddick. (Both, DC.)

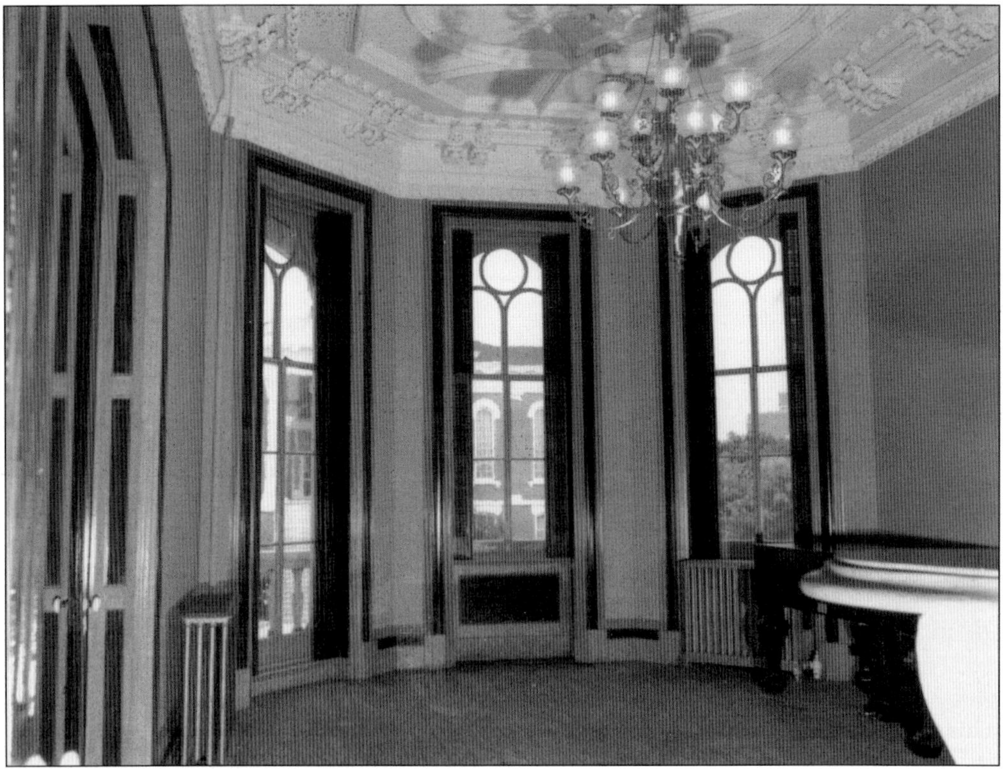

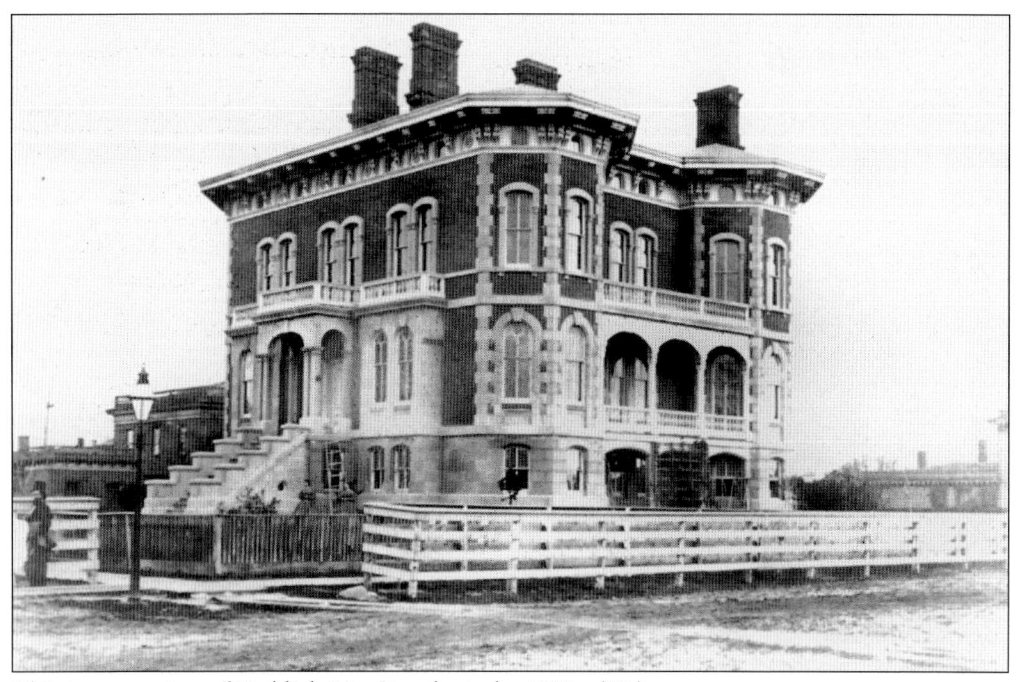

This is a rare view of Reddick Mansion from the 1870s. (JR.)

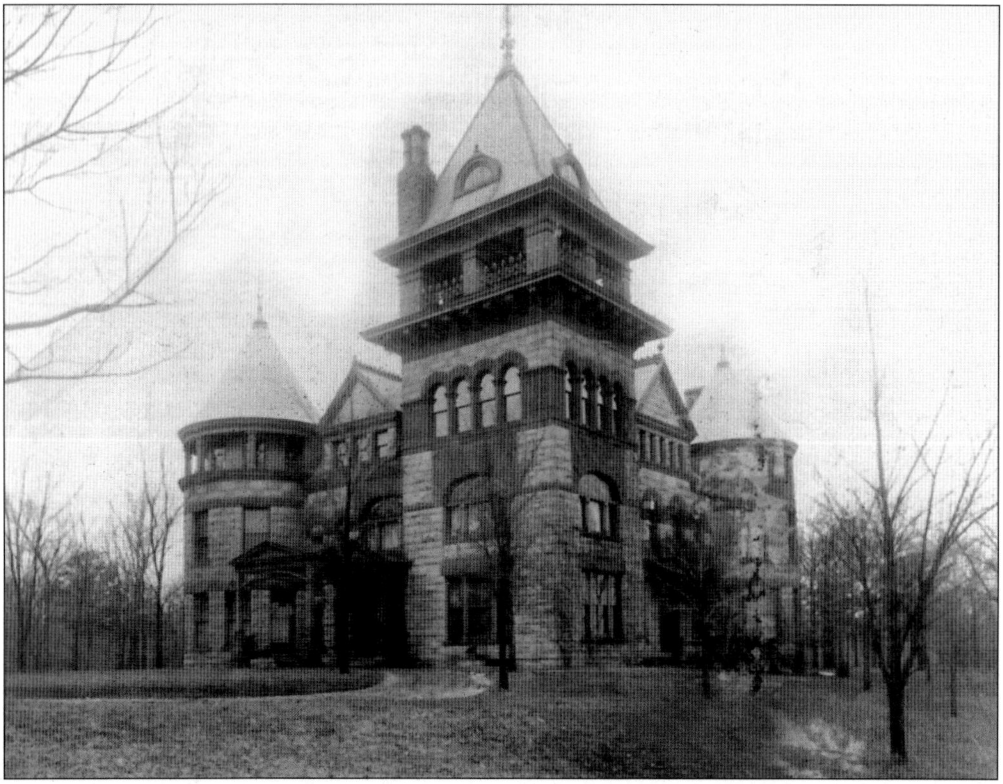

This mansion on the north bluff was built by Frederick Sherwood in the 1890s. He sold the house to W.D. Boyce in 1903. The mansion burned down in 1908. (JR.)

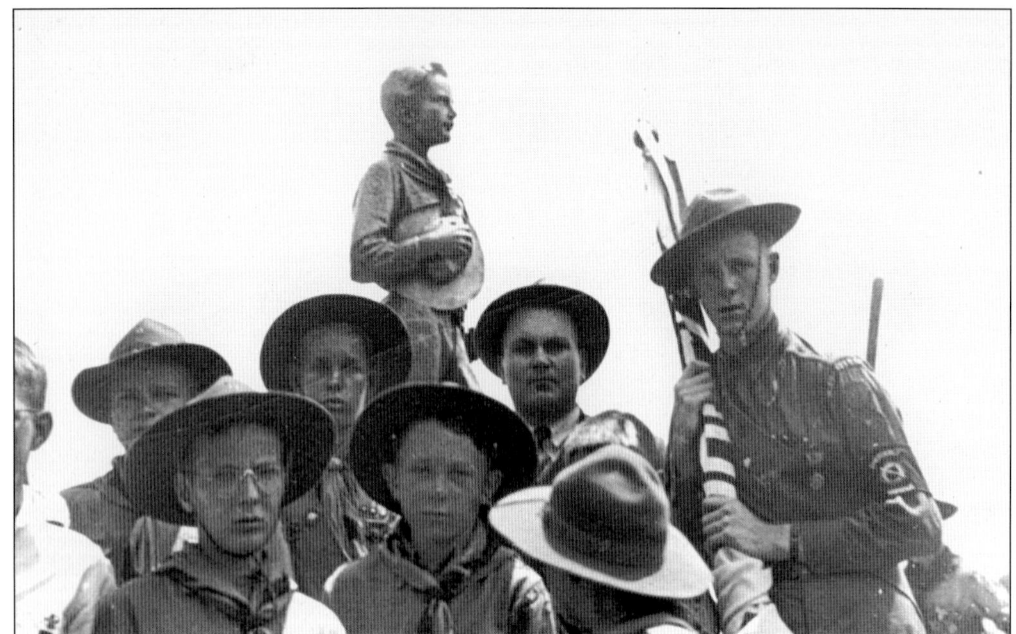

Ottawa was the home of William Dickson Boyce, who founded the Boy Scouts of America in 1910. In the above picture, Boy Scouts and leaders from all across the country are gathered on June 21, 1941, for the dedication of the Boy Scout memorial statue in Ottawa Avenue Cemetery, near Boyce's grave. In the picture below, Boy Scouts march in the Ottawa centennial parade in 1931. The Ottawa Scouting Museum opened in 1997 at 1100 Canal Street. (Both, Ottawa Scouting Museum.)

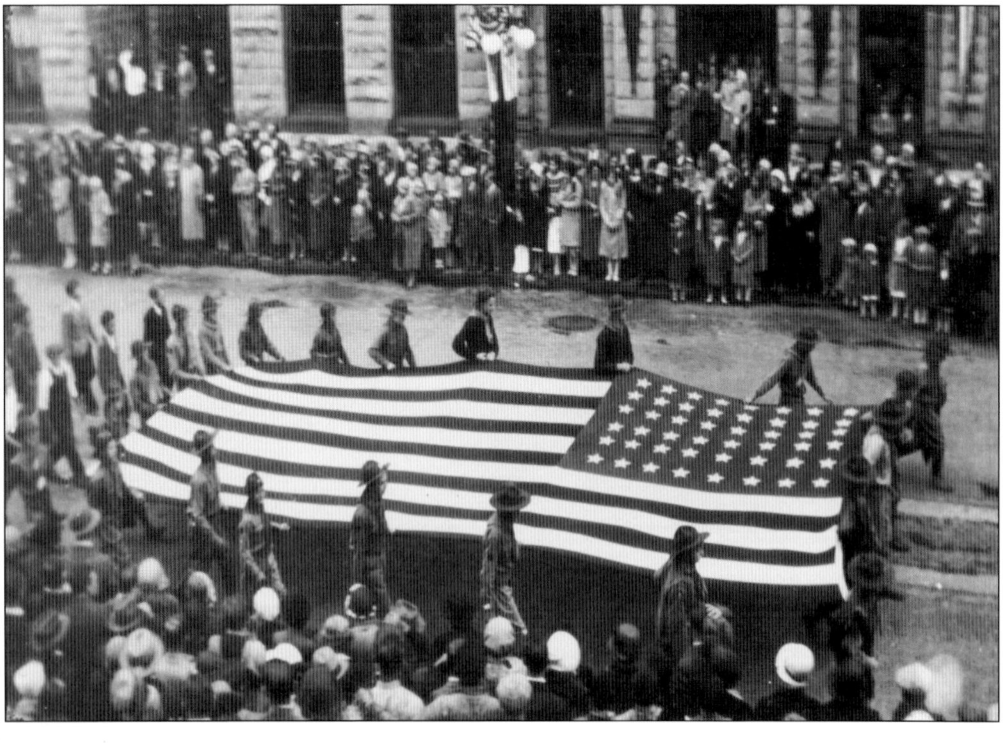

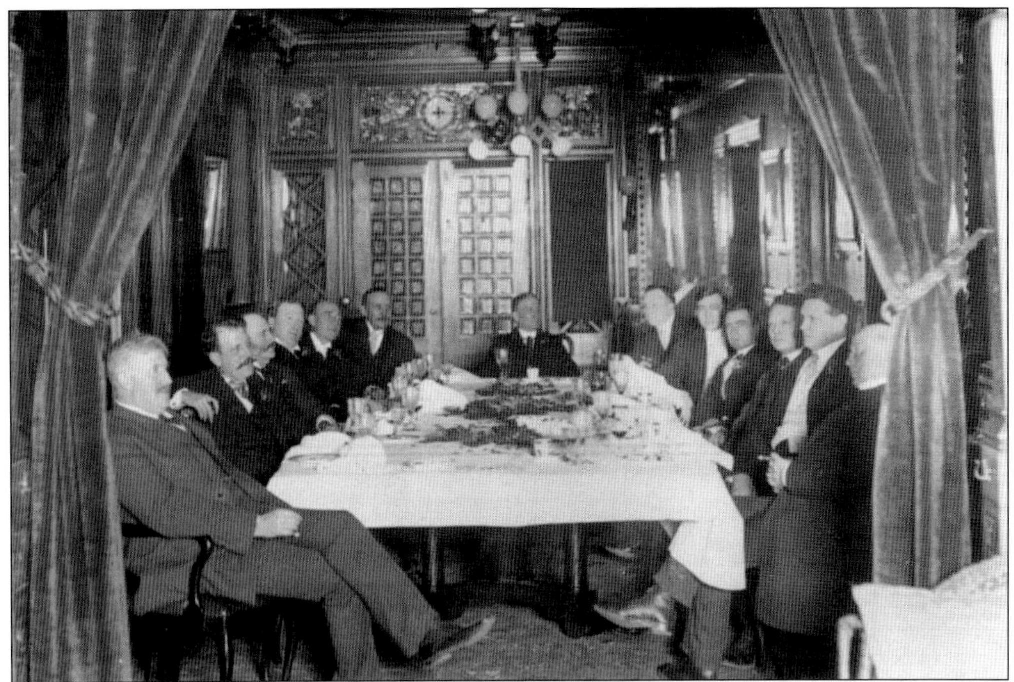

W.D. Boyce (far left in the above picture) frequently entertained guests in his Ottawa mansion. These pictures are from 1905. There were probably not any merit badges given to the men and women for smoking a hookah pipe, as pictured below. (Both, JR.)

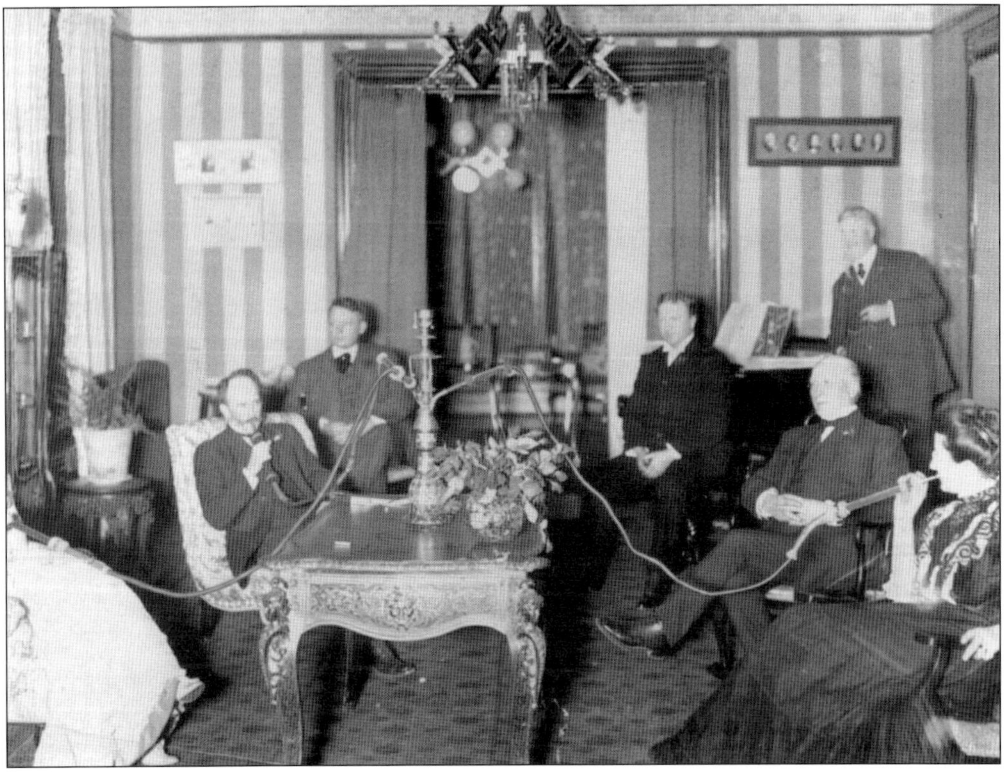

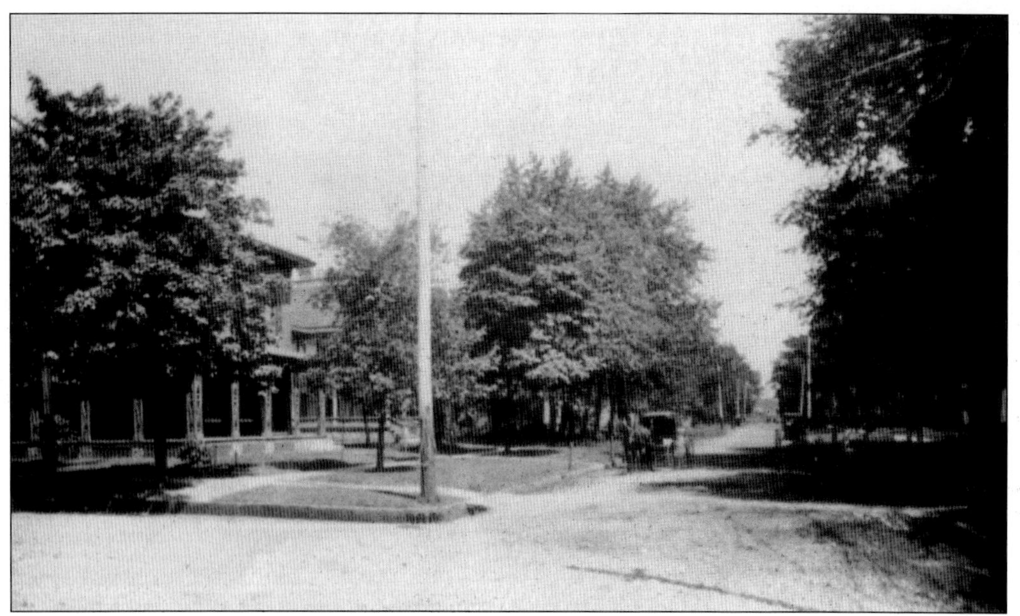

The beautifully illustrated *Art Work: Ottawa and Vicinity*, published in 1893, had this view of Paul Street, looking north from Jackson Street. (JR.)

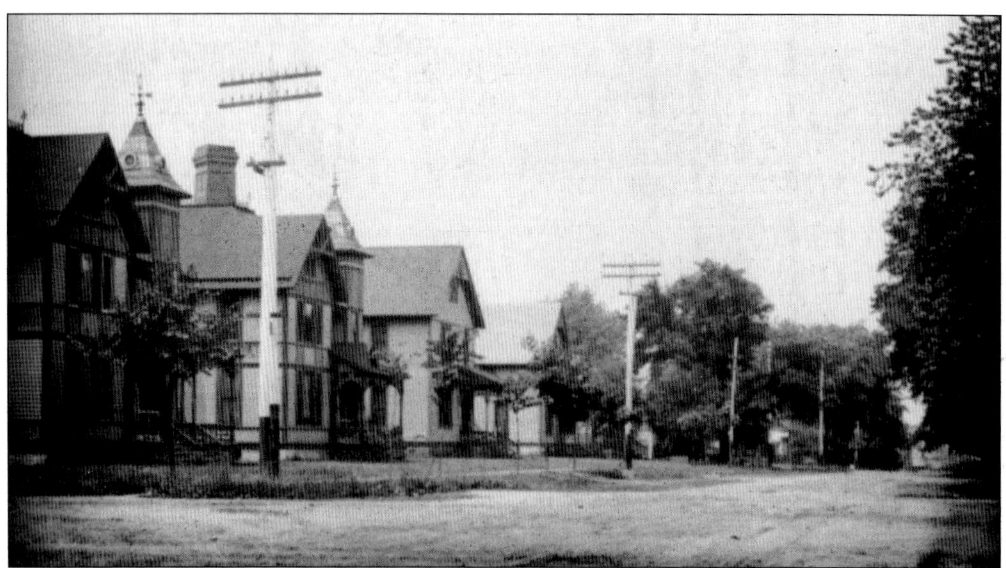

This 1893 view shows Pearl Street in Ottawa, looking west. (JR.)

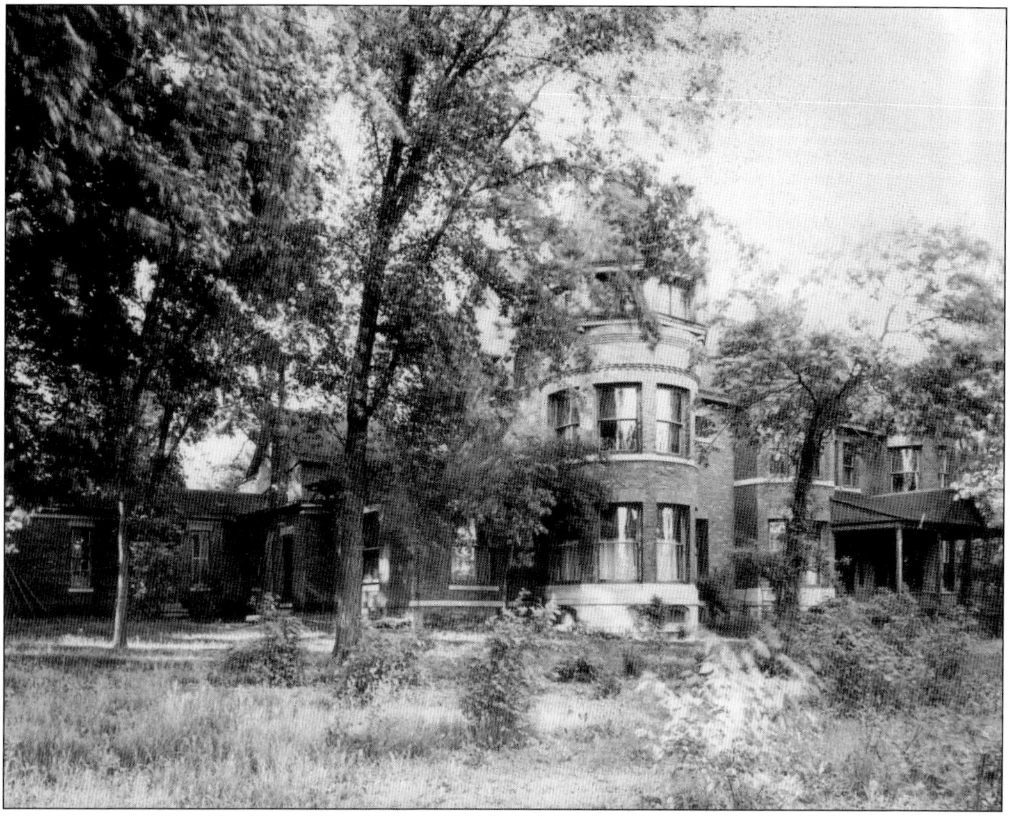

The once proud mansion of Delia Field, wife of Marshall Field III, on Caton Road is now gone. Delia was the daughter-in-law of Ottawa judge and Illinois Supreme Court justice John Dean Caton. (JR.)

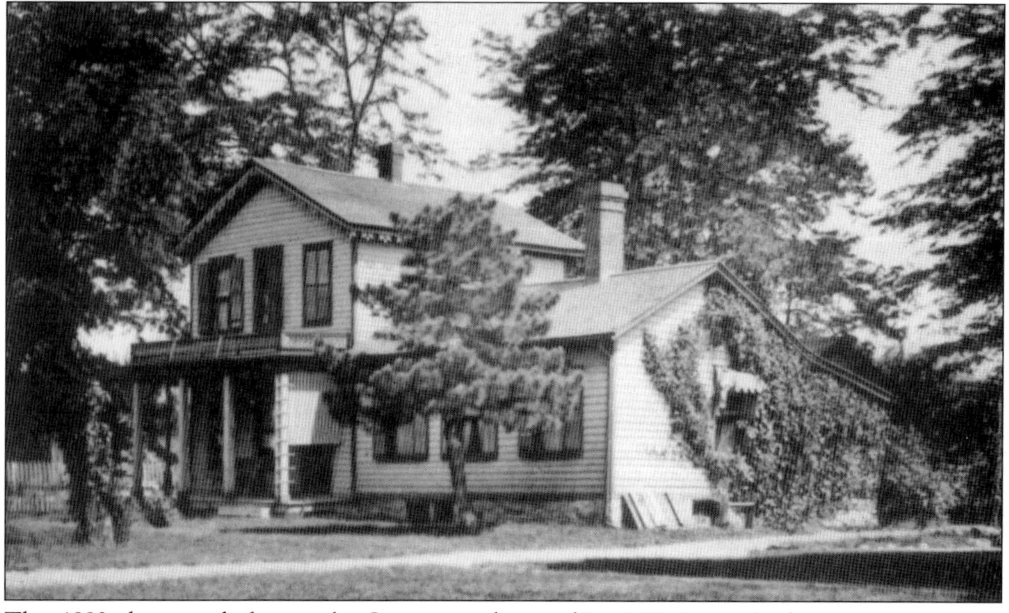

This 1893 photograph depicts the Ottawa residence of Dr. E.W. Weiss. (JR.)

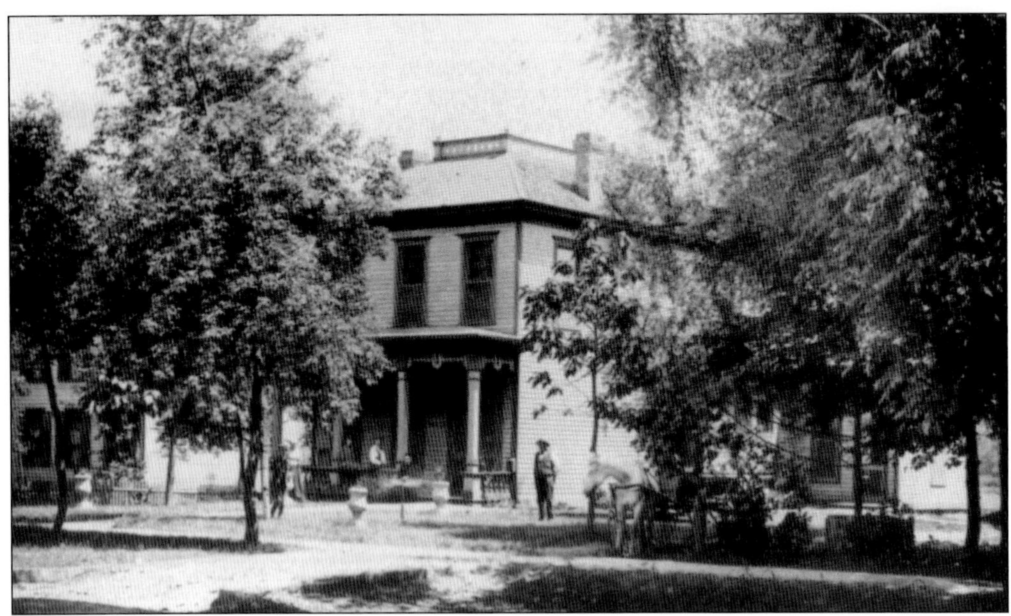

This was the house of W.H. Gilman, at 525 East Main Street, as seen in 1893. (JR.)

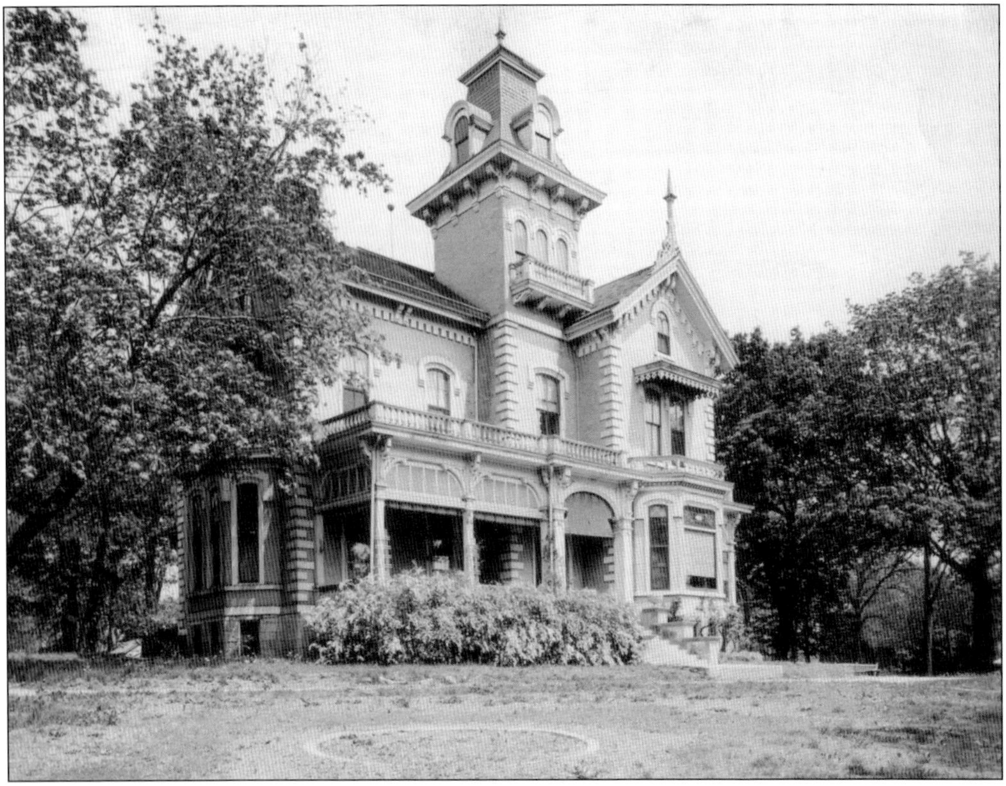

The Lorenzo Leland mansion was on the north bluff of Ottawa. Leland was clerk of the Supreme Court. The house is now gone. (JR.)

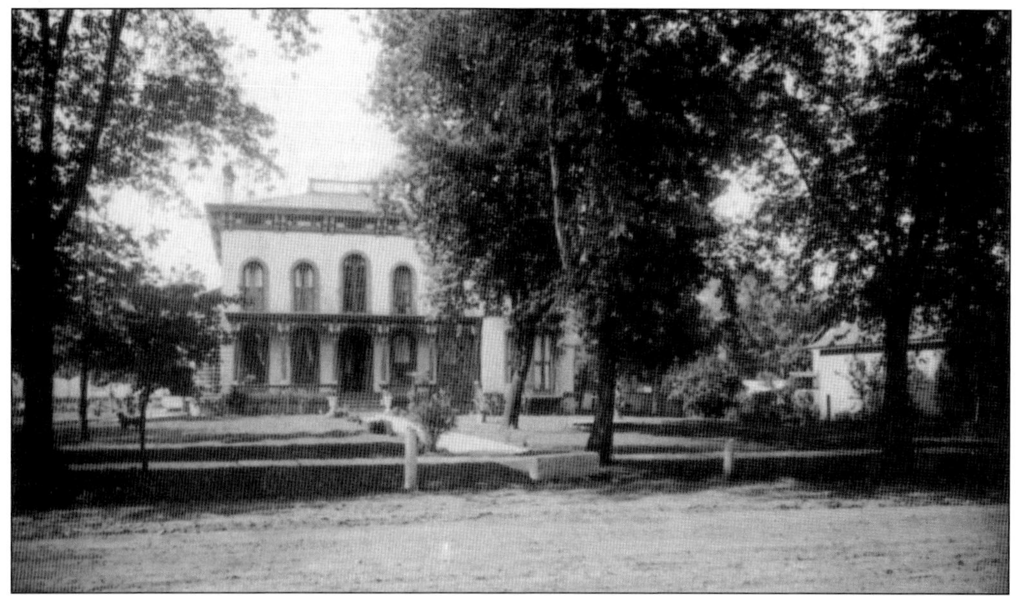

The home of Washington and Phoebe Bushnell, at 616 East Pearl Street, was photographed in 1893. Washington Bushnell was attorney general of Illinois. The house was built in 1872 and originally had 33 rooms and six baths. (JR.)

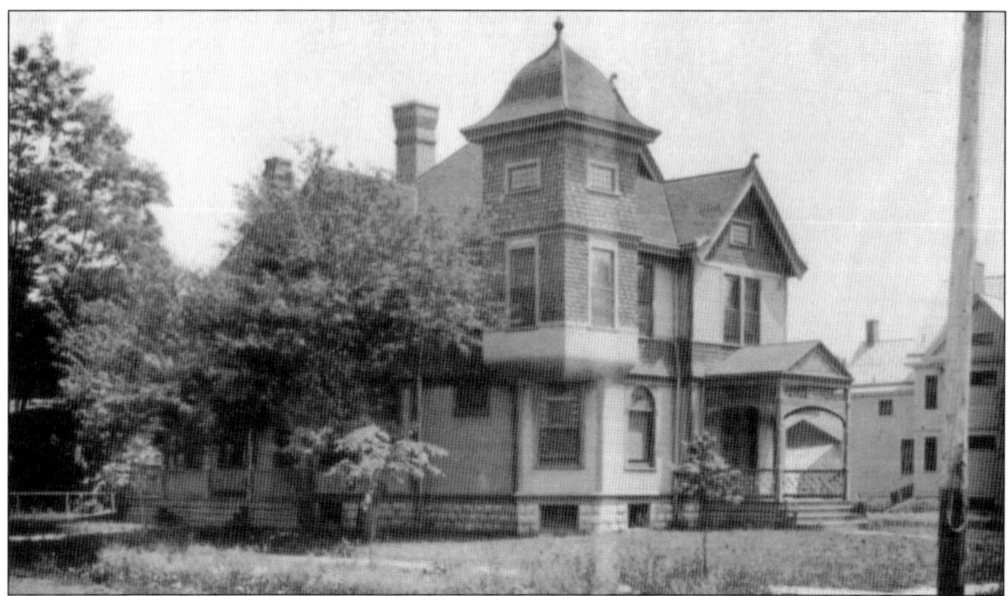

The Green family lived here in 1893. (JR.)

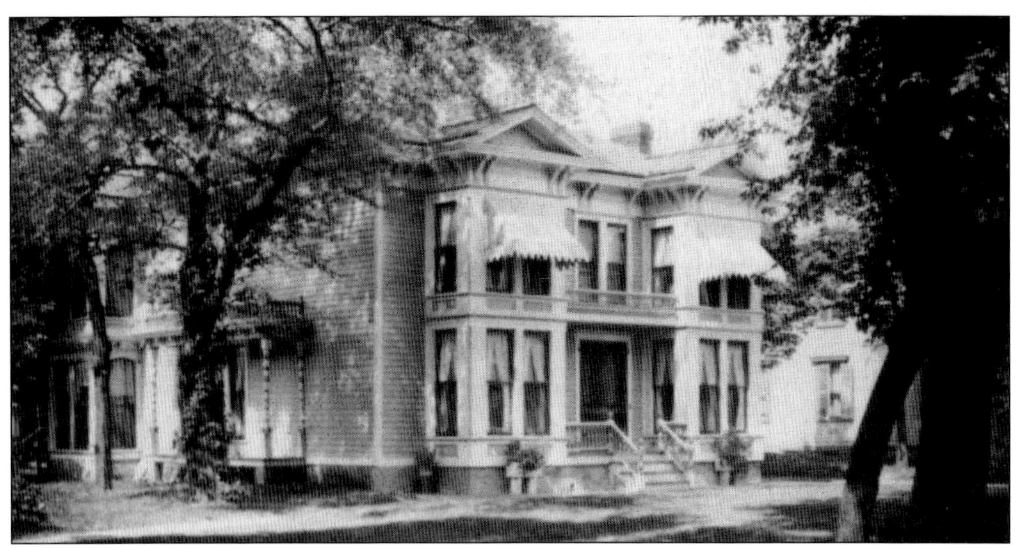

This is an 1893 view of the home of Andrew Lynch, at 304 Congress Street. Lynch owned a boot shop and dry goods store at 121–125 West Main Street. (JR.)

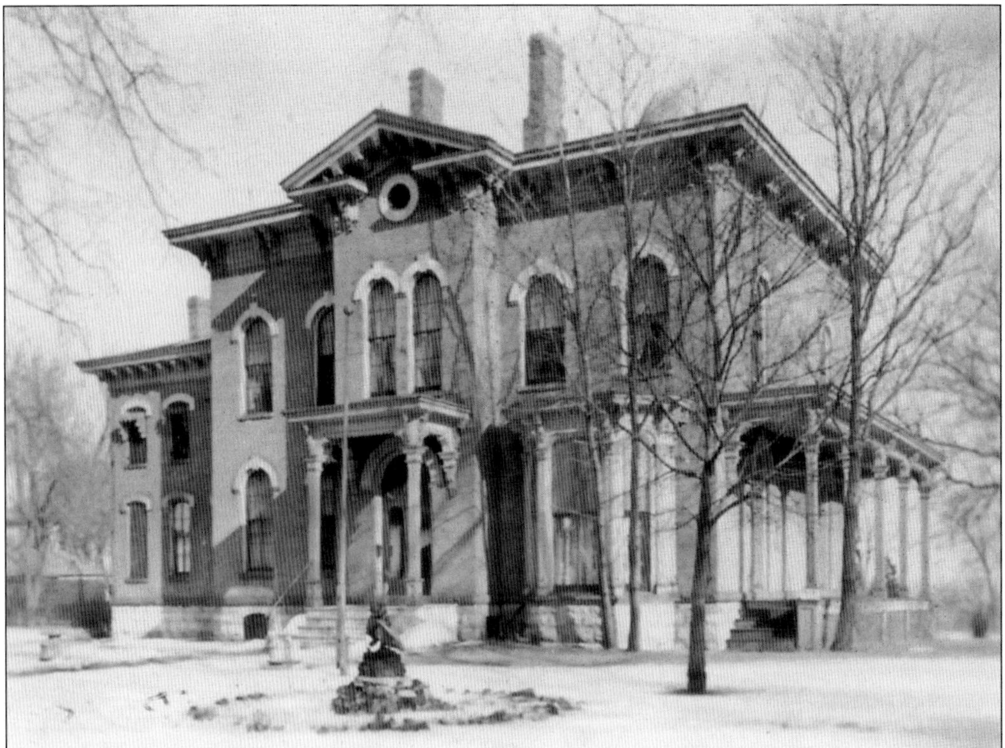

The house of Congressman Burton Cook, at 902 Paul Street, is now gone, replaced by the Doughtery high rise building. Cook held Lincoln's coat at the 1858 debate in Ottawa and gave the speech renominating Lincoln in 1864. (JR.)

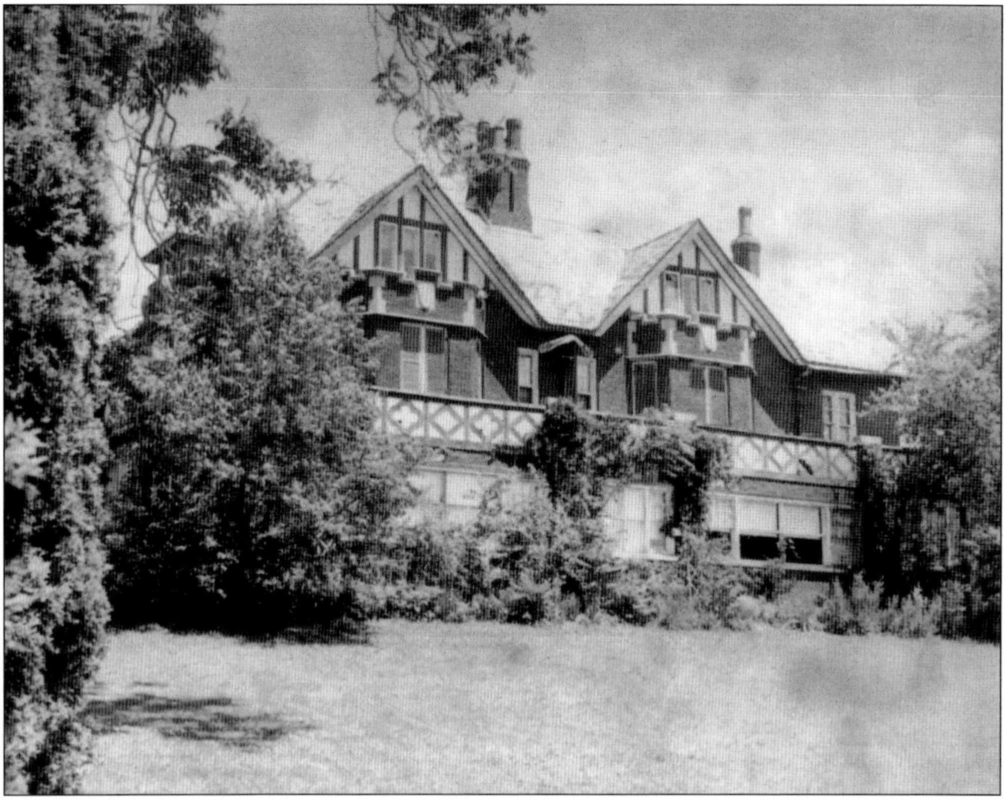

Reynolds Manor was a fabulously decorated house on Ottawa's north bluff. Dr. H.J. Reynolds renovated it into 15 apartments in the 1940s as "luxury havens for socialites." His second wife, Elfrieda Nolan, an eccentric artist, painted scenes on walls throughout the house. The house was razed in 1997. (JR.)

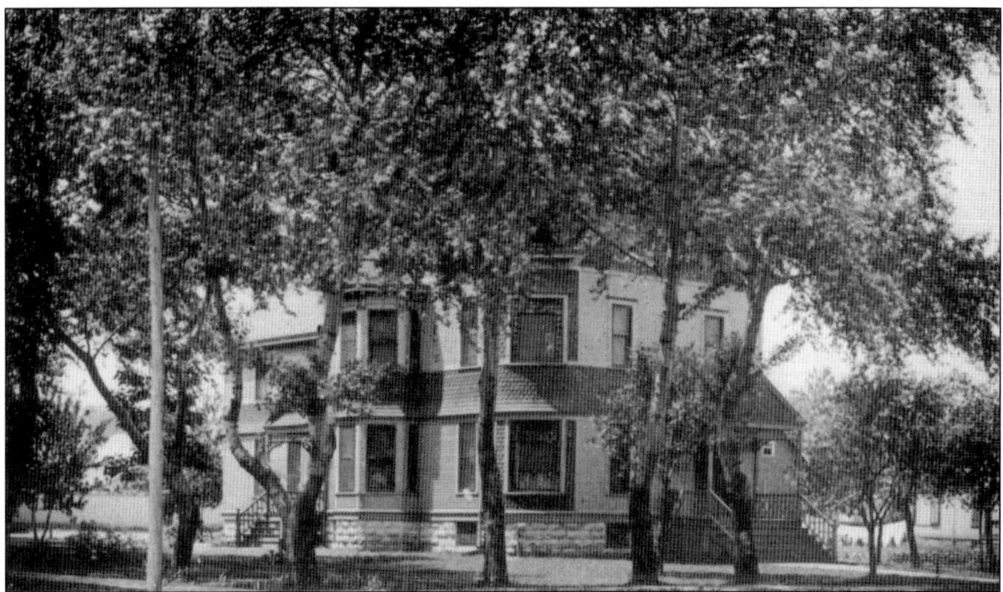

This is the home of C.D. DeLapp, at 400 North Fillmore Street, as seen in 1893. (JR.)

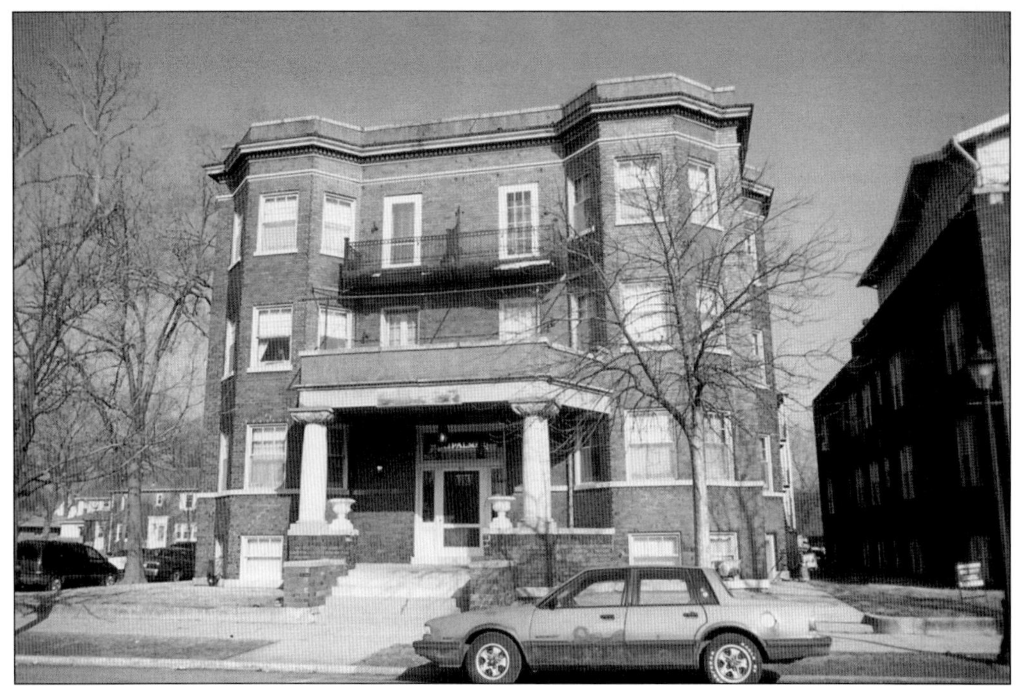

The Palmer Apartments (above) on Columbus Street was Ottawa's finest apartment building when it was constructed. The Masonic Temple (below) was built in 1910 on Columbus Street, across from Washington Square Park. The Masons came to Ottawa in 1840, and a lodge was chartered in 1846. (Both, JR.)

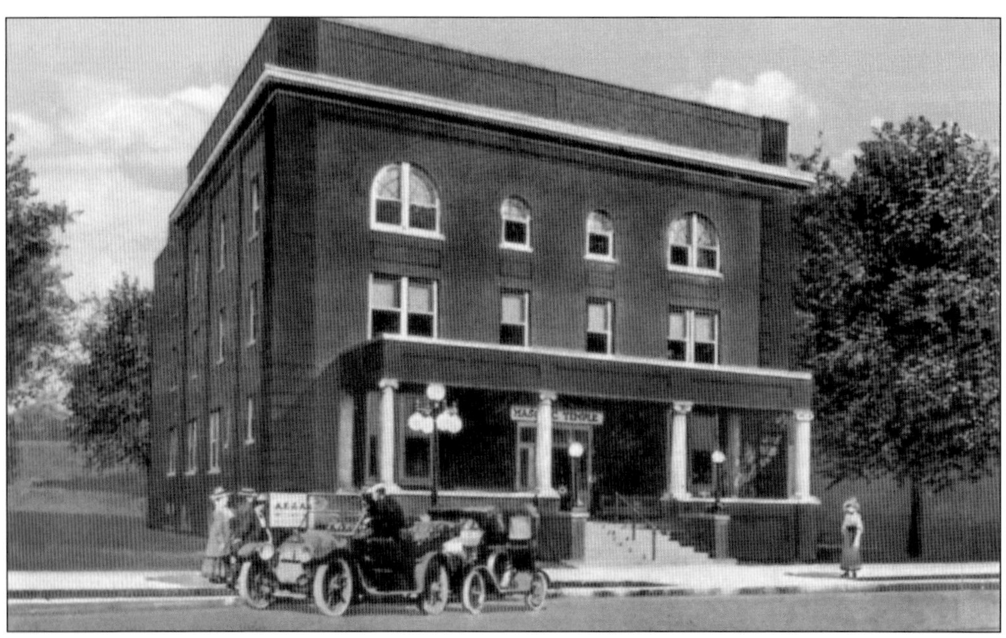

Three

Churches and Schools

The number of churches in Ottawa testifies to the religious commitment of its citizens. Missionaries were conducting worship services here as early as 1823, when the first settlers began arriving. Many of Ottawa's largest churches trace their beginnings back more than a century: First United Methodist in 1832, Christ Episcopal in 1837, First Congregational in 1839, First Baptist in 1841, St. Columba in 1841, Evangelical United Methodist in 1864, Epworth Methodist in 1853, St. Francis in 1859, Zion Lutheran in 1860, First Presbyterian in 1868, Trinity Lutheran in 1892, and St. Patrick's in 1893.

The education of young children also began early. A school district was established in 1855, and two large schools were built in the 1860s—Columbus School (on the site of today's Masonic Temple) and Lincoln School (at Madison and Clay Streets). A few years later, several schools were added—Franklin School (Erie and Superior Streets), Washington School (York and Congress Streets), Jefferson School (Columbus and DeLeon Streets), Lincoln School (Madison and Sanger Streets), and Shabbona School (Glover and State Streets).

By the end of the century, there was a need to replace the schools with larger buildings, and Lincoln School was replaced in 1898, Washington School in 1905, Jefferson School in 1910, and Shabbona School in 1912, all on their former sites. Columbus School was built in 1905 on Guion Street.

In the 1950s, McKinley School and Central School were added. Shepherd Junior High was built in 1969. Washington, Columbus, and Shabbona were closed and razed in the 1970s.

Ottawa's high school building burned in 1876. Two years later, school resumed when the township took over the duties. A large high school building was constructed on Columbus Street in 1879. When there was a need for bigger facilities, the present high school building on East Main Street was constructed in 1916. Major additions were made in 1932, 1962, 1976, and 2004.

Marquette High School got its start in 1857, when the Sisters of Mercy founded St. Xavier's Academy and St. Joseph's Convent. A school was built in 1889, and it burned in 1900. A new building was constructed in 1901. The school added a wing in 1949, which has since been expanded to replace the old building. The school changed its name to Marquette in 1949.

As far as higher education, Brown's Business College operated from 1888 to 1930, and Pleasant View Luther College from 1896 to 1936.

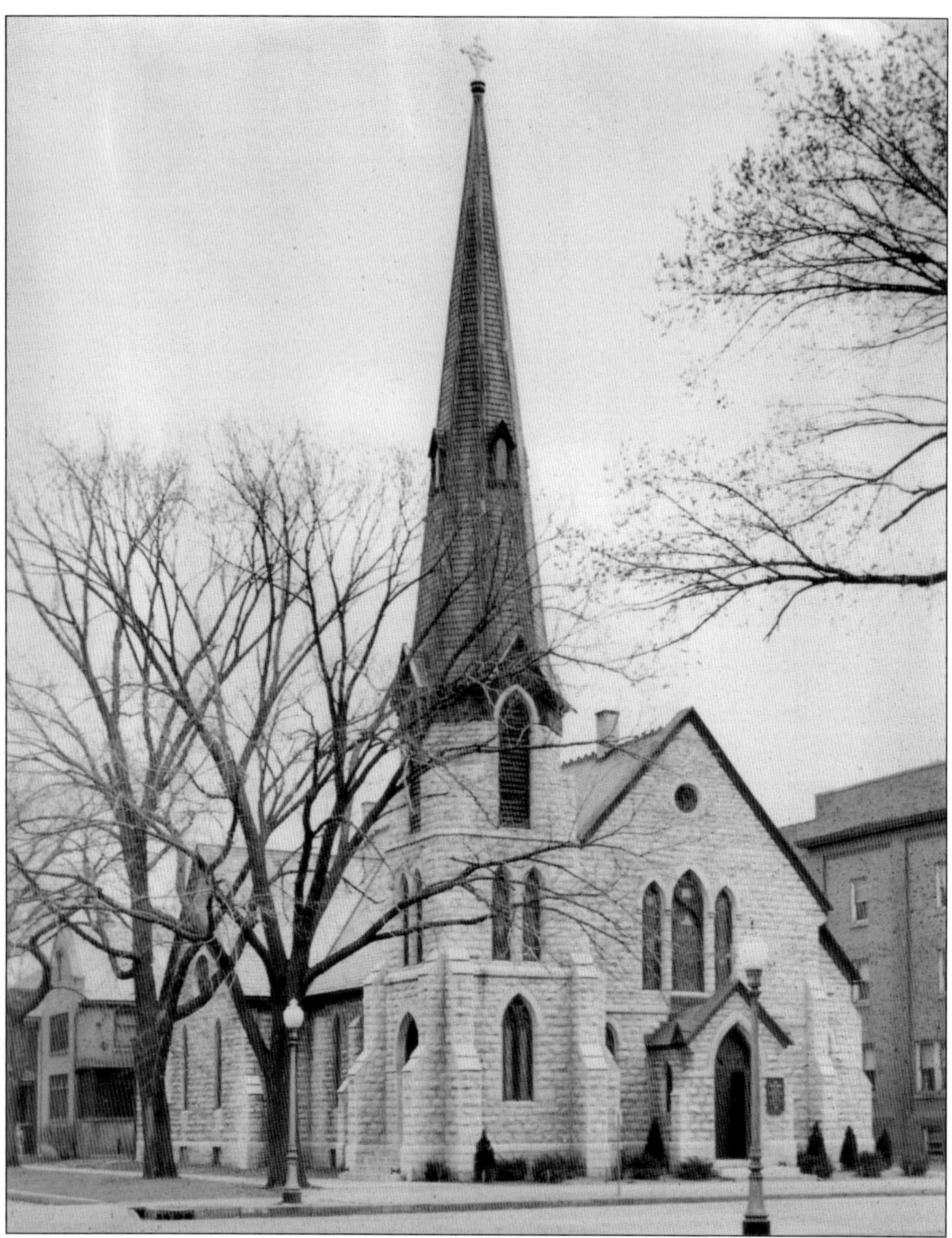

Christ Episcopal Church of Ottawa was founded in 1837. Worshippers met in several locations until the present church was built in 1871 on Columbus Street at Lafayette Street. The style was Gothic, and the material was Joliet limestone. Inside are many beautiful painted glass windows. One is in memory of Civil War general W.H.L. Wallace, made in 1872 by famed German artist Julius Hubner. It is the only work by Hubner in the United States. Several large panels show the resurrection of Christ, while a smaller panel shows the life of General Wallace. It is considered one of Ottawa's treasures. (JR.)

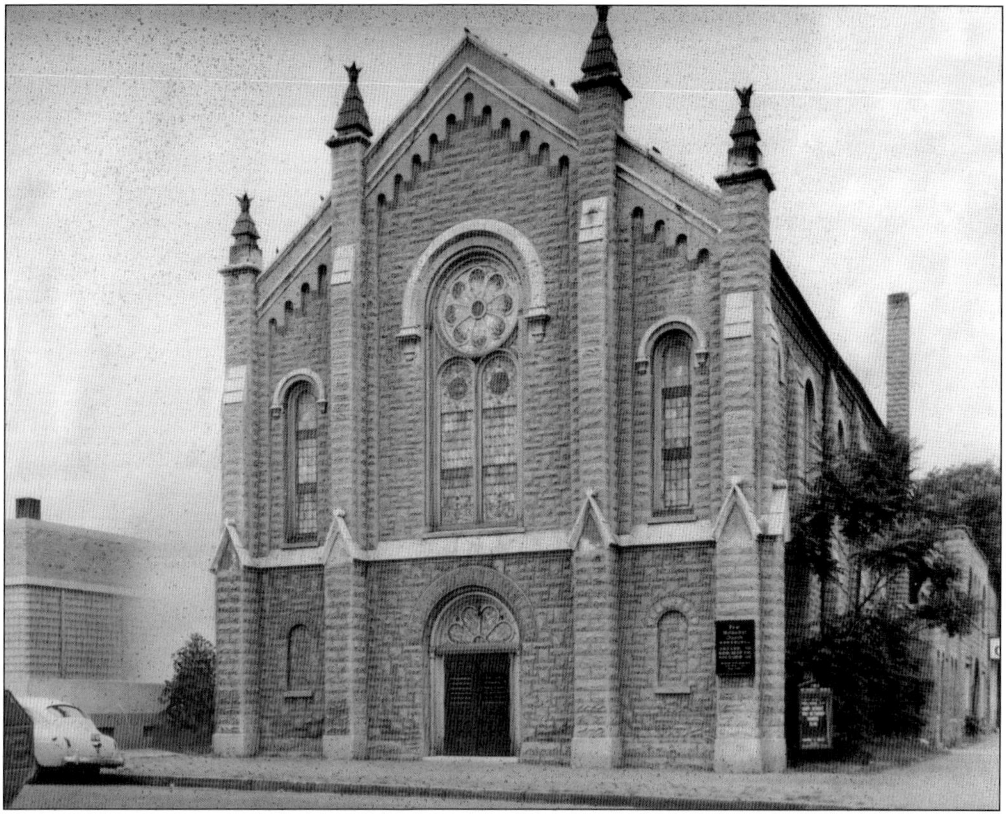

First Methodist Church started in Ottawa in 1833. The present building (above) was constructed in 1866. The picture below shows a streetcar bringing crowds to the Rock River religious conference at the church on October 5, 1889. (Both, JR.)

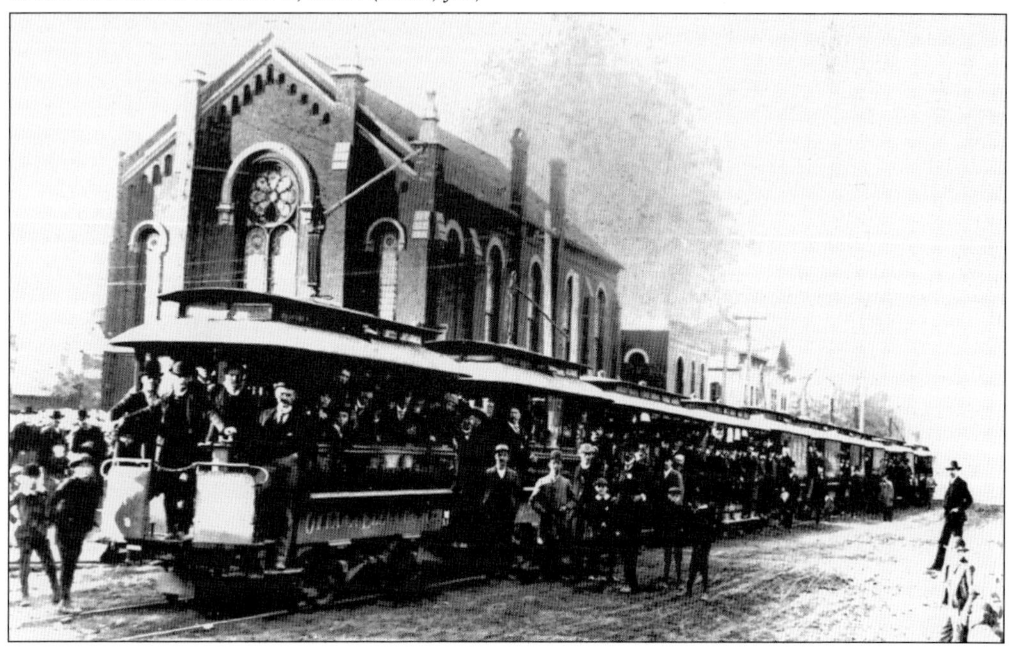

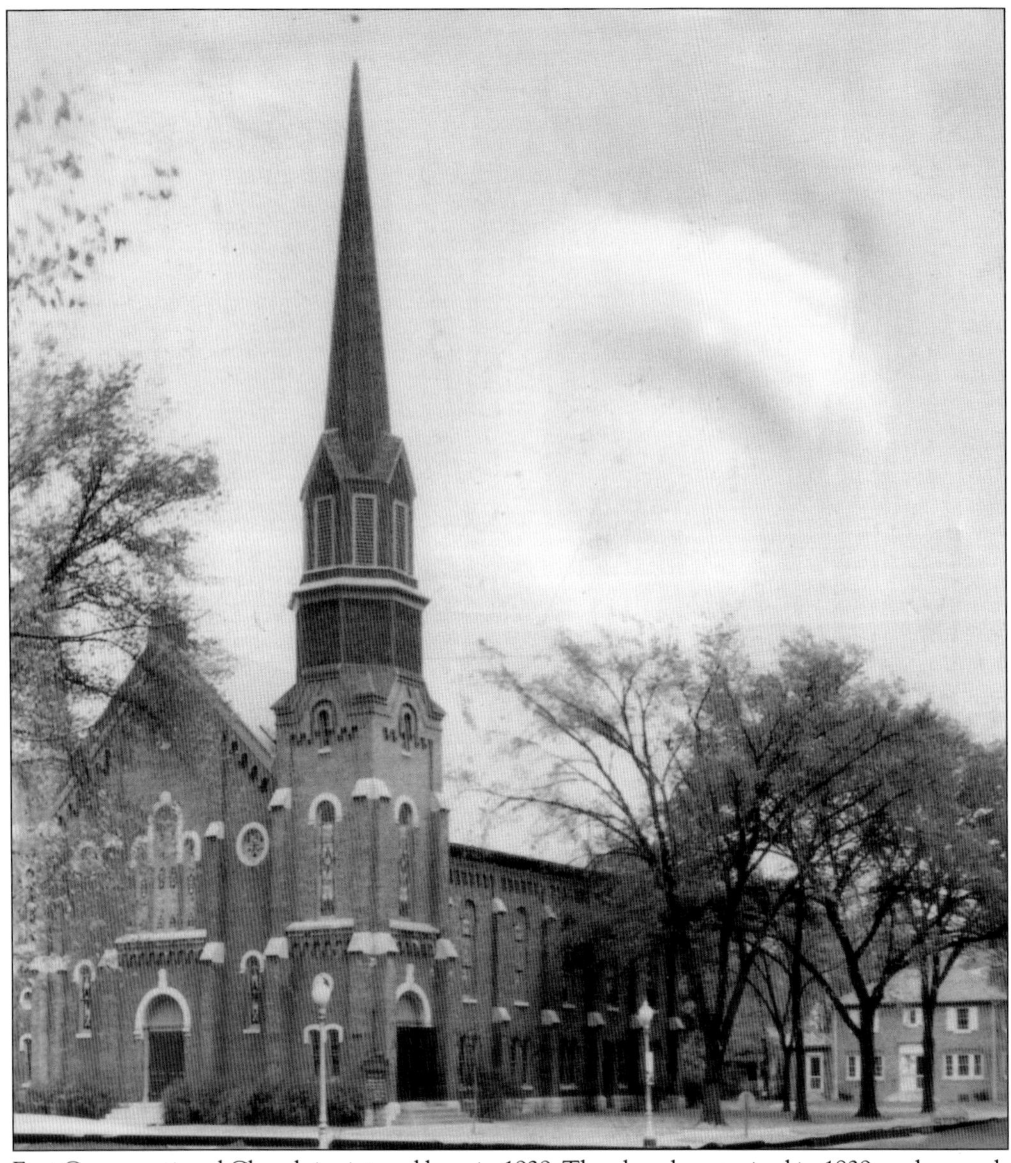

First Congregational Church is pictured here in 1939. The church organized in 1839, and a wood-frame building was constructed in 1846 on Columbus Street at Jackson Street. The present brick church was built in 1870 on the site where the first structure once stood. (JR.)

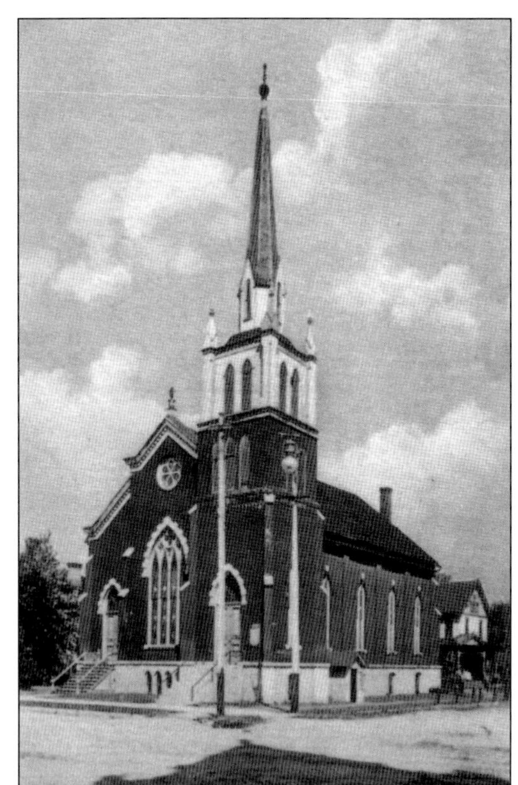

First Presbyterian Church began on Ottawa's south side in the 1860s. The present church was built in 1870 on Columbus Street at Jefferson Street. The view on the right is from 1893; the picture below is from 1979, when the church was without its steeple. The steeple has since been restored. (Both, JR.)

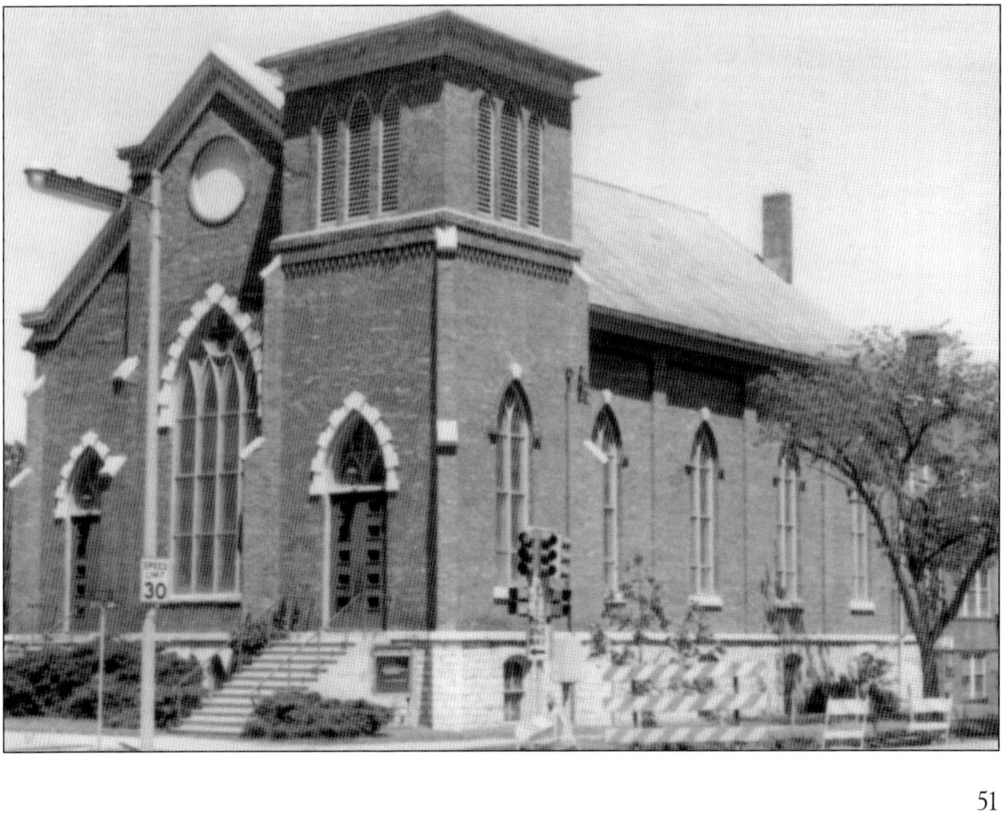

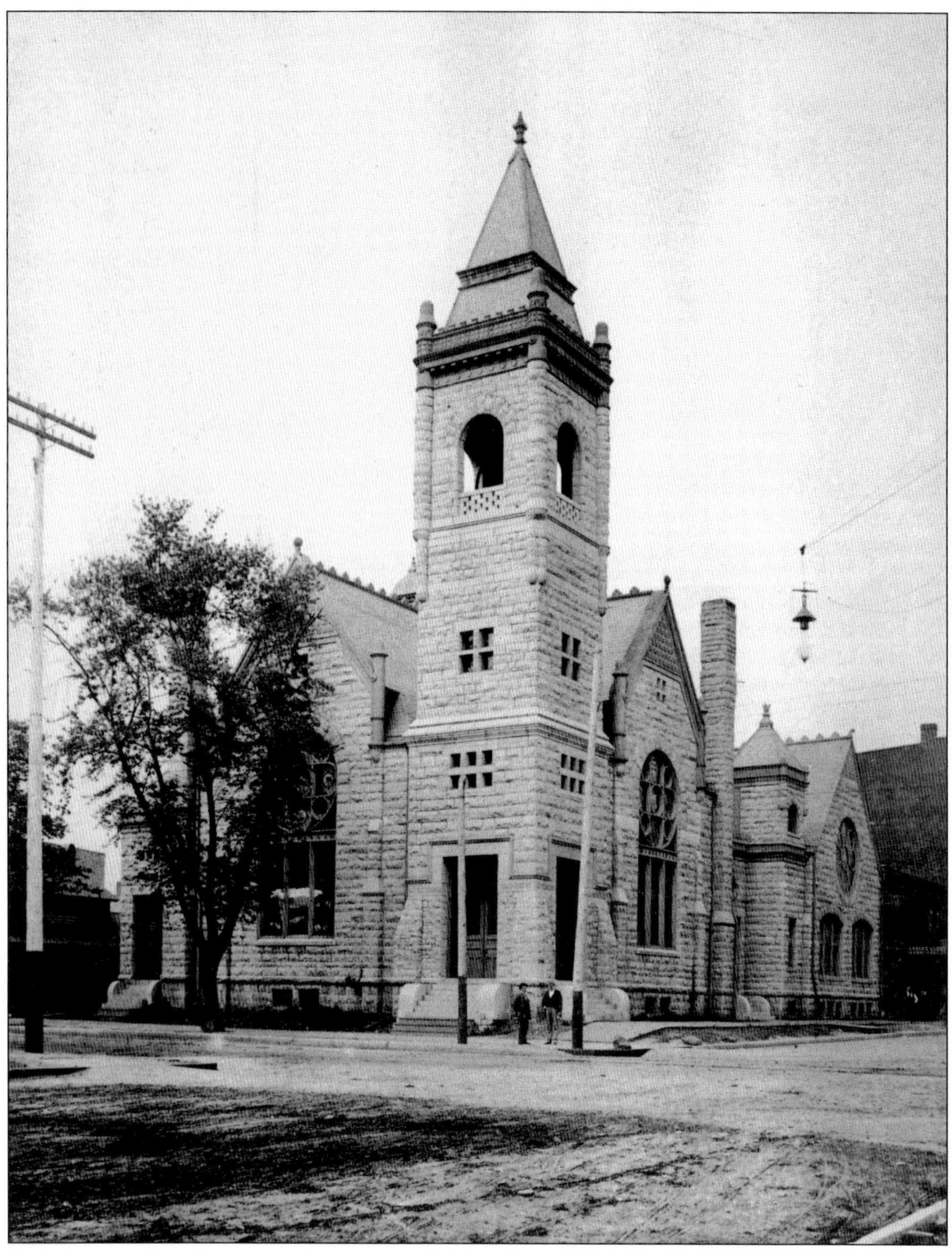

First Baptist Church organized in 1841. The first church was built on the northeast corner of LaSalle and Jackson Streets. A second church building went up in 1867 on Jefferson Street, where the Elk's building is today. The church (pictured here in 1893) was built in 1890 and 1891 on the southwest corner of Jefferson and Columbus Streets. It burned down on August 26, 1959. The church was rebuilt in 1961 on McKinley Road. A gas station was later constructed on the former site, and a drive-up banking facility was built there in 2006. (JR.)

At right is another look at the First Baptist Church, with its clock tower, in the 1950s, just before it burned down. Trinity Lutheran Church was organized by Norwegian immigrants in 1892. The congregation was affiliated with Pleasant View Luther College until a church was built in 1910 at Glover and Guthrie Streets. The present church building (below) was constructed in 1958 at 717 Chambers Street. (Both, JR.)

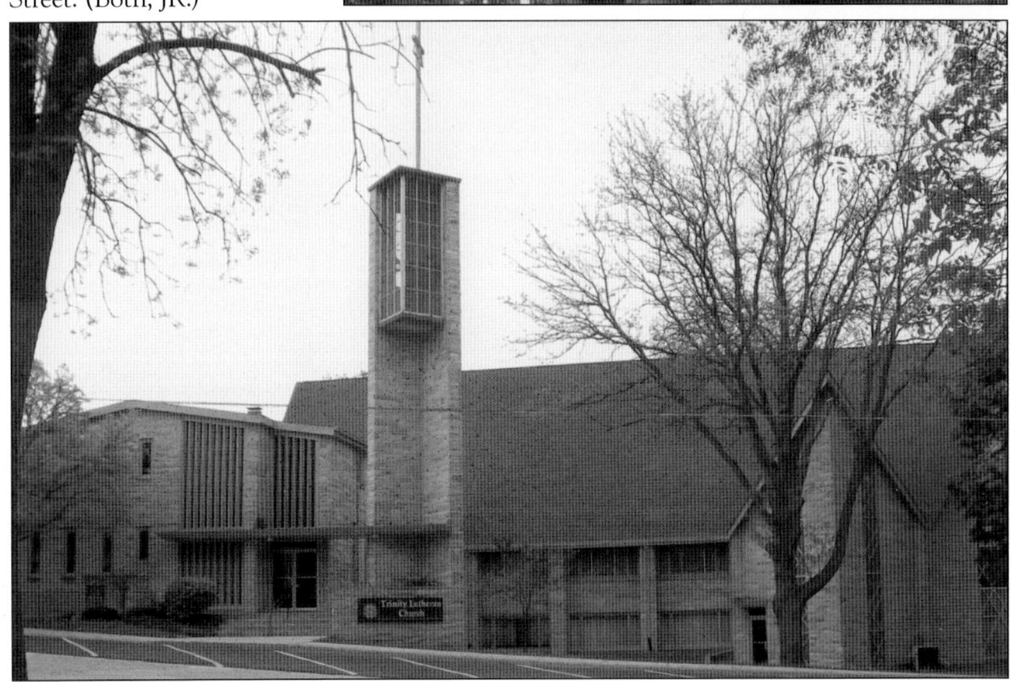

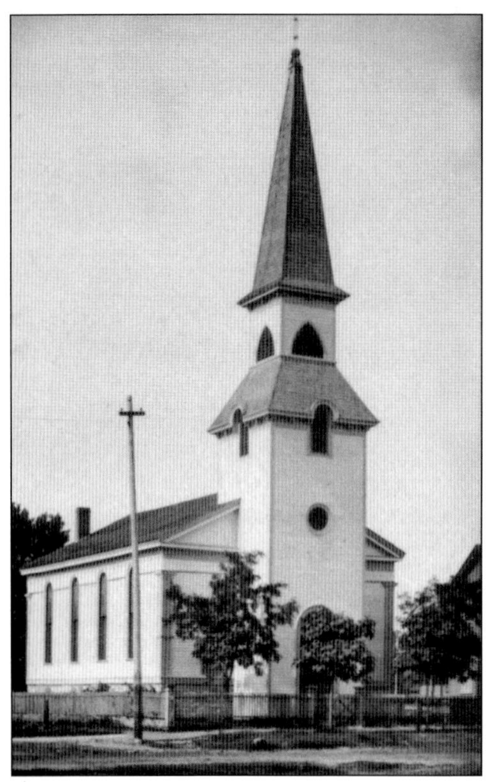

Zion Evangelical Church started in 1865. The congregation bought a church building from the Methodists on LaSalle Street, near Jefferson Street. In 1880, the building was moved to the corner of Jefferson and Mulberry Streets and was enlarged and improved.

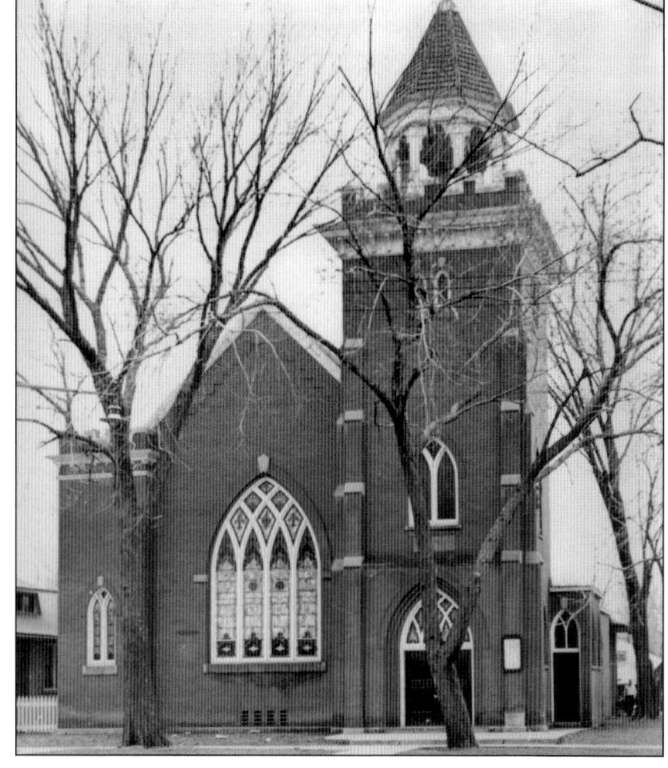

A new brick building was constructed in 1903 at the corner of Madison and Sycamore Streets. Zion Evangelical Church merged with Trinity Evangelical Church in 1927. They needed a larger building, and it was completed in 1931 at 1116 Illinois Avenue. The congregation was United Brethren for a few years until it became Methodist in 1968. The former Zion building on Madison Street has been the home of Bethel Lutheran Church since 1938. Today, the steeple is gone. (Both, JR.)

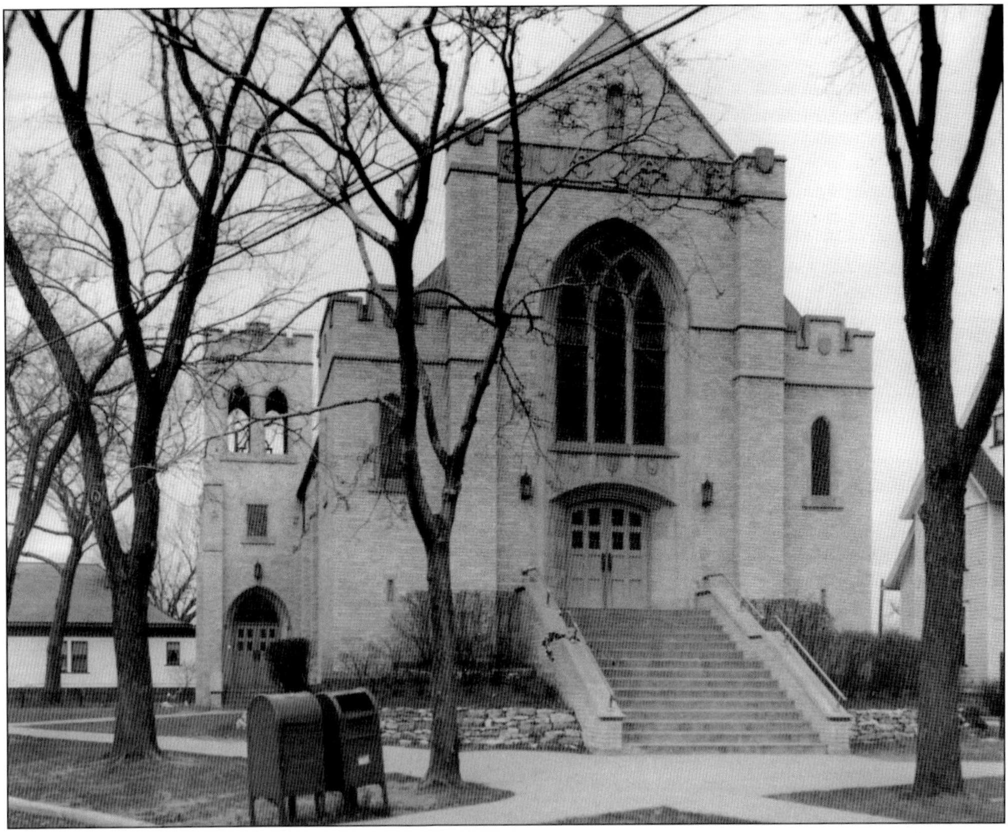

Evangelical United Methodist Church, at 1116 Illinois Avenue, is pictured above in the 1940s and below at worship in the 1950s. (Above, JR; below, DC.)

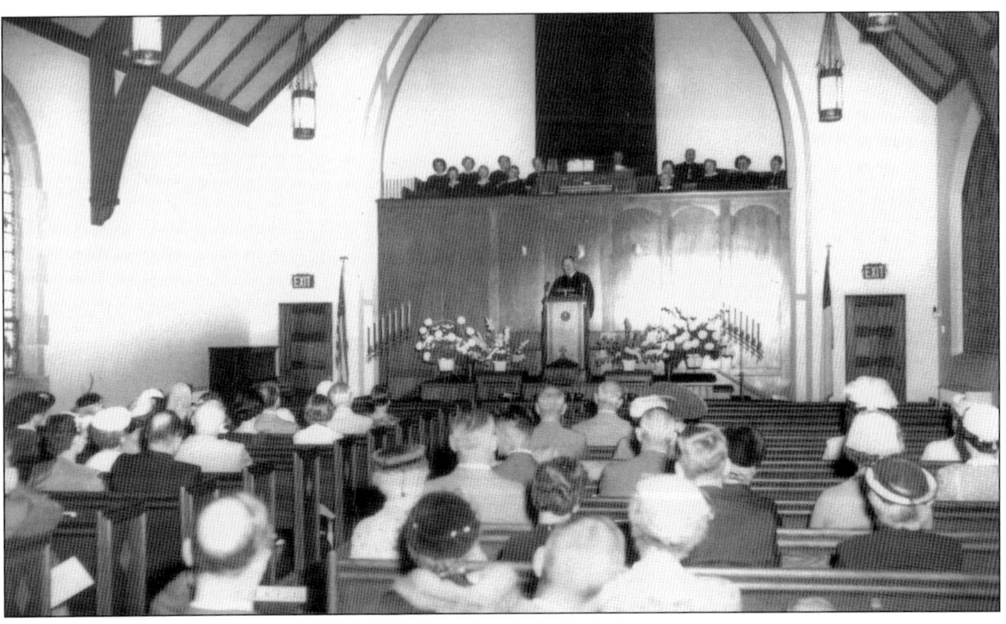

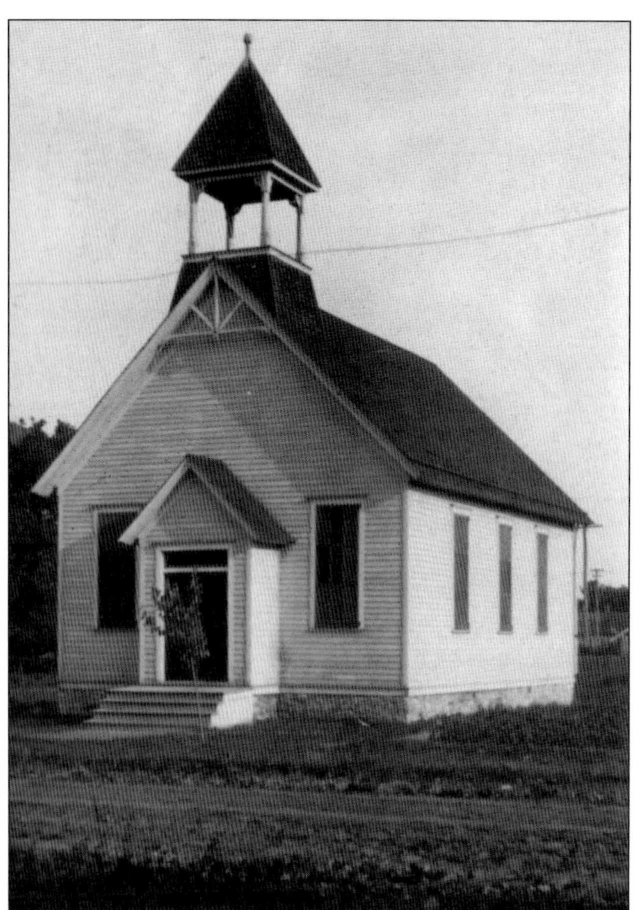

The Davis Memorial Swedish Methodist Episcopal Church was built in 1892 on the corner of Post and Prairie Streets. Hans Pearson, a Swedish immigrant who made a lot of money in his new homeland of Ottawa, donated the funds to build a church for his countrymen. He named it after Dr. Samuel Davis, of Oak Park, a prominent clergyman.

Difficulty in crossing the Illinois River is what led Methodists in South Ottawa to form the Second Methodist Episcopal Church in 1853, when a church was built at Campbell and Catherine Streets. The church took a new name, Epworth Methodist Church, in 1909. A new church building was constructed on Gentleman Road in 1965. (Both, JR.)

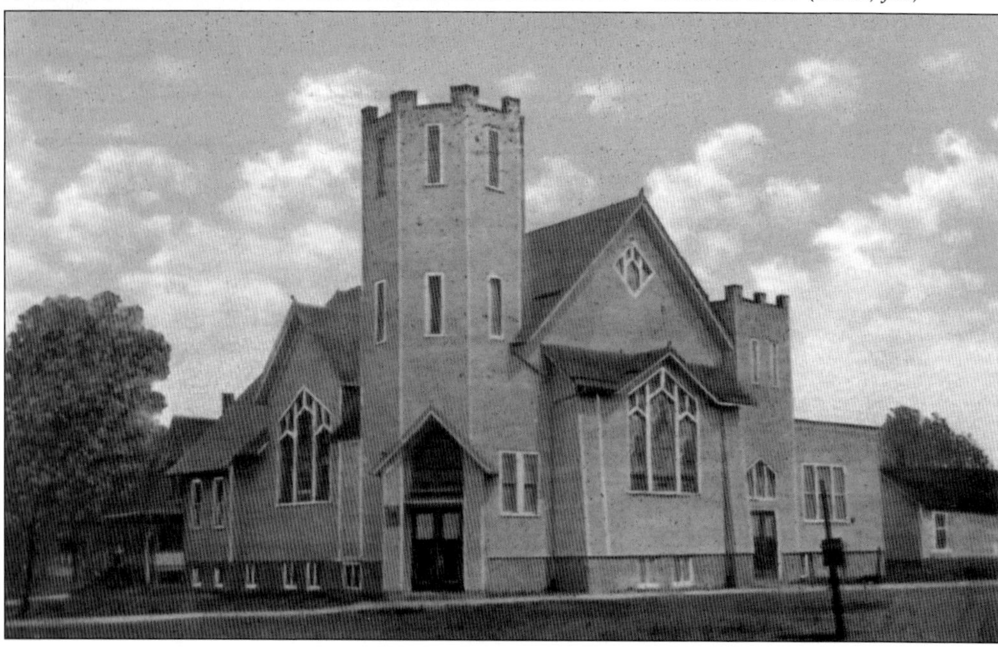

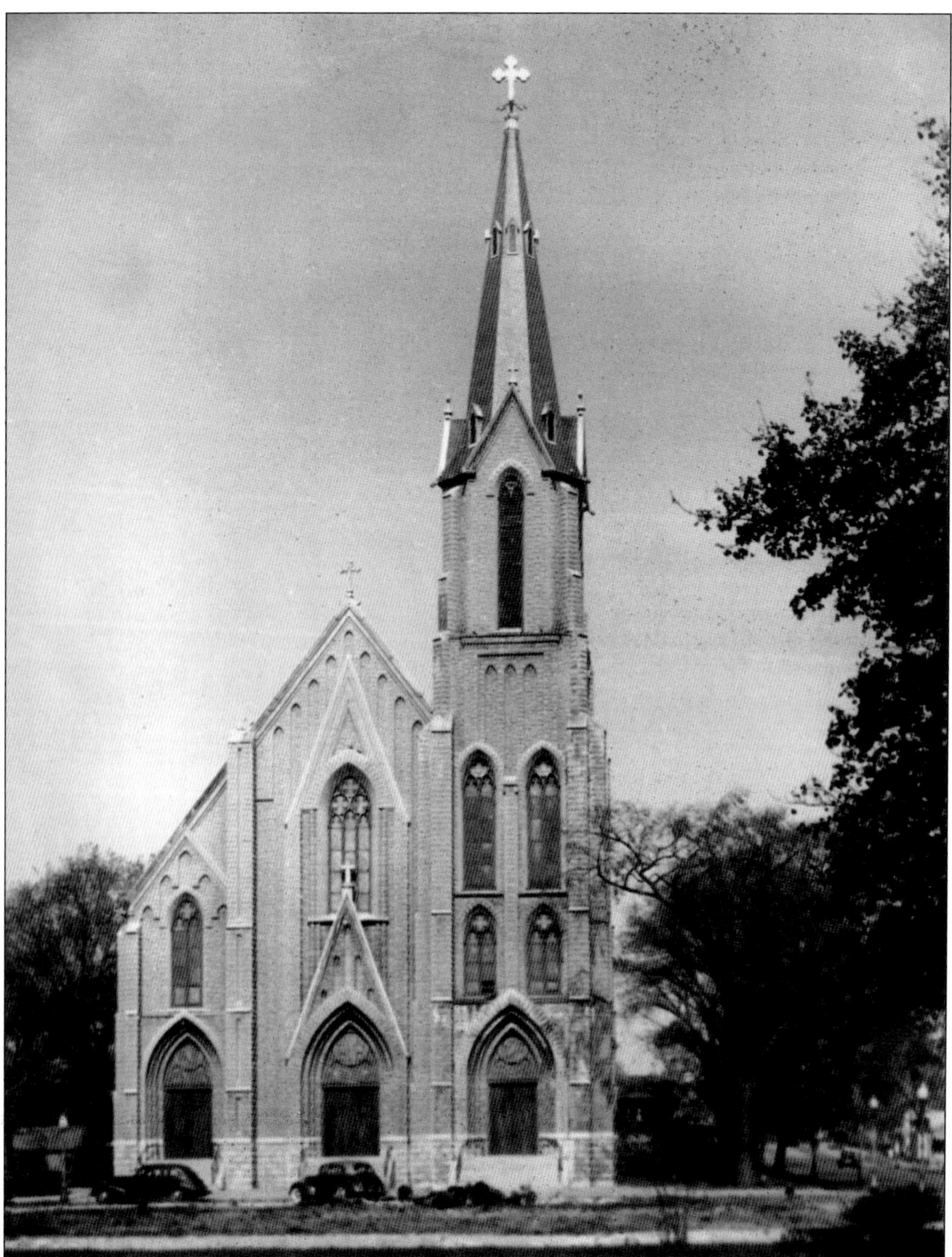

St. Columba Catholic Church got its start when visiting priests came from LaSalle in 1838. A wood-frame church was built in 1841 on the 300 block of West Jefferson Street. Another church building went up on LaSalle Street a few years later, and it burned down in 1851. A third church building was constructed in 1852. Work started in 1877 on the fourth and present church building (above) on Washington Street at Columbus Street, and it was completed in 1884. A Catholic school was built farther down the block in 1892. (JR.)

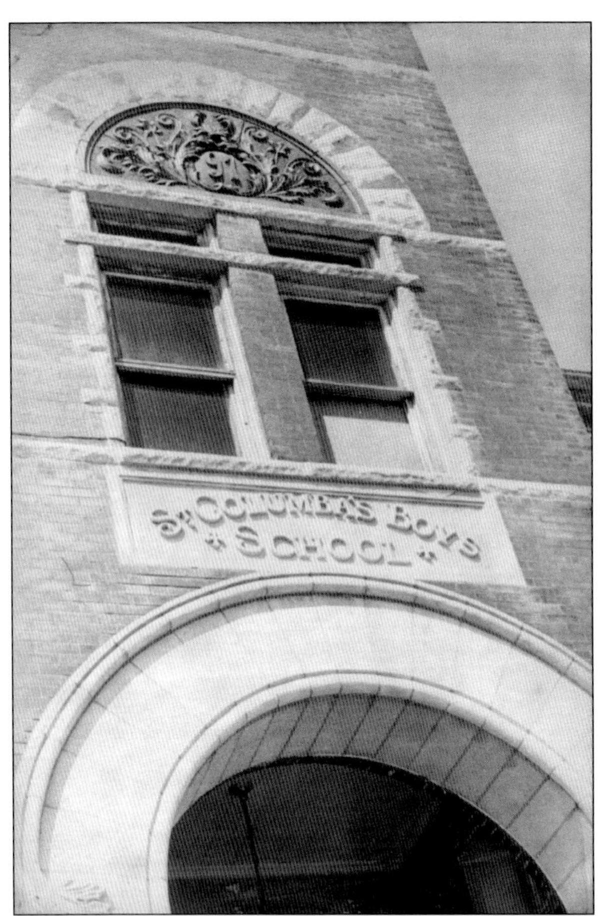

St. Columba School opened in 1892 on Washington Street at LaSalle Street. A high school addition was built in 1913. It was originally a school for boys but later became coeducational. A new school was built in 1963. When the old building was razed in 1981, an addition to the present school was built on the site. St. Columba School is now called Marquette Academy. St. Columba School and Church are pictured together in the postcard below, even though the postcard printer got the name wrong. (Both, JR.)

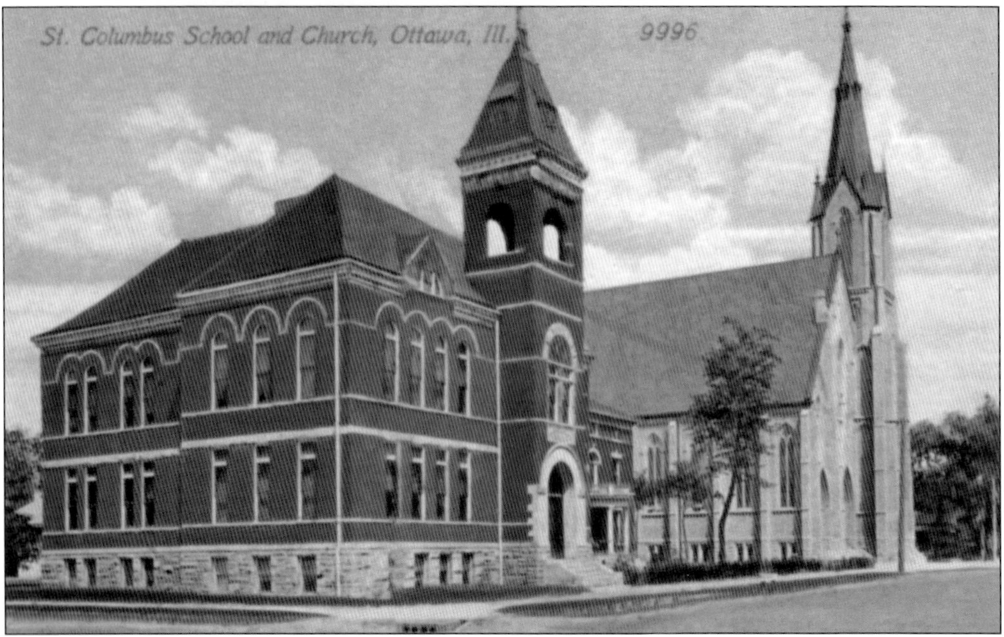

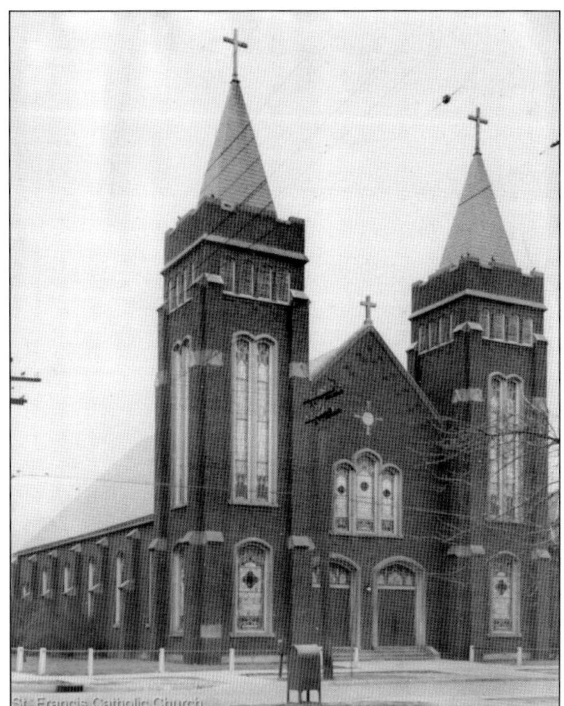

St. Francis Catholic Church was started in 1859 by German Catholics, and a wood-frame church was built at Sanger and Jackson Streets. The present brick church was built in the same location in 1916. A school was built in 1913 and closed in 1970. The church's First Communion class of 1966 is pictured below. (Both, Saleda family.)

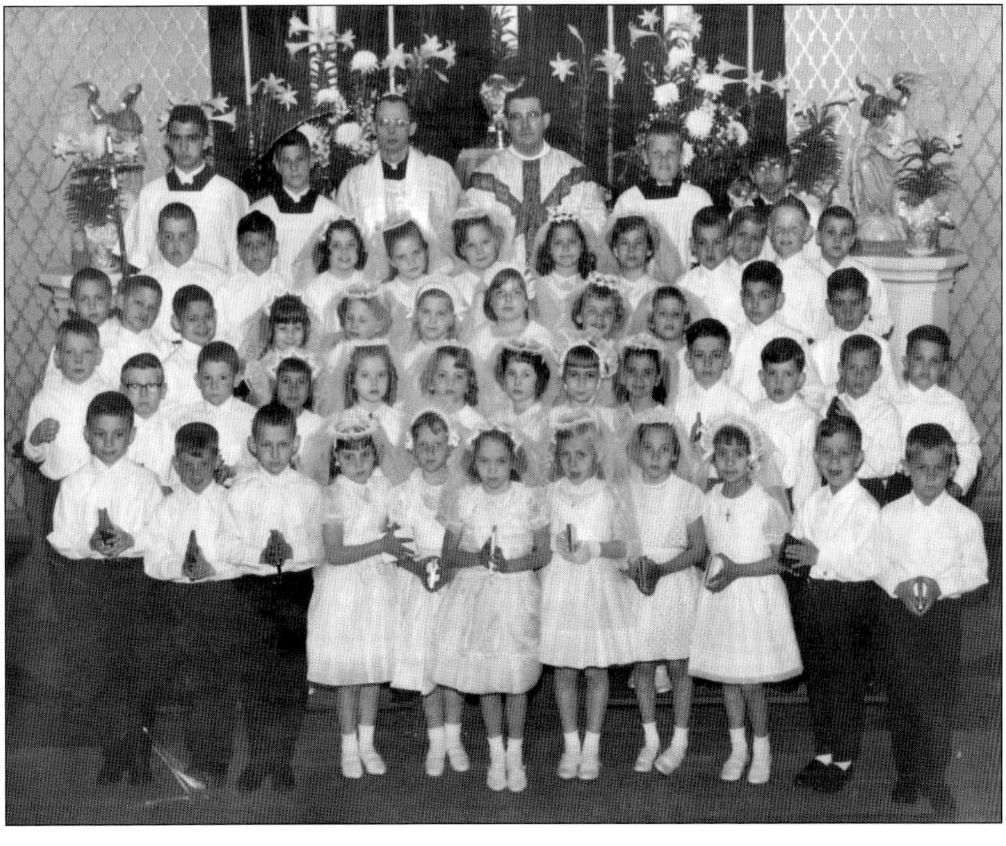

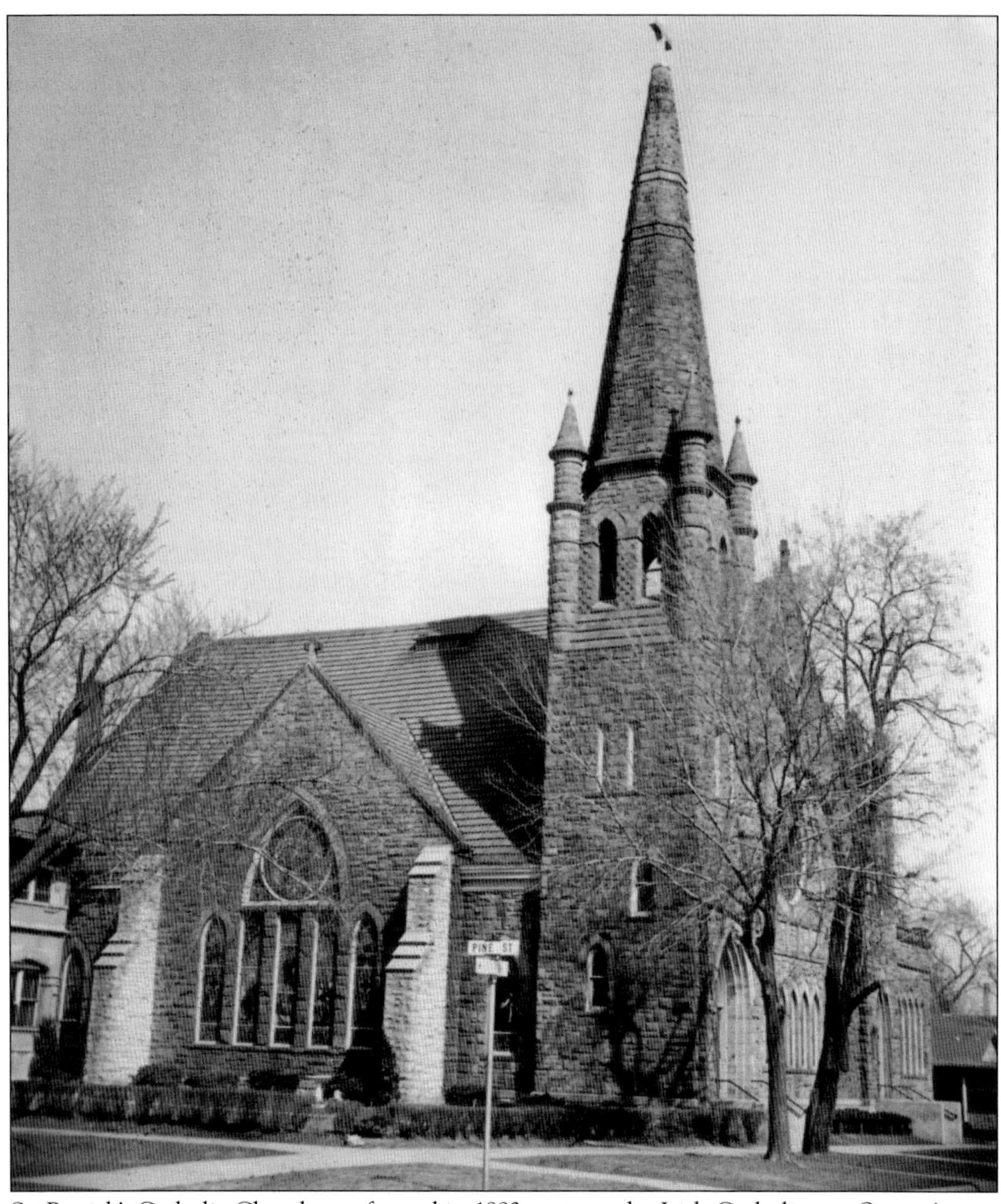

St. Patrick's Catholic Church was formed in 1893 to serve the Irish Catholics on Ottawa's west side. The cornerstone of the church, on the northeast corner of Jefferson and Pine Streets, was laid on September 24, 1893. Services were held in St. Hilda's Chapel until St. Patrick's was completed in 1898. A school was built across the street in 1913. Thousands of people came to Ottawa for a unique event on September 1, 1913, when three Catholic schools were dedicated on the same day: St. Patrick's, St. Columba, and St. Francis. St. Patrick's added a gymnasium in 1957. A major renovation to the church was done from 1984 to 1986. (JR.)

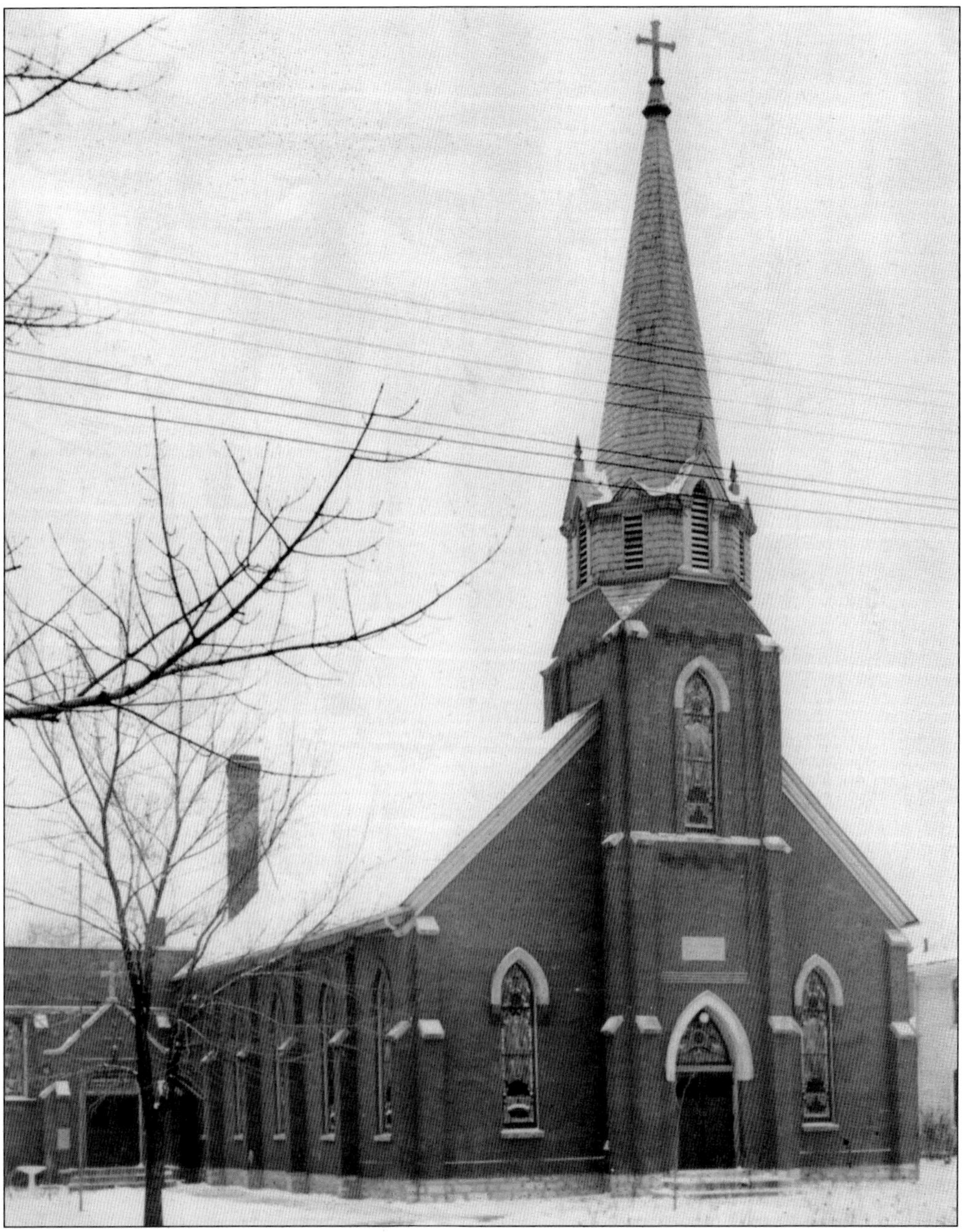

Zion Evangelical Lutheran Church was founded in 1860 by 17 German immigrant families. A Lutheran Day School opened in 1862 and operated until 1947. A preschool started in 1985, which continues today in addition to regular Sunday school, Bible study, and other Christian education. The church is located at 622 West Jefferson Street. (JR.)

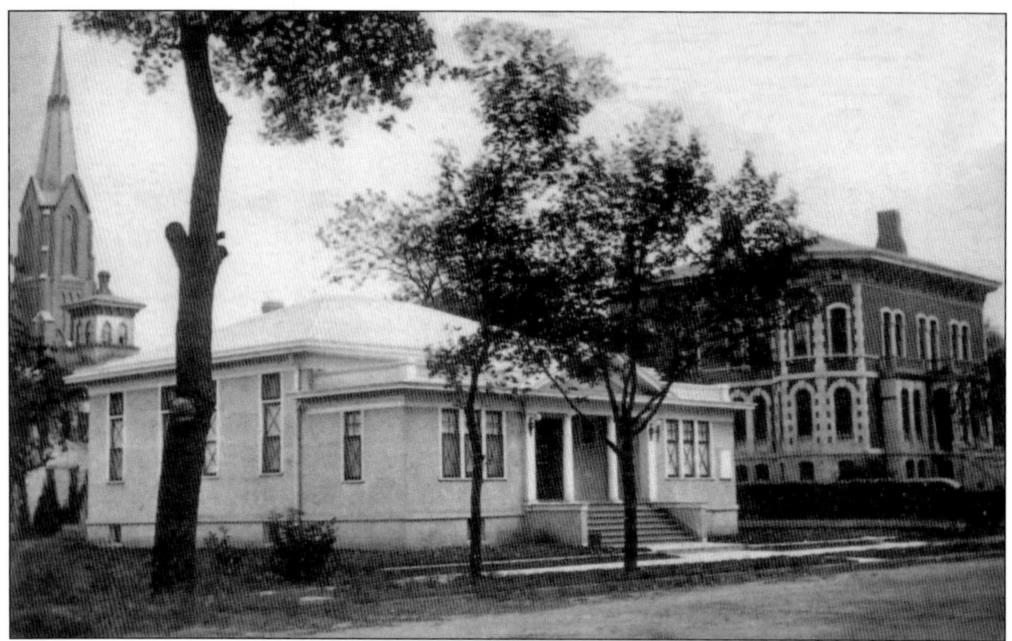

The First Church of Christ, Scientist, came to Ottawa in 1897. This church was built on Lafayette Street in 1907. The property was sold in 1964 and became an office building. Christian Scientists met in a house on State Street until disbanding in 1974. (JR.)

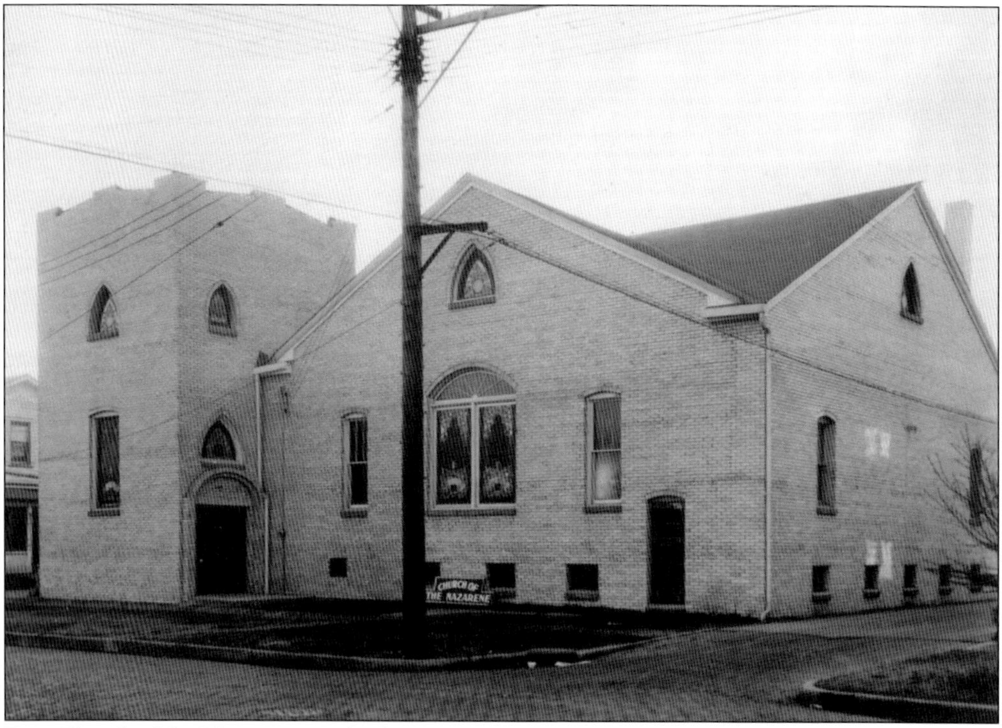

First Church of the Nazarene was built at 215 West Washington Street in 1925. The congregation built a new church on North Route 23 in 1970. The old building now is Illinois Valley Evangelical Free Church. (JR.)

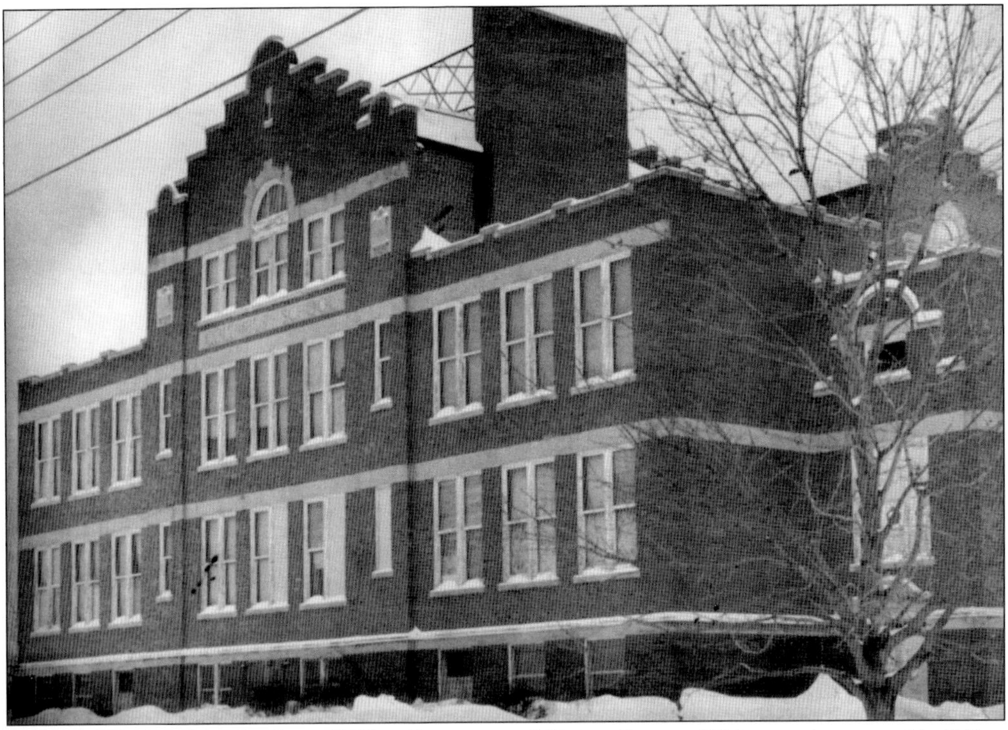

Columbus School was built in 1905 at Superior and Guion Streets. This was the second building for Columbus School, and it was torn down in the 1970s. The Ravlin Congregate High Rise later was built on this location. (JR.)

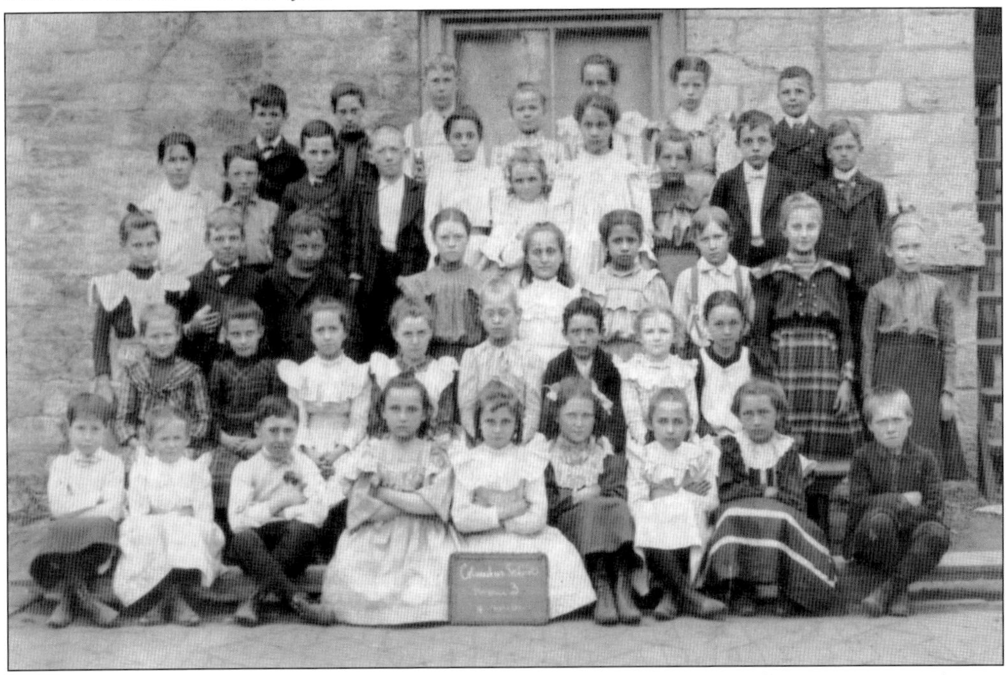

This is room three of Columbus School, as pictured on April 30, 1901. This picture was taken at the school's first site, on Columbus Street, where the Masonic Temple was built in 1910. (DC.)

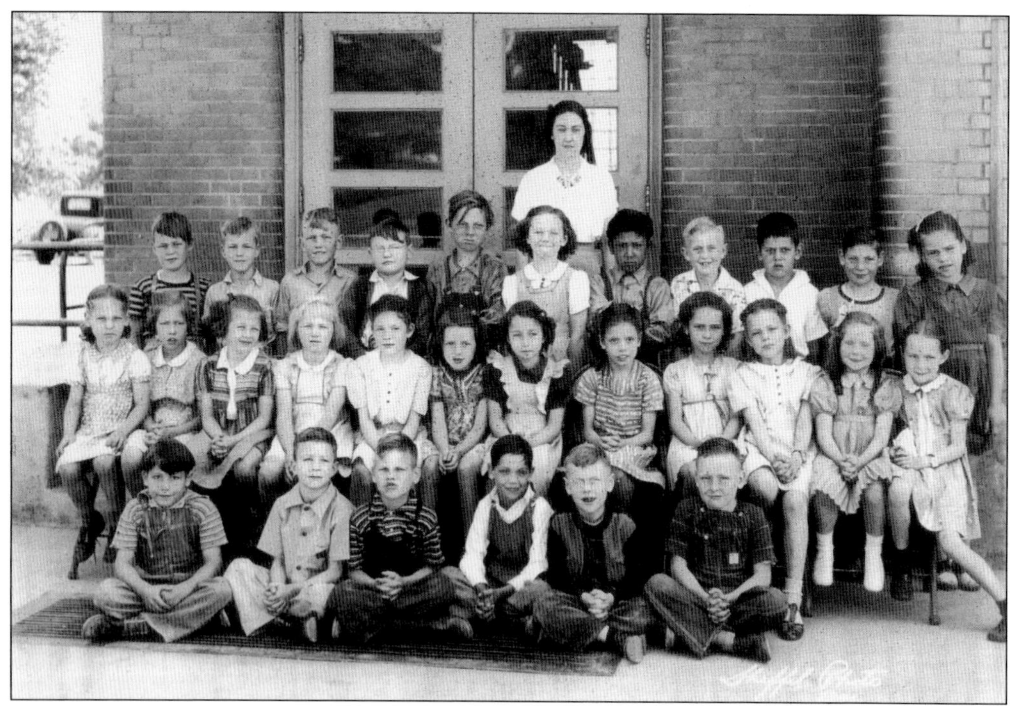

Here, students at Jefferson School, at 1709 Columbus Street, are pictured seven years apart. In the picture above, from 1941, the students are second graders, and below they are in the eighth grade in 1947. (Both, DC.)

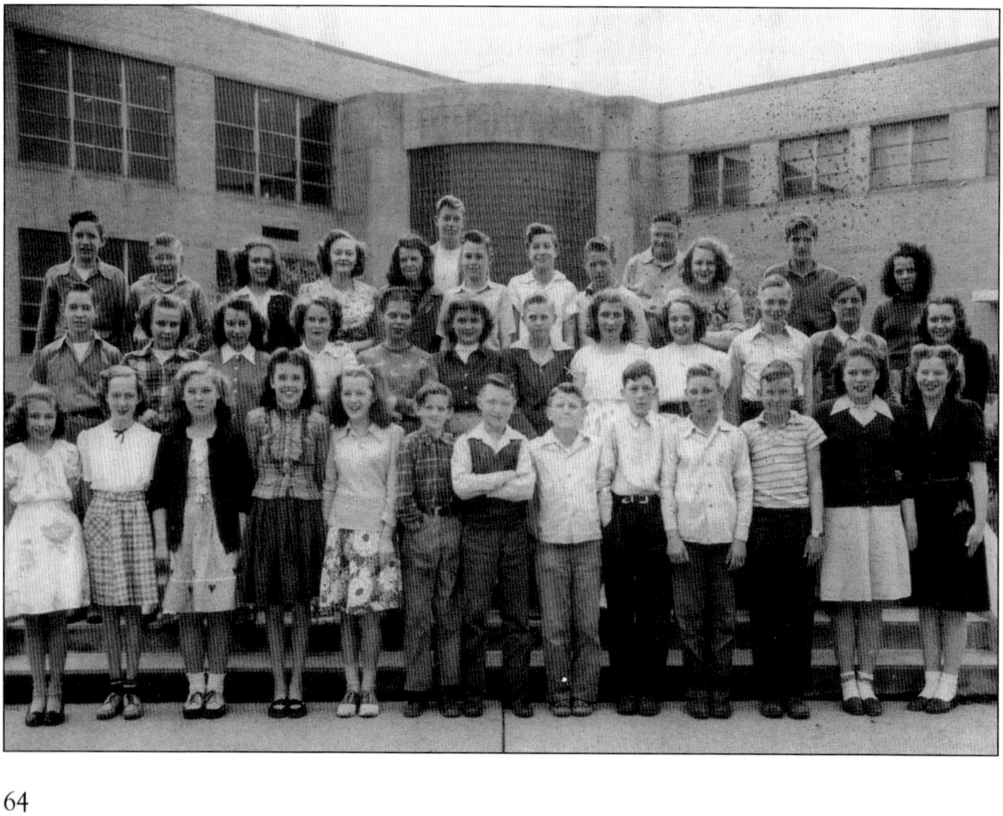

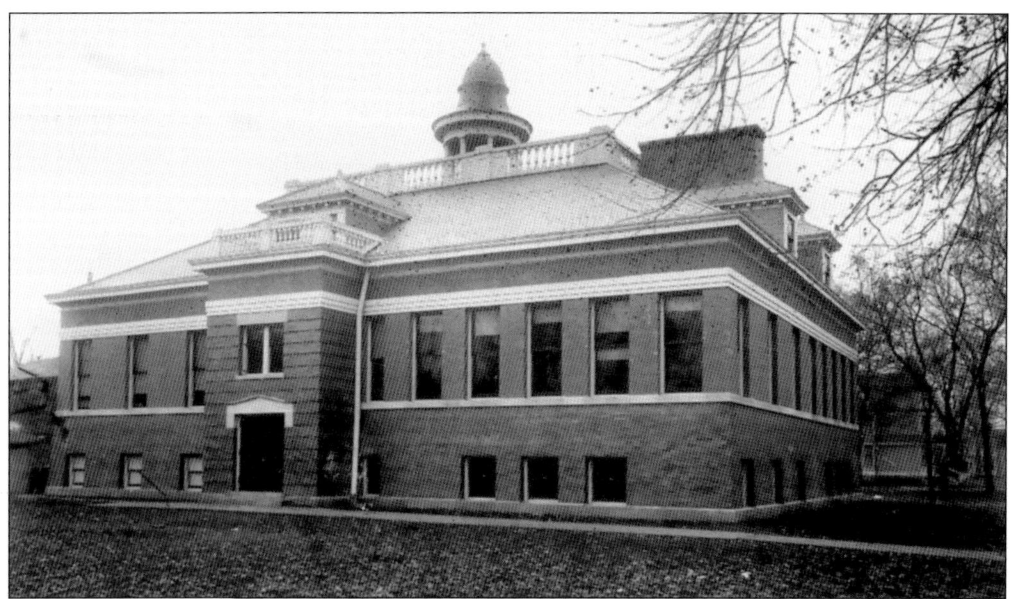

Washington School, commonly known as East Side School, was built in 1906 at York and Congress Streets. The site is now a playground. It was designed by Ottawa architect Jason Richardson, who also designed Shabbona School. Today, Richardson's office building is Dettore's Town Lanes. (JR.)

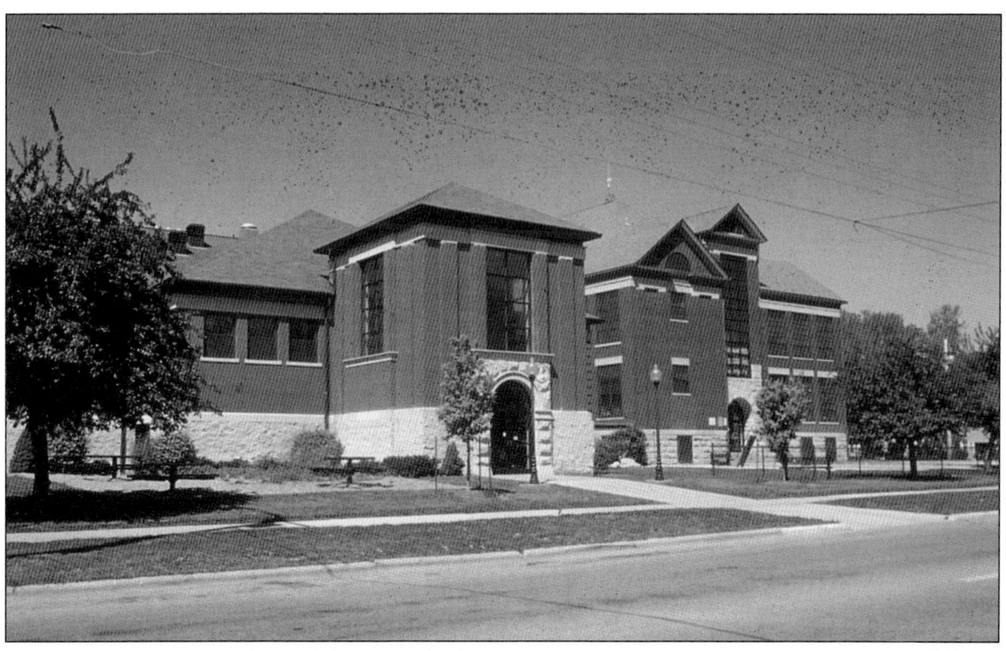

Lincoln School, on Madison Street, was built in 1898 on the site of the previous Lincoln School, which had been constructed in the 1860s. This school still serves the community, and it recently underwent remodeling and updating. (JR.)

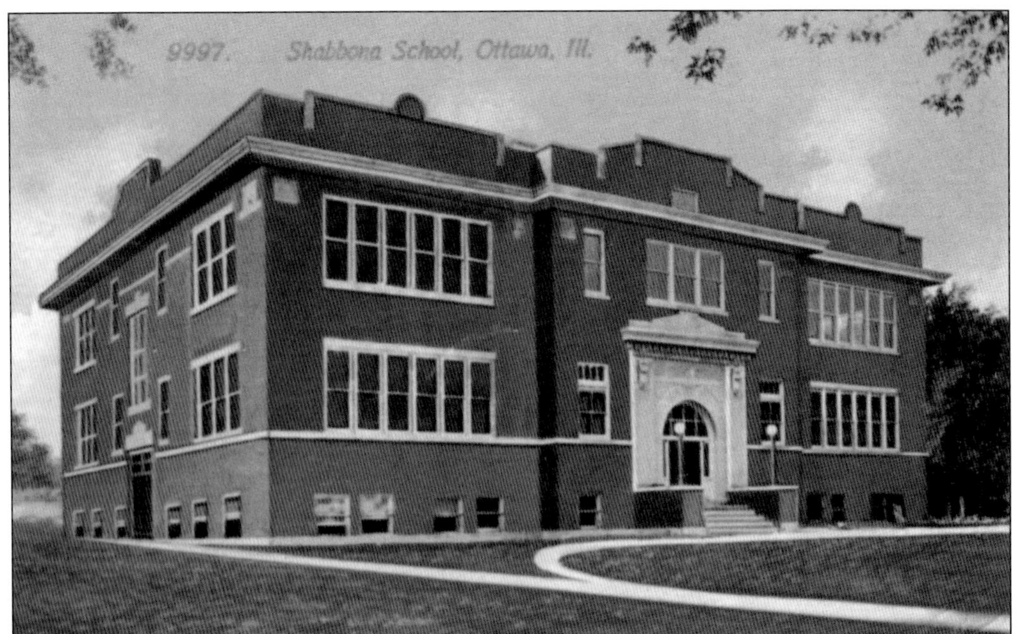

Shabbona School was built in 1912 at Glover and State Streets. Today, the school is gone and a park is on the site. (JR.)

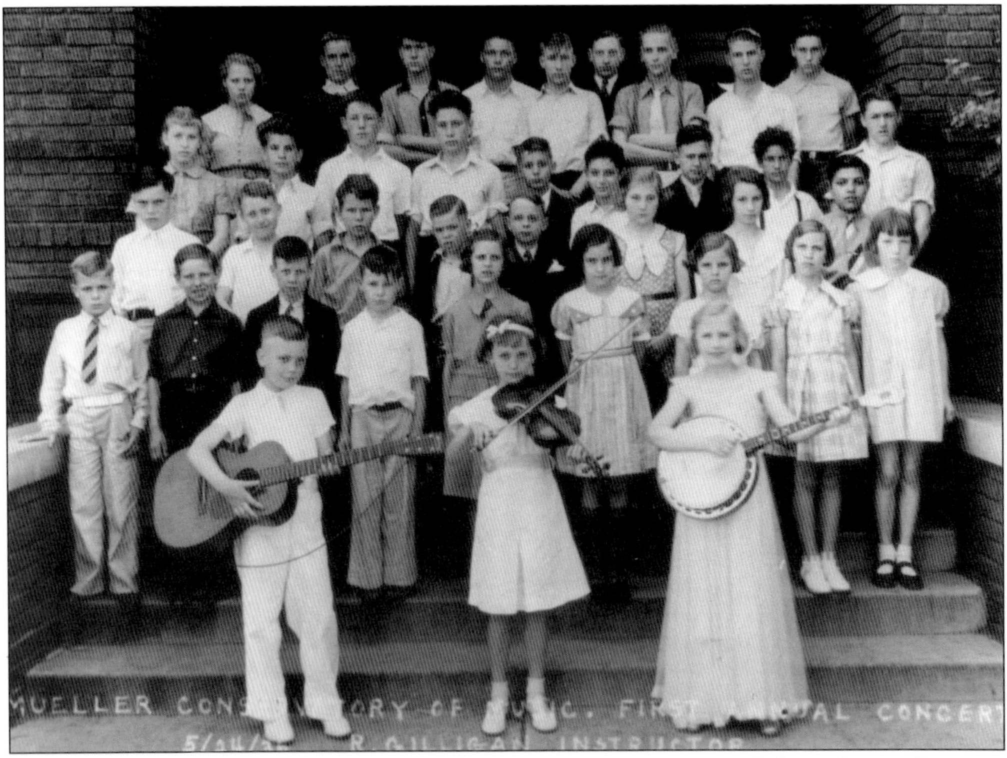

Mueller Conservatory of Music was located in room 301 at 102 West Madison Street. It was in business for a few years in the 1930s. This picture is from its 1936 class. Dorothy Clemens is the girl shown second from the right in the third row. (DC.)

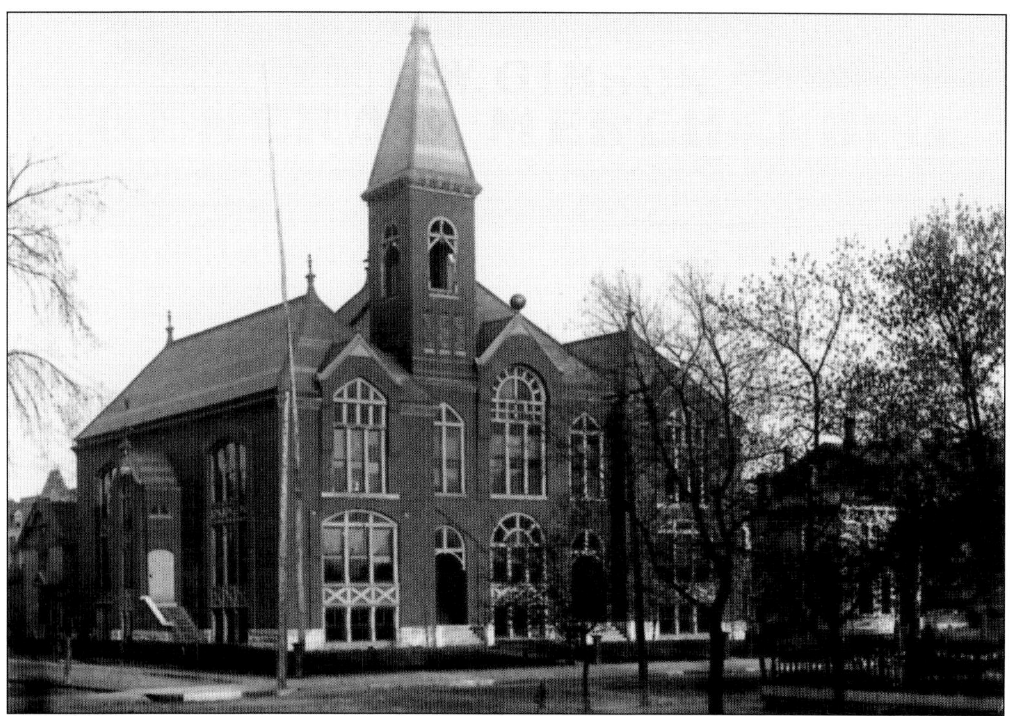

The Ottawa Township High School (OTHS) building (above) was constructed in 1879 on Columbus Street, on the southeast corner with Washington Street, and opened on January 5, 1880. The growth of Ottawa created a need for bigger facilities, and the present building (below) was completed in 1916. A Manual Arts building and new gymnasium were built in 1931 and 1932, another major addition was completed in 1962, and a third gymnasium was built in 1976. A fourth addition was completed in 2004. (Both, JR.)

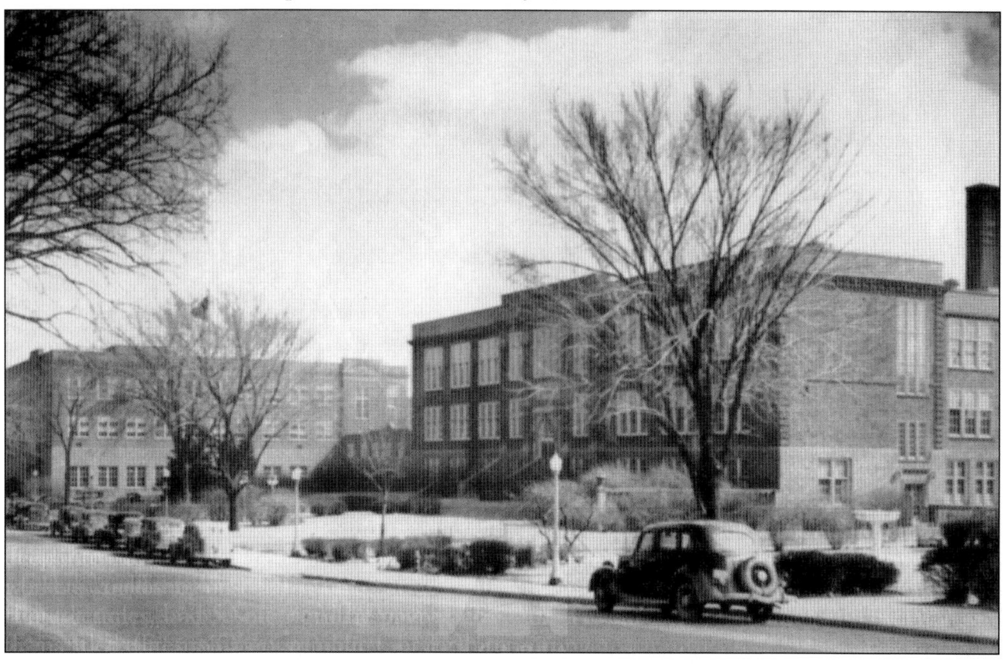

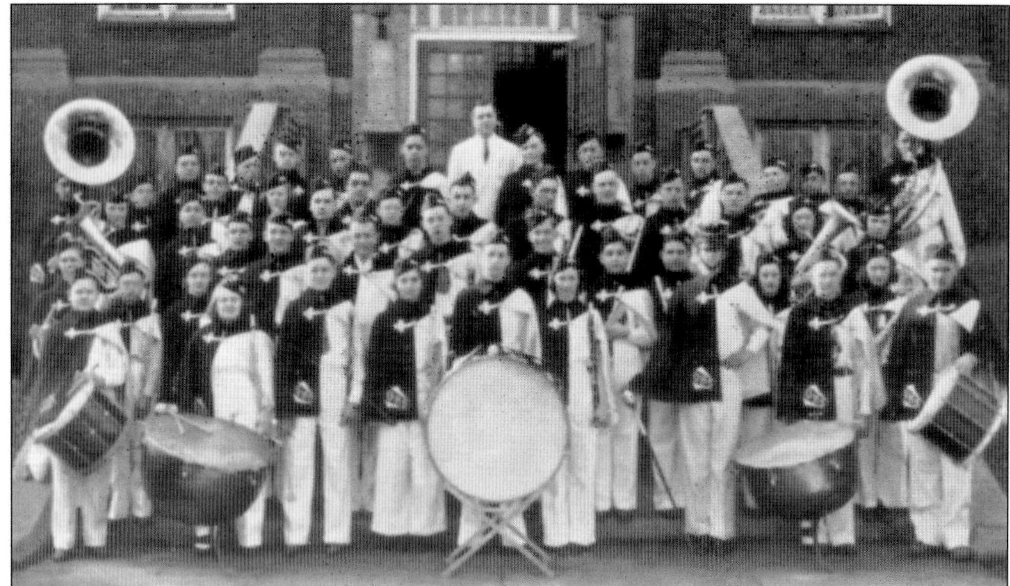

The OTHS music program's statewide reputation for excellence began with John Kinnison, director of grade school bands from 1951 to 1983, and Ray Makeever, director of high school bands from 1950 to 1984. Under Makeever, the band earned 31 consecutive First Division ratings. As of 2011, OTHS has the second-most music department state championships in Illinois, with 16 (including the last 15 years); Herscher High School has 31. (Ottawa and Herscher are in different classes.) In 2011, Sarah Reckmeyer is the band director and Roger Amm is the choral director. The band is pictured above in 1938 with Arthur Hentrich as director. (Both, Saleda family.)

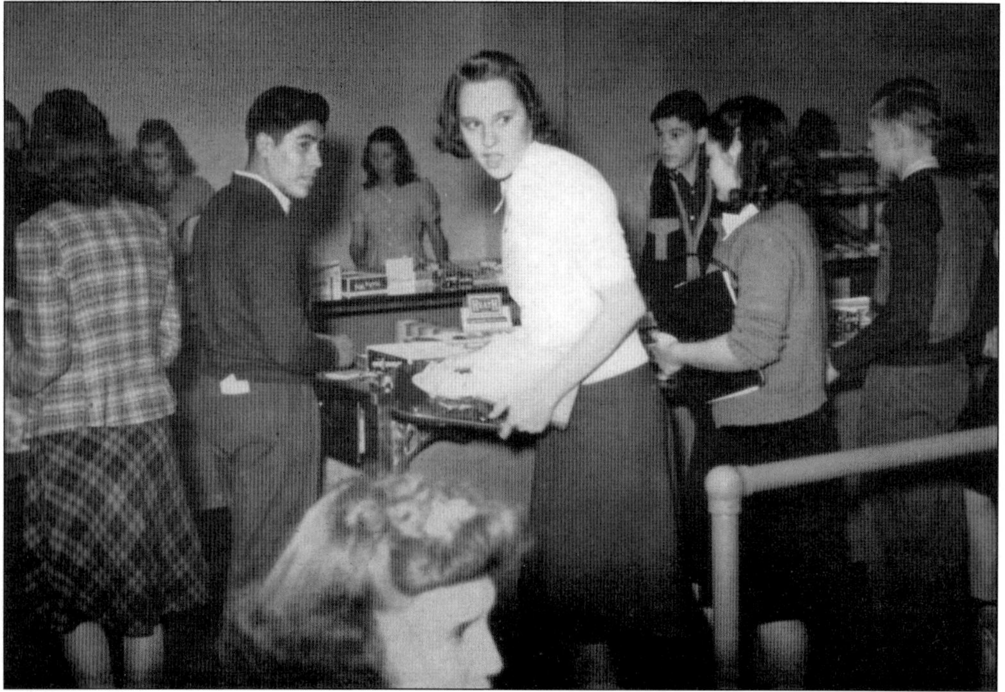

This is a candid photograph of a lunchtime scene in the OTHS cafeteria in 1941.

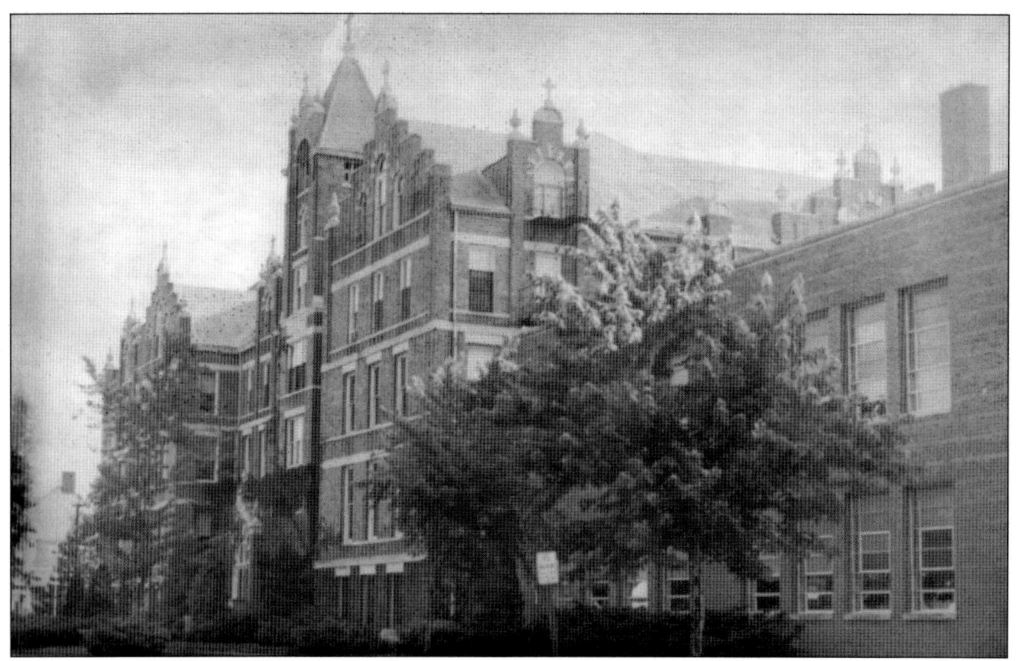

In 1857, a Catholic high school opened in Ottawa when the Sisters of Mercy came from Ireland and founded St. Xavier's Academy and St. Joseph's Convent. The school (pictured above) was built in 1901 at Washington and Paul Streets. In 1913, St. Xavier's Academy became a girls' school. In 1946, both boys and girls were admitted and the school's name was changed to Ottawa Catholic High School. The school was renamed Marquette High School (pictured below, under construction) when a new building was constructed in 1949. (Both, JR.)

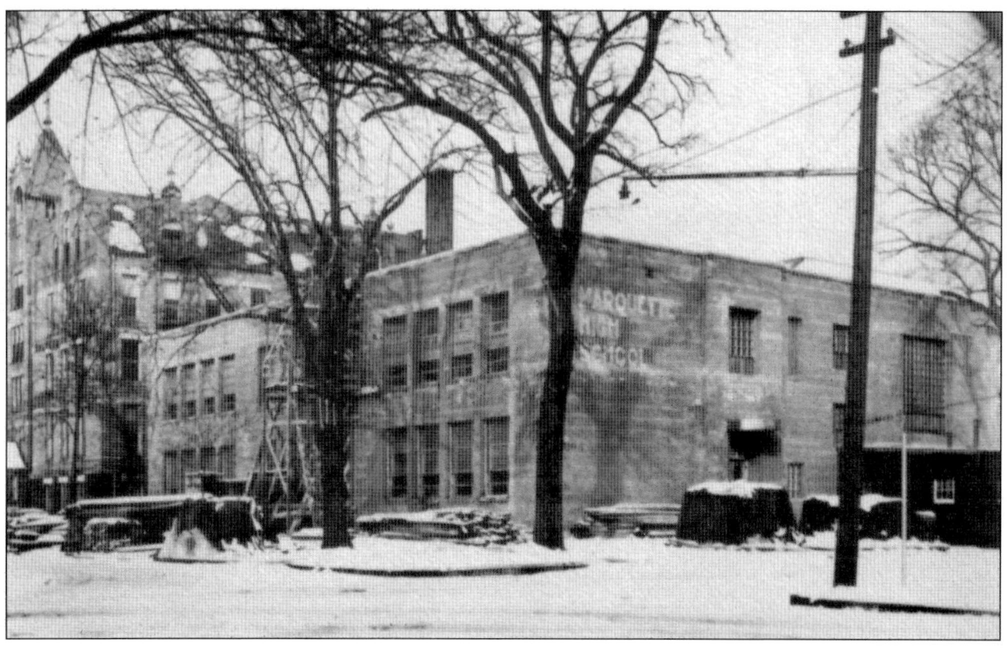

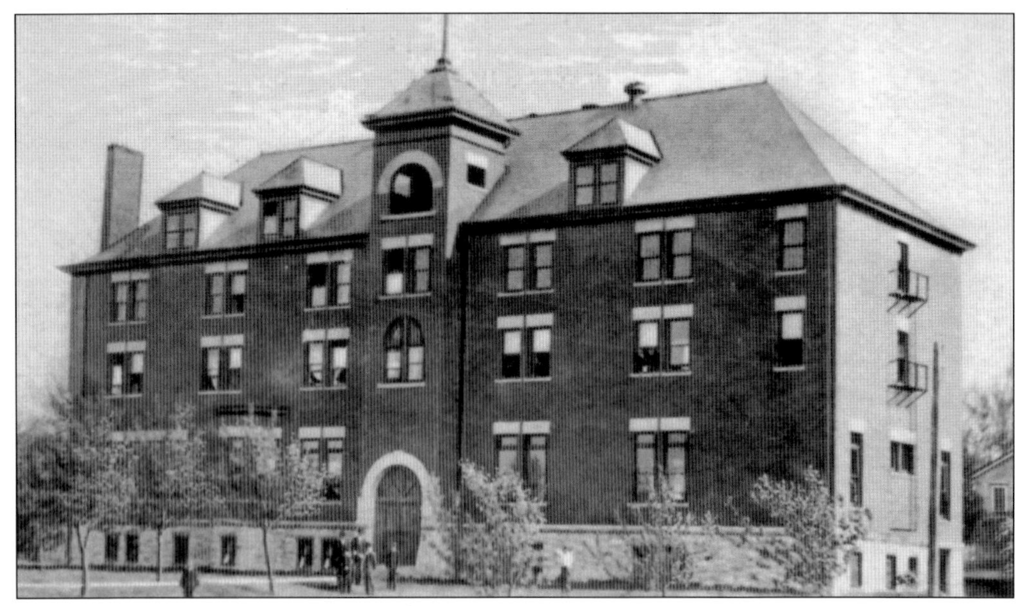

Pleasant View Luther College opened in 1896 on College Avenue on Ottawa's south side. It was founded by Norwegian Lutherans, who began settling in the Ottawa area in 1834. The college closed in 1936, during the Great Depression, and reopened in 1937 as Pleasant View Luther Home, a care facility for the elderly. Additions were built in 1957 and 1962. The original college building was torn down in 1962. The Alfred Nelson Gymnasium (pictured below) was torn down in 1975, and a modern multistory health center was built on the spot. (Both, JR.)

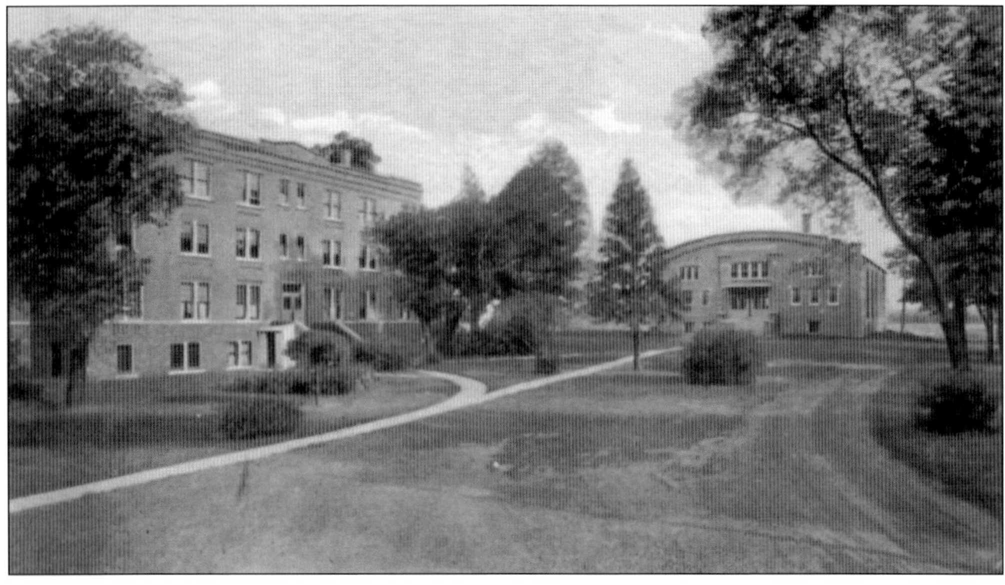

Four

Sports and Recreation

Starved Rock, Matthiessen, and Buffalo Rock State Parks are popular attractions for local people and for thousands of tourists who travel great distances. Starved Rock has a fabulous dining hall, a hotel with a pool, and cabins. The canyons, waterfalls, bluffs, and park land are as beautiful as can be found in any region of the state, but the Ottawa area offers a lot more, including abundant fishing and boating on the Fox and Illinois Rivers.

Ottawa has had some memorable sports moments. In June 1858, a legendary baseball game between Ottawa and a visiting team from Marseilles ended with Ottawa winning 224-207. The score after the first inning was 81-75. The worst loss of the Ottawa Township High School basketball team came in 1916, when it lost to Morris 72-2.

Under Coach Bill Novak, the OTHS football team had undefeated seasons in 1957, 1959, 1961, 1962, 1965, 1966, 1967, 1969, and 1971. Novak's teams went 167-46 during his tenure, from 1947 to 1971. Novak is in the Illinois Sports Hall of Fame, along with other legendary Ottawa coaches Gil Love (basketball), Dean Riley (basketball), June Gross (track), Tom Henderson (tennis), and John Love (basketball).

A few legendary places are gone. Blackhawk Beach, two miles west of Ottawa on Route 71, was an abandoned quarry. The high-quality beach for swimming opened in 1925. When the Libbey-Owens-Ford factory began dumping waste nearby in 1959, the water was polluted, and the beach was closed. Majestic Park, a popular amusement site near Ottawa in the early 1900s, is also gone. There was a driving park with a racetrack and grandstand, located on East Norris Drive, at the present-day site of the swimming pool.

A county fair was held in Ottawa beginning in 1846. Fairgrounds were built off West Main Street and later near Ottawa Avenue Cemetery. Fairs were discontinued from 1881 until 1912.

Still around and still very popular is the 4-H Fair. It started in the early 1930s on the Norris Drive fairgrounds and was held in various locations before finding a permanent home in South Ottawa Township on 4-H Road. Camp Tuckabatchee was opened by the Ottawa Camp Fire Girls in 1927, providing swimming, horseback riding, camping, canoeing, sports, and other activities.

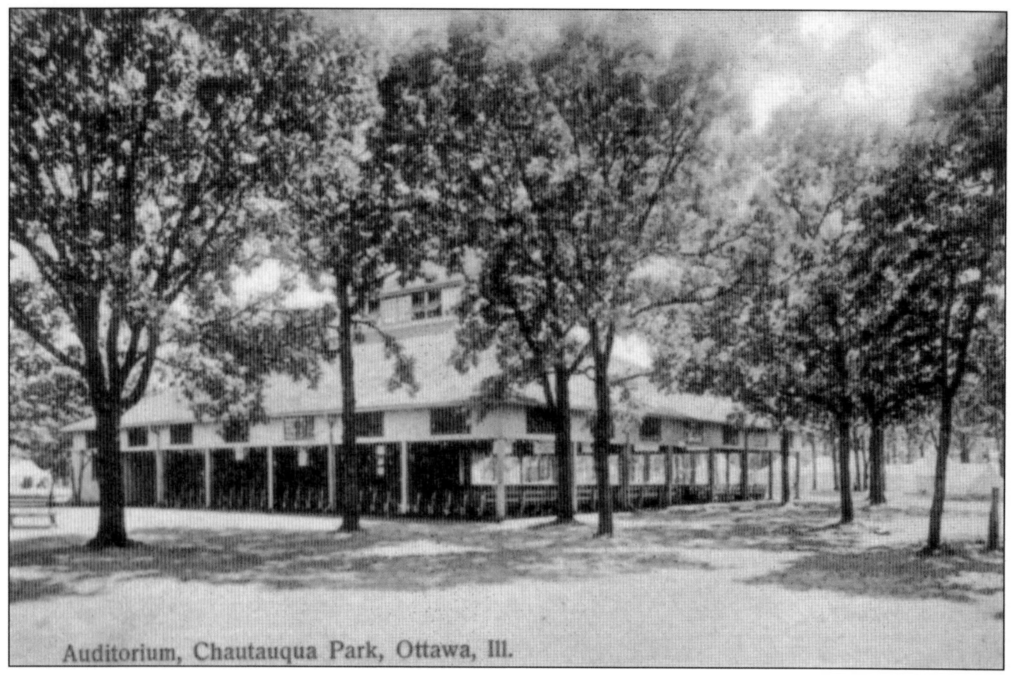

The Chautauqua Movement was very popular in the early 1900s. Lecturers, orators, humorists, musicians, and other entertainers put on an assortment of intellectual, educational, and amusing fare. The first Chautauqua was in 1902 in a grove two miles west of town. Thousands of people attended each year, and hundreds of people camped out for the 10-day event. A pavilion was built in 1904 with seating for 1,500. The annual event continued until the Depression years of the early 1930s. (Both, JR.)

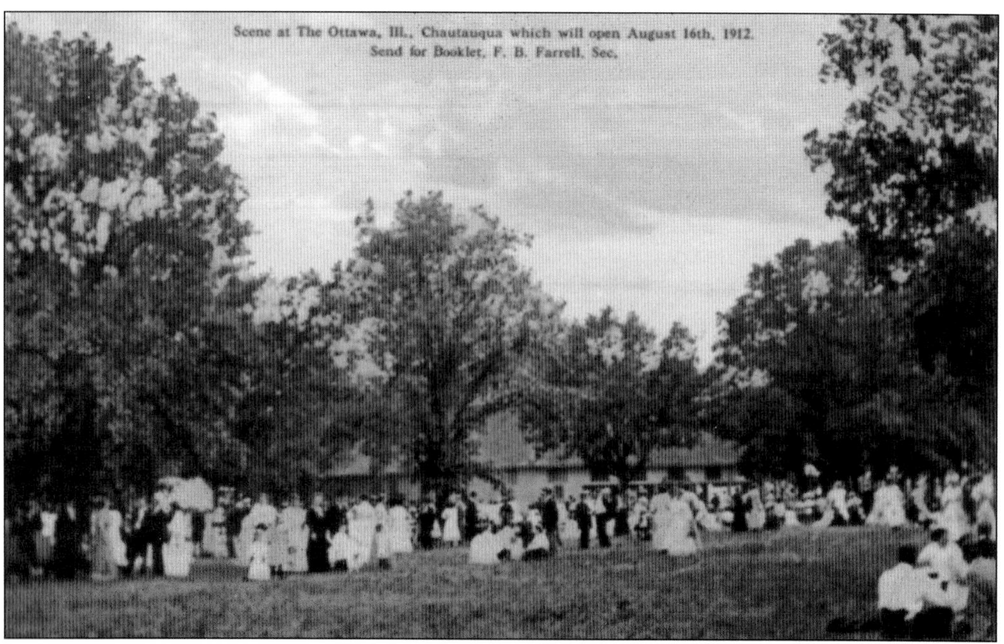

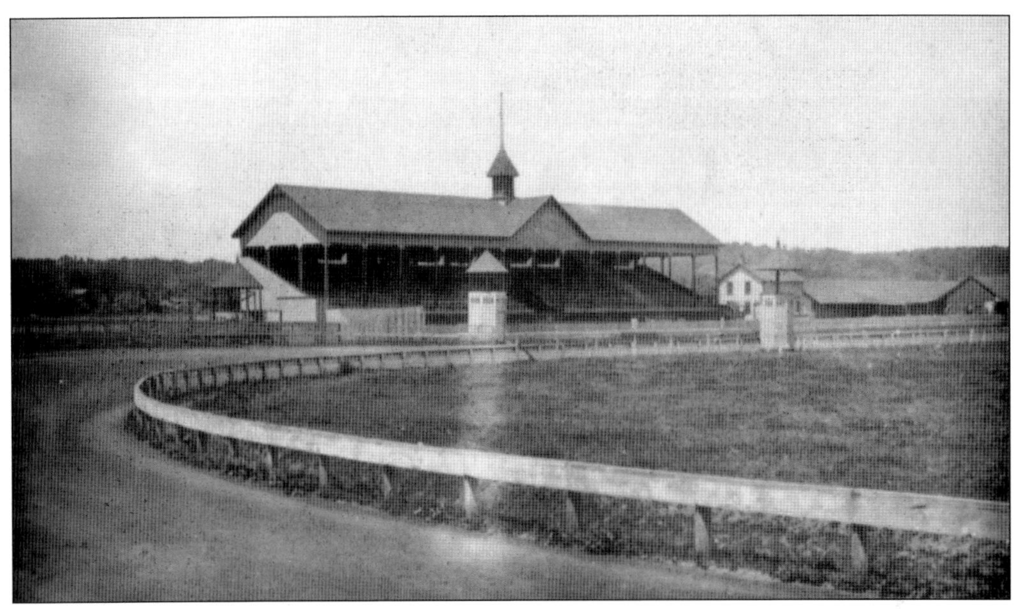

The first LaSalle County Fair was in 1853 on the courthouse grounds. The first fairgrounds were built in 1860, west of town. Ottawa hosted the Illinois State Fair in 1872, 1875, and 1876. The state fair started in 1853 and was held in different cities in order to make it easier for people to attend. It finally settled permanently in Springfield in 1892. County fairs ended in 1881 but resumed in 1912. Even without a fair, horse racing was always popular. The Ottawa Driving Park, a racetrack with a grandstand, was built on East Norris Drive in 1887. (Both, JR.)

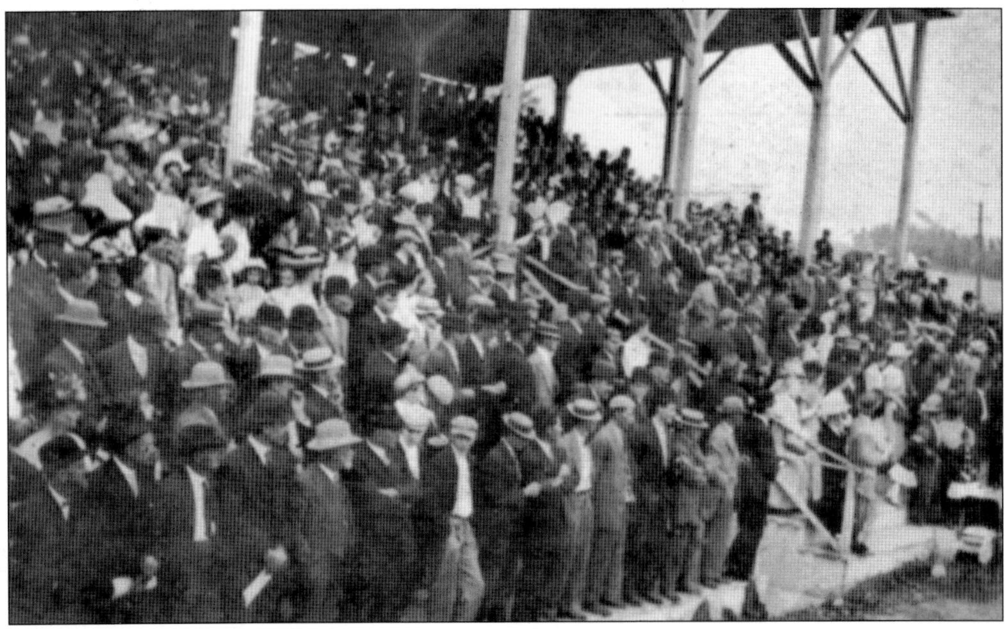

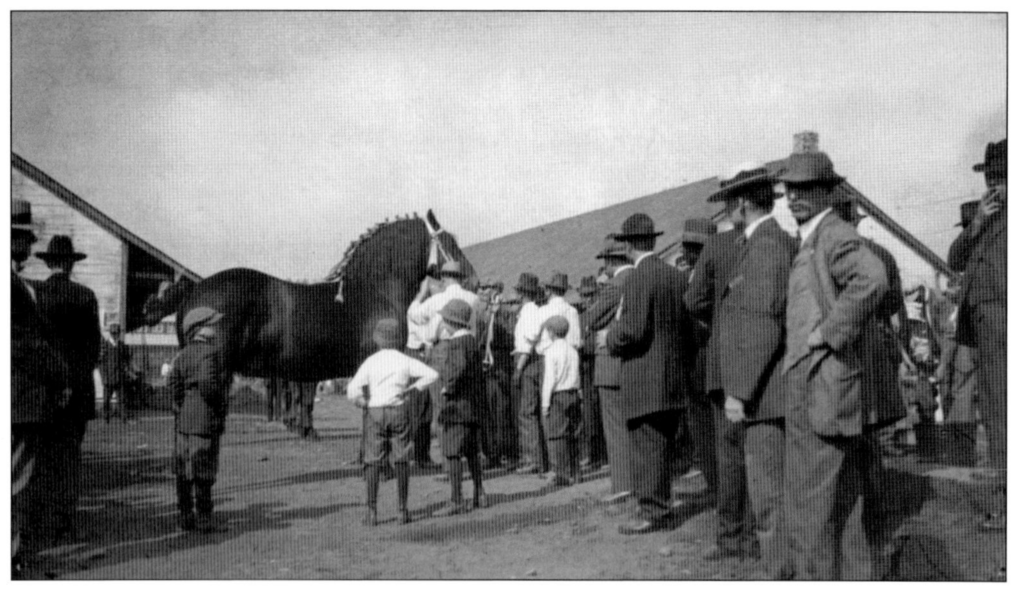

In 1912, the county fair was revived and the facilities of the driving park were purchased by the County Fair Association. The pictures on this page are from 1912. A racetrack, grandstand, and other facilities were built on East Norris Drive. The site is the present-day location of Riordan Pool and the baseball diamonds. (Both, JR.)

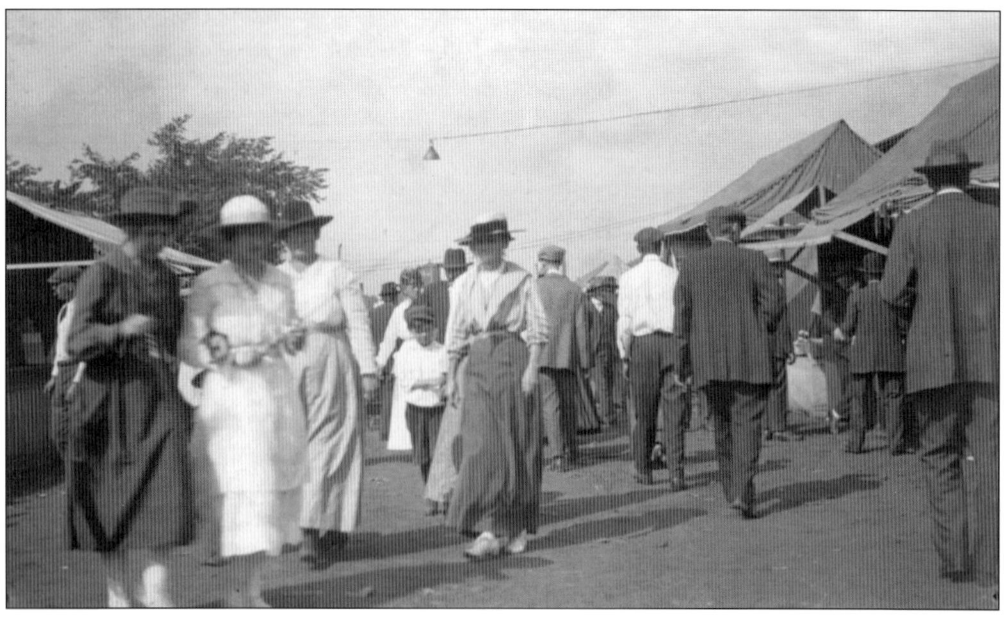

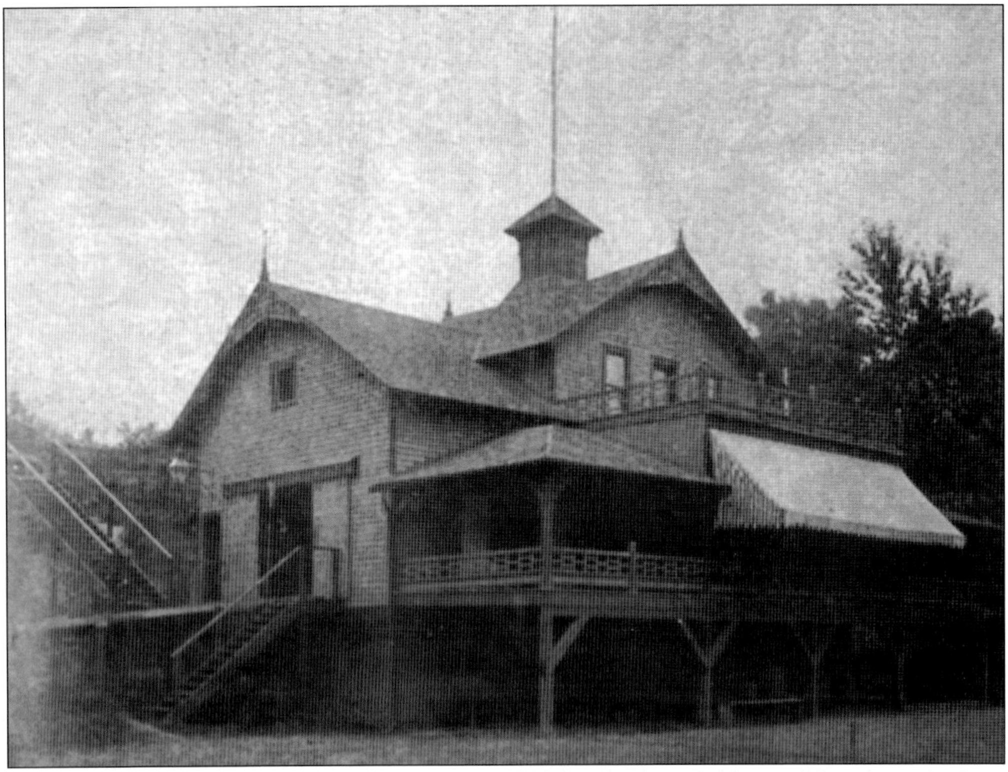

The Ottawa Boat Club began in 1885 as a social club. The first clubhouse (above) was built in 1886 on the south bank of the Illinois River, near the present-day tennis courts in Allen Park. Ottawa Boat Club's present-day building (below) was constructed in 1903 at the south edge of Columbus Street on the west bank of the Fox River. The cascades were from the I&M Canal feeder canal emptying into the river. (Both, JR.)

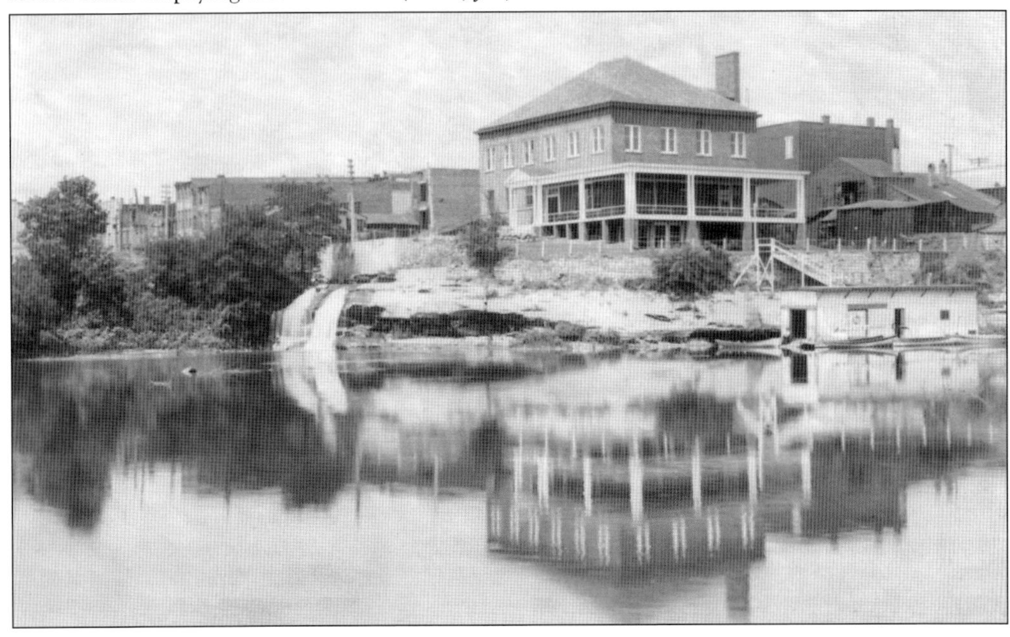

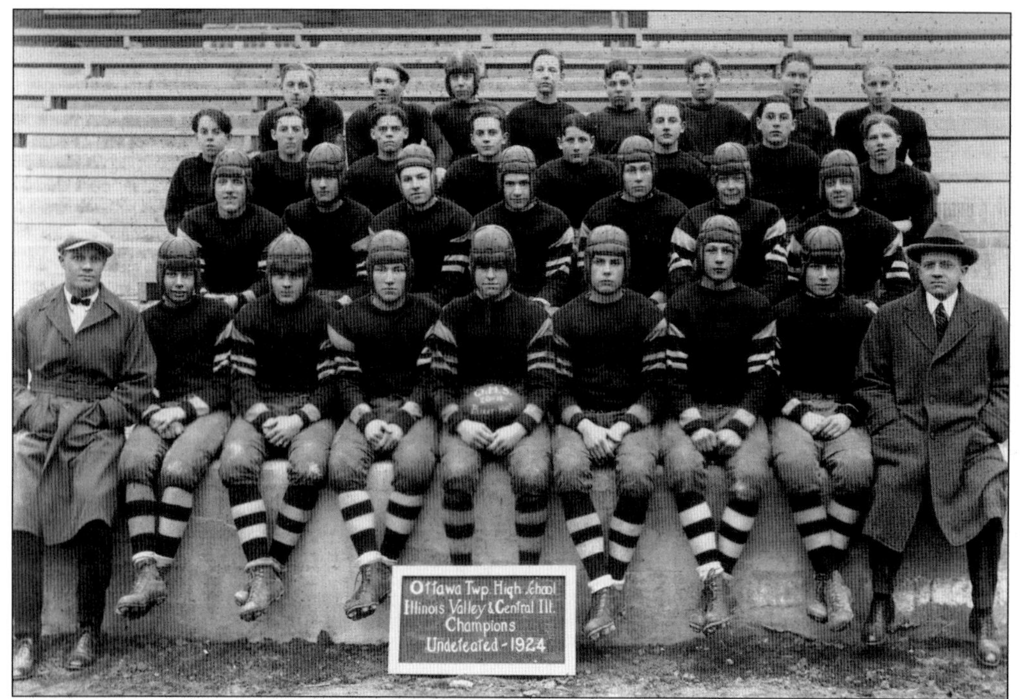

Ottawa Township High School's 1924 football team was undefeated and conference champions. (JR.)

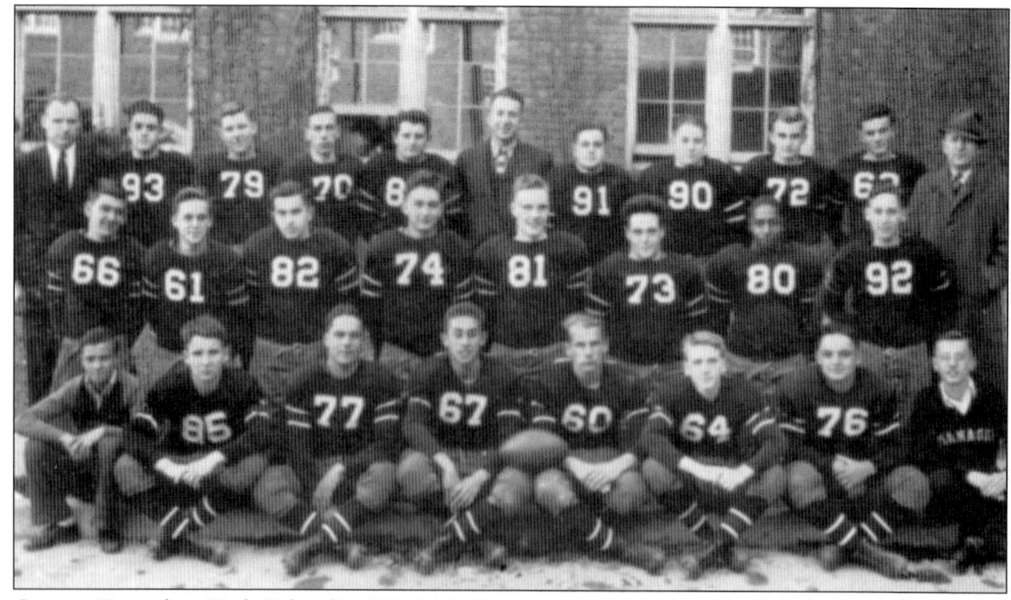

Ottawa Township High School's 1939 football team is pictured above. (Saleda family.)

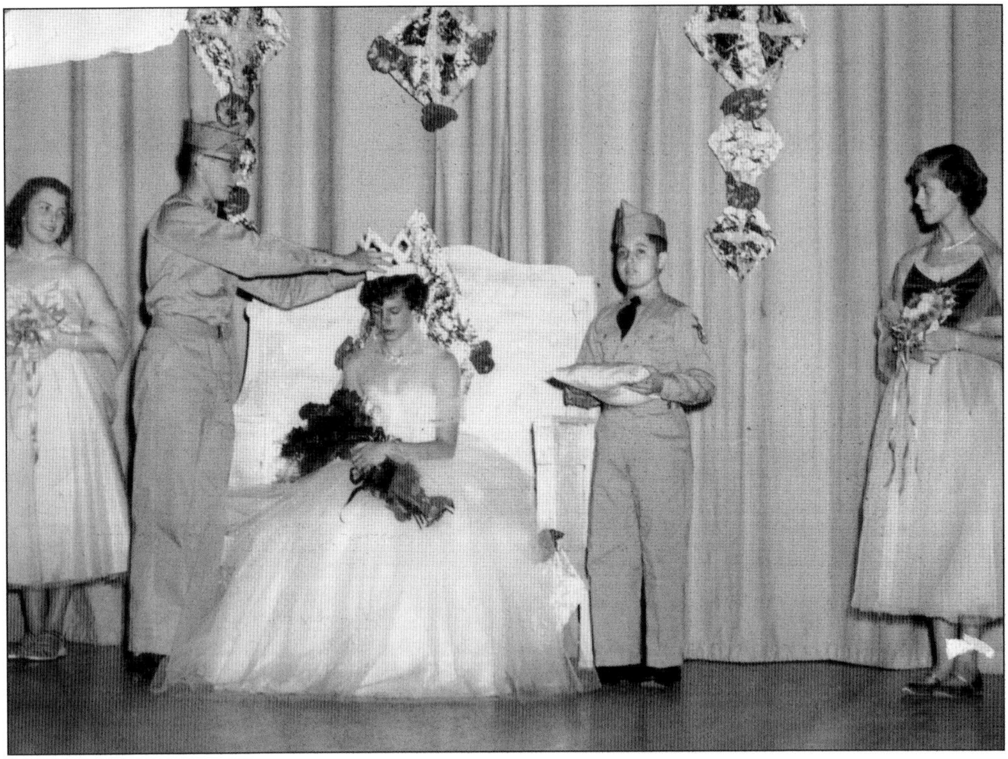

Margaret Formhals was crowned Ottawa Township High School's homecoming queen in 1952. A float from the 1952 homecoming parade is pictured below. (Both, DC.)

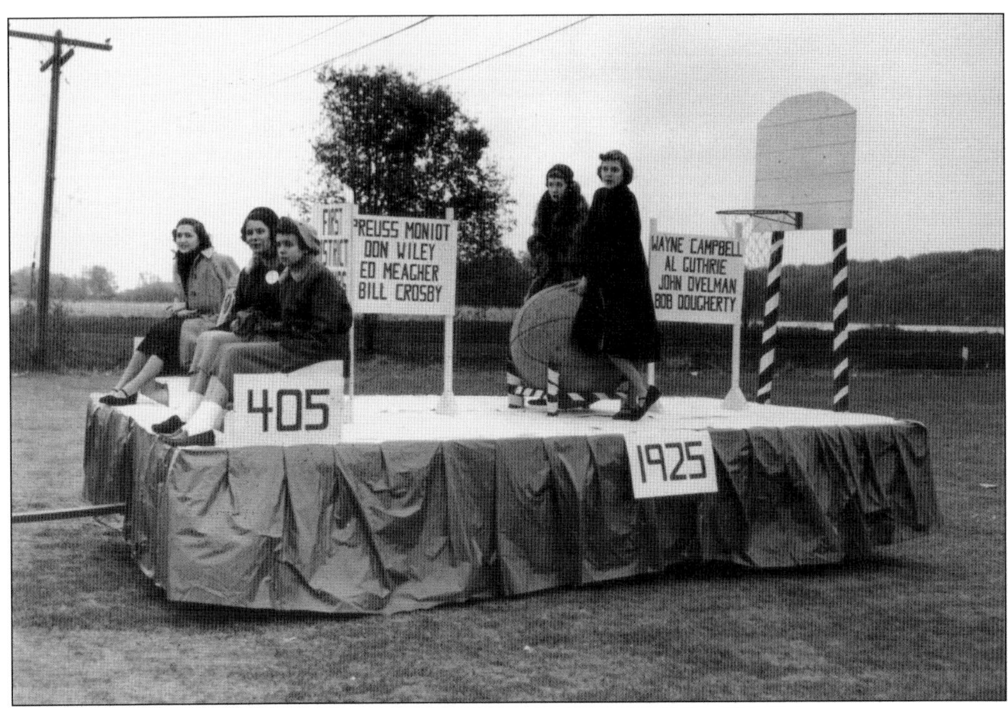

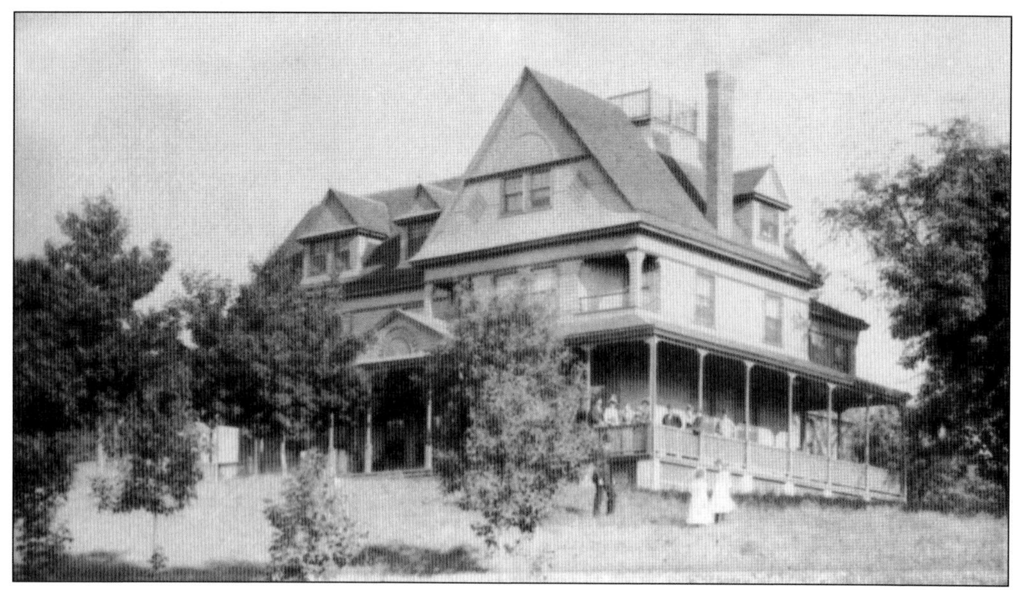

The most popular area tourist attraction is Starved Rock State Park. The name comes from an Indian legend—Potawatomi and Fox Indians attacked the Illinois Indians in 1769 and trapped them on top of the Great Rock, where the Illinois Indians eventually starved to death. The rock was a fort for French explorers from 1682 to 1702. The land was bought from the US government by Daniel Hitt in 1835 for $85. In 1890, Hitt sold the property to Ferdinand Walther, who developed it as a resort and built a large hotel (above). It became a state park after Walther sold the land to the State of Illinois in 1911. (Both, JR.)

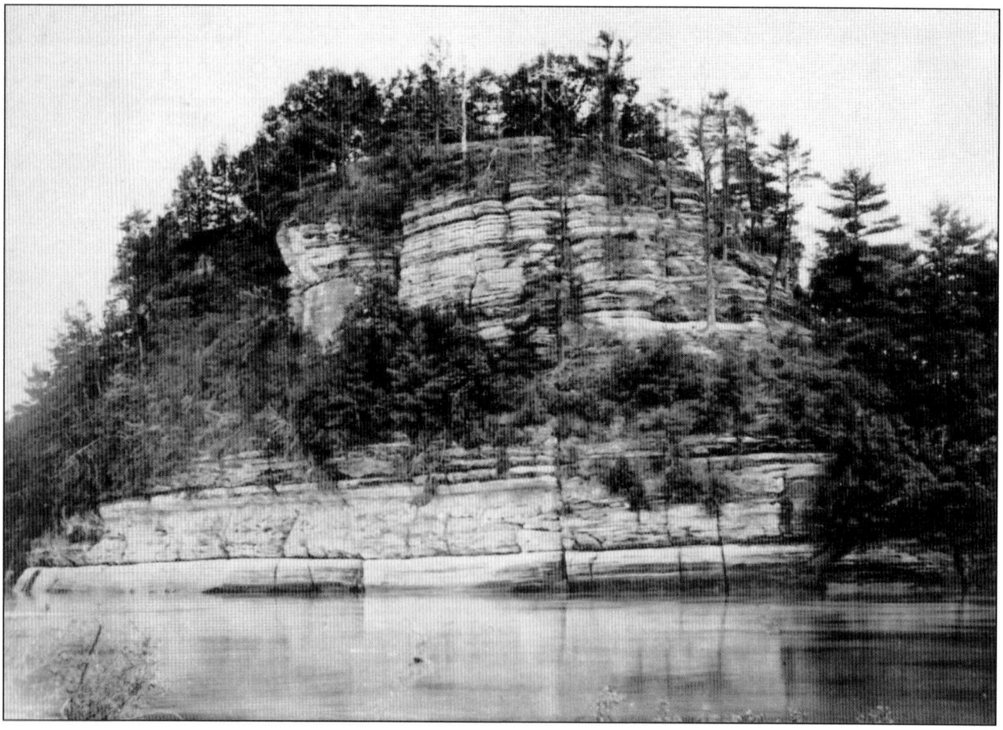

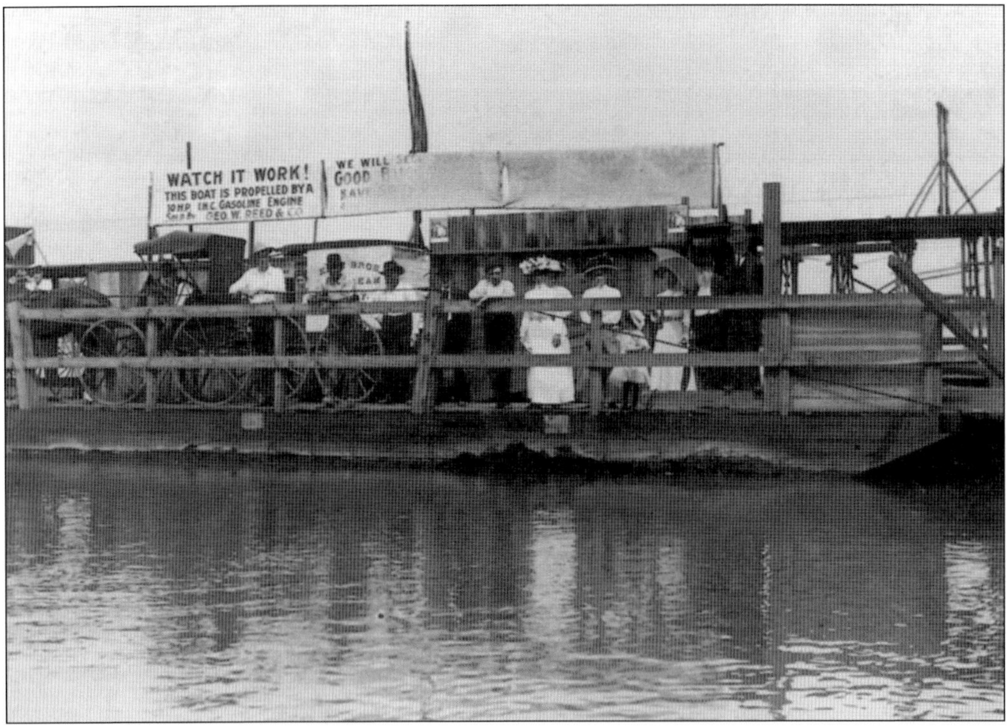

River ferrys, such as the ones pictured here in the 1890s, took passengers on excursion cruises along the Illinois River, often ending at Starved Rock. (Both, JR.)

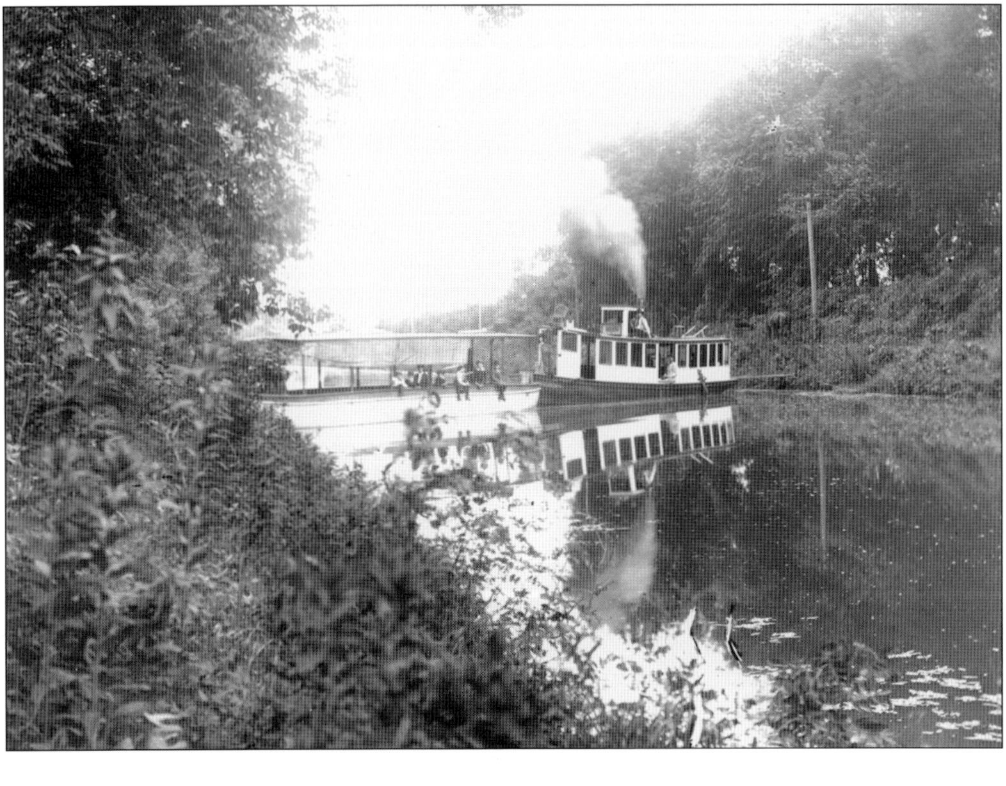

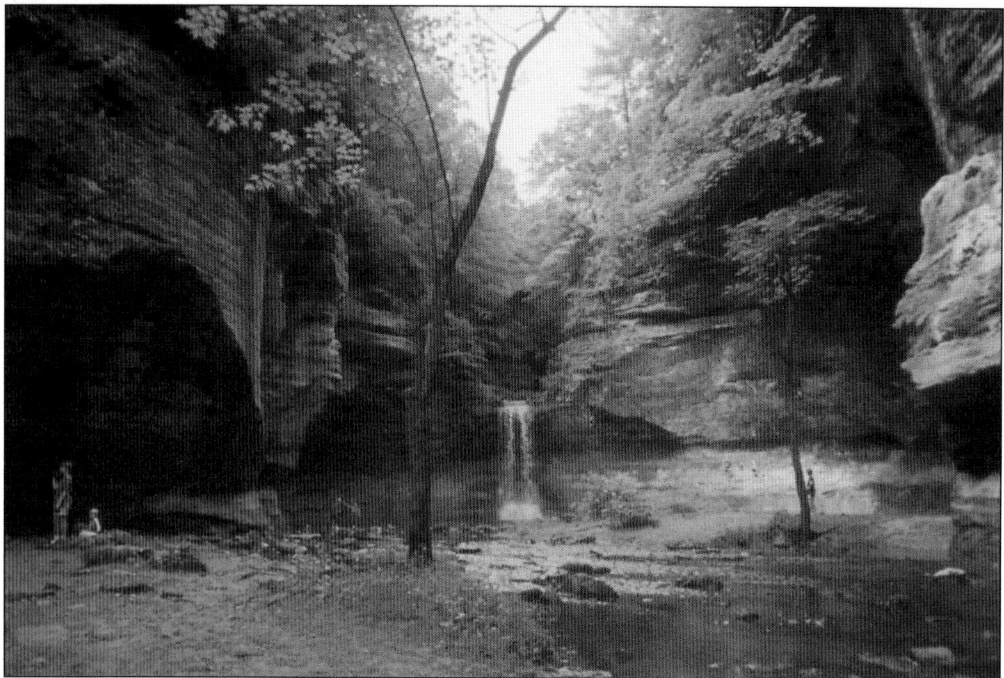

Matthiessen State Park is adjacent to Starved Rock. Frederick Matthiessen, an industrialist and philanthropist from LaSalle, purchased the land in the late 1800s and built trails, bridges, stairways, and dams and called the area Deer Park. After Matthiessen's death, the park was donated to the state; it was renamed for Matthiessen in 1943. (Both, JR.)

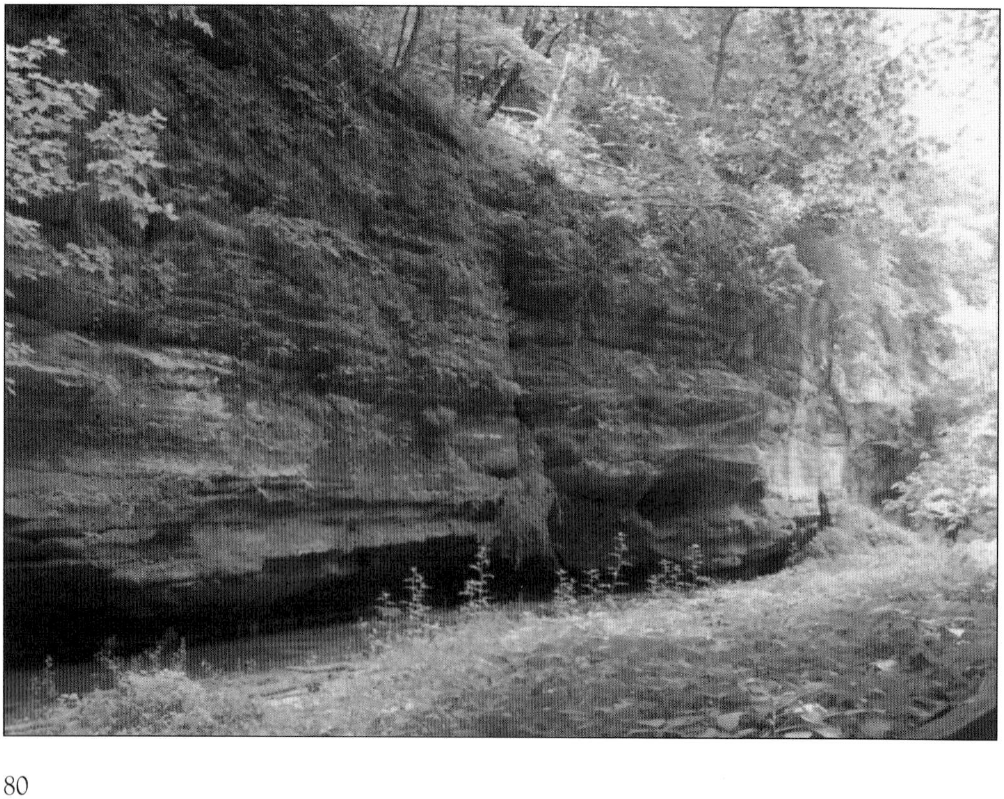

Five

War and Remembrance

The military history of the Ottawa area goes back to the wars between Indian tribes with the most legendary battle occurring at Starved Rock.

On May 20, 1832, an Indian raiding party attacked settlers at Indian Creek, north of Ottawa, killing 16 people. Chief Shabbona warned settlers of the impending attack, but they refused to go to Fort Johnston for safety.

Capt. Abraham Lincoln was stationed at Fort Johnston for 10 days in 1832 during the Black Hawk War. Lincoln is known to have stayed in Ottawa five times. He spent five days in Ottawa in June 1852, in a legal case with the I&M Canal. Lincoln attended several sessions of the Supreme Court in Ottawa, staying at T. Lyle Dickey's mansion on the north bluff. Lincoln spoke at Washington Square Park on behalf of presidential candidate John C. Fremont in 1856, two years before his famous debate.

The Civil War reached Ottawa, and several houses became part of the Underground Railroad, sheltering runaway slaves on the way to Canada. One was the house of John Hossack, at 210 West Prospect Avenue. Amos Ebersol's farmhouse, four miles south of Ottawa, also sheltered escaping slaves.

A total of 5,942 men from LaSalle County fought in the Civil War, and the names of the 810 men who died in the war are on a memorial in Washington Square Park. Of that number, 160 were from Ottawa.

Another memorial in the park lists 28 Ottawa men killed in World War I, 146 killed in World War II, 7 killed in Korea, and 13 killed in Vietnam.

The first three casualties of World War II died at Pearl Harbor on December 7, 1941. Marine Cpl. James McCarrens and Navy Cook Third Class Herman Koeppe were aboard the USS *Arizona*; Seaman Robert Halterman was on the USS *Oklahoma*. The Ottawa VFW post is named for these three men.

At nearby Seneca, a shipyard built 157 landing ship tanks (LSTs) between 1942 and 1945. The LST, a large, flat-bottomed ship that carried invading troops onto beaches, was essential for the landing of men and supplies at Normandy, North Africa, and throughout the South Pacific. Chicago Bridge & Iron set up the shipyard in a former cornfield at the edge of the Illinois River, where the ships were launched upon completion. As many as 11,000 men worked there at its peak.

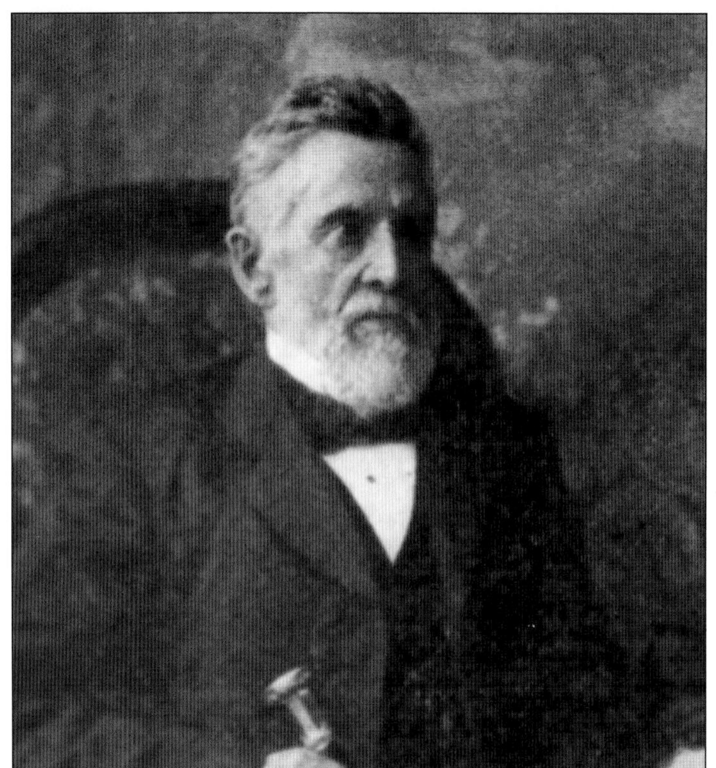

Several houses in the Ottawa area were used as part of the Underground Railroad, sheltering runaway slaves. John Hossack (pictured here) was a strong abolitionist who hid slaves in his house. In 1859, Hossack and another man grabbed Jim Gray, a runaway slave, from a marshal outside an Ottawa court room. They put him in a waiting buggy and sped away up LaSalle Street. Hossack and two other men served brief jail sentences. Hossack's daughter married John Scott, who helped start the Carson, Pirie, Scott store. Pictured below is Hossack's house on West Prospect Avenue. (Both, JR.)

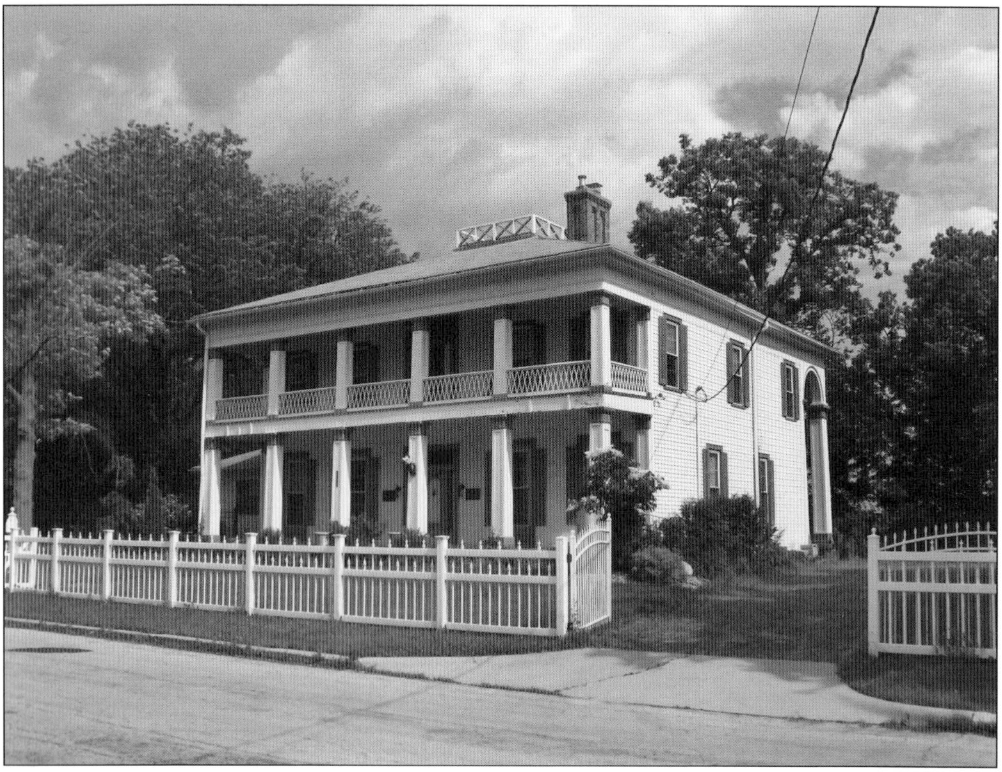

A legless Civil War veteran poses for a portrait at the Ottawa studio of W.E. Bowman. Below is the Eames house at Superior and Paul Streets. Local lore claims that this picture was taken in 1858 after the Great Debate, and that Douglas and Lincoln are the men in front wearing top hats. If true, it would be the only known photograph of the two men in Ottawa. The picture is too grainy to authenticate, but it sure makes for a great debate. (Both, JR.)

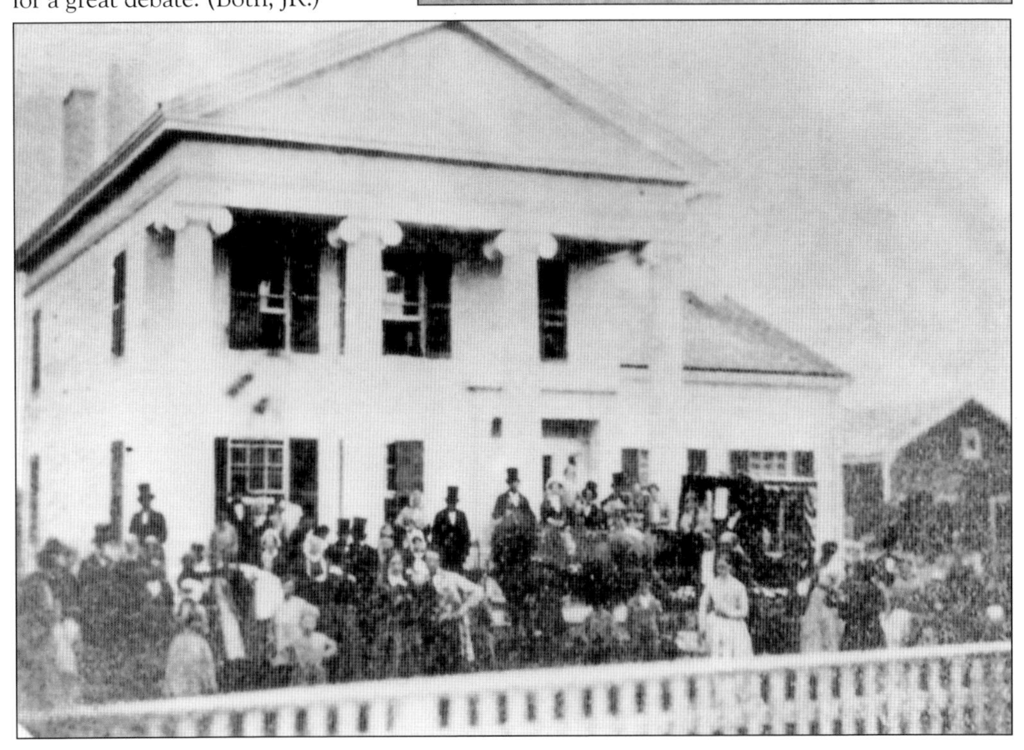

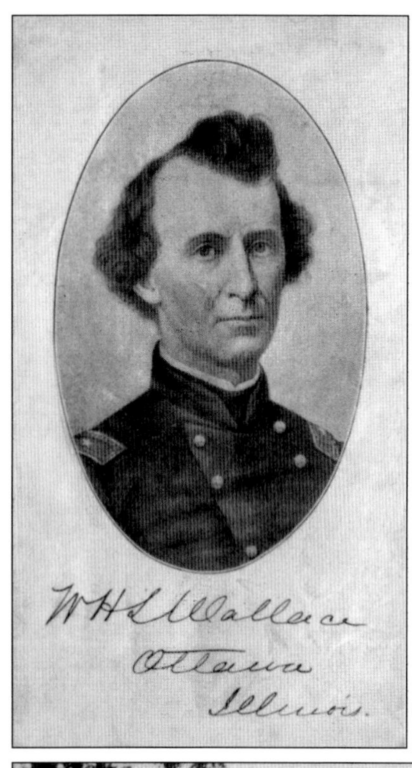

William Hervy Lamme Wallace was born in Ohio in 1821 and came to Ottawa with his family at age 13. He became a lawyer and married Ann Dickey, the daughter of prominent Ottawa lawyer T. Lyle Dickey. Both Wallace and Dickey sometimes partnered in legal cases with their friend Abraham Lincoln. Dickey also served valiantly in the Civil War. Below is the W.H.L. Wallace house in Ottawa, built in the 1850s and called "The Oaks." The next several pages contain pictures of the inside of the house from a time when the Wallace family still lived there. The house was converted into apartments in the 1940s. (Both, JR.)

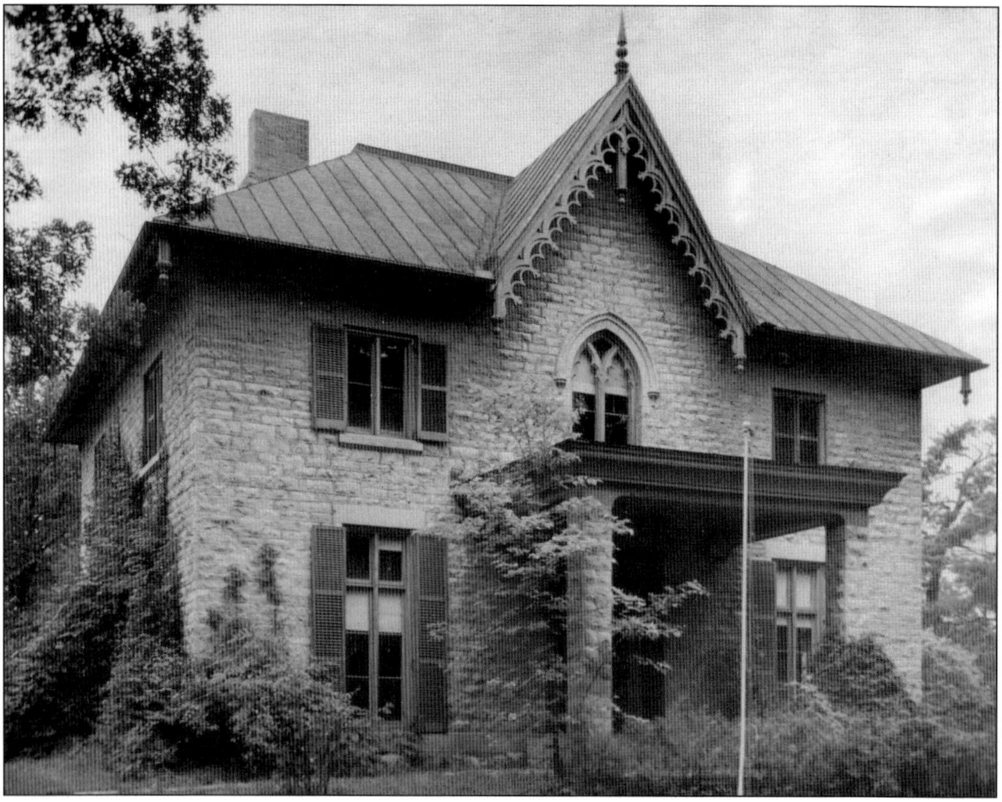

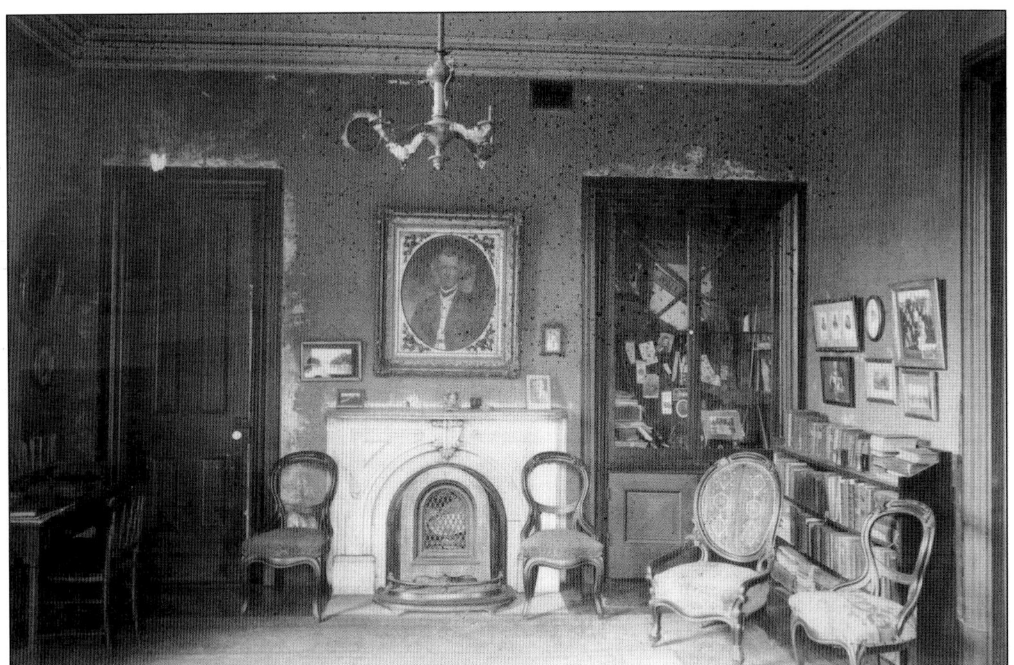

W.H.L. Wallace of Ottawa was a veteran of the Mexican War. His heroics in the Civil War garnered several promotions, and he was named a general. Gen. W.H.L. Wallace was killed in the Battle of Shiloh on April 10, 1862. Wallace was the highest-ranking Union officer killed at Shiloh. (Both, JR.)

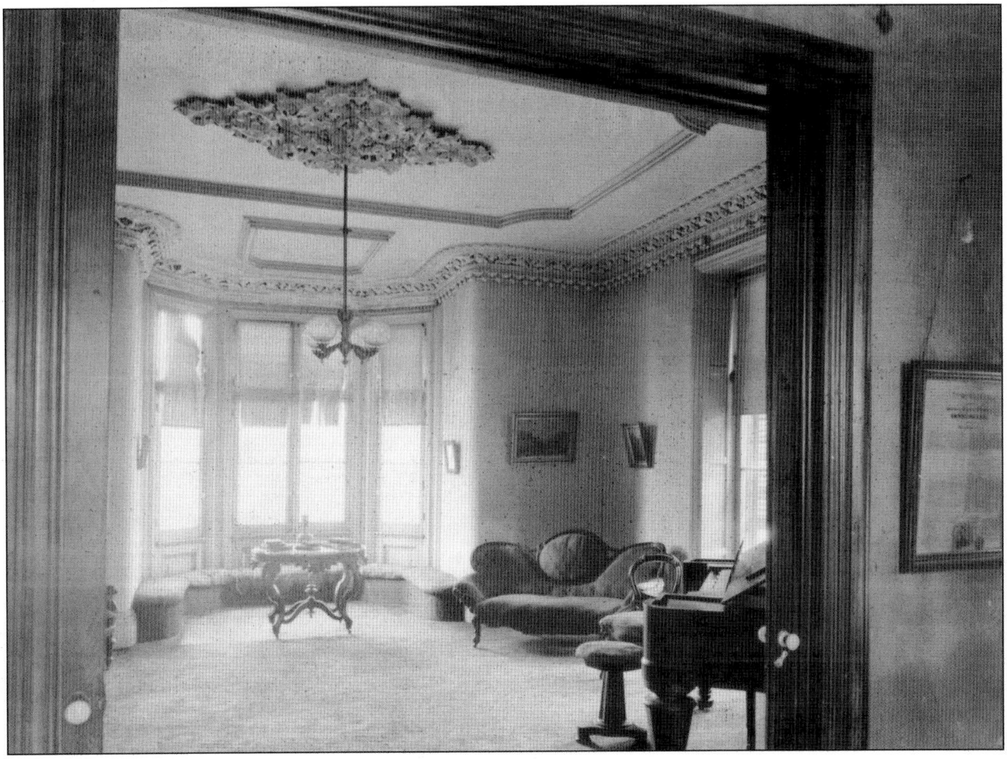

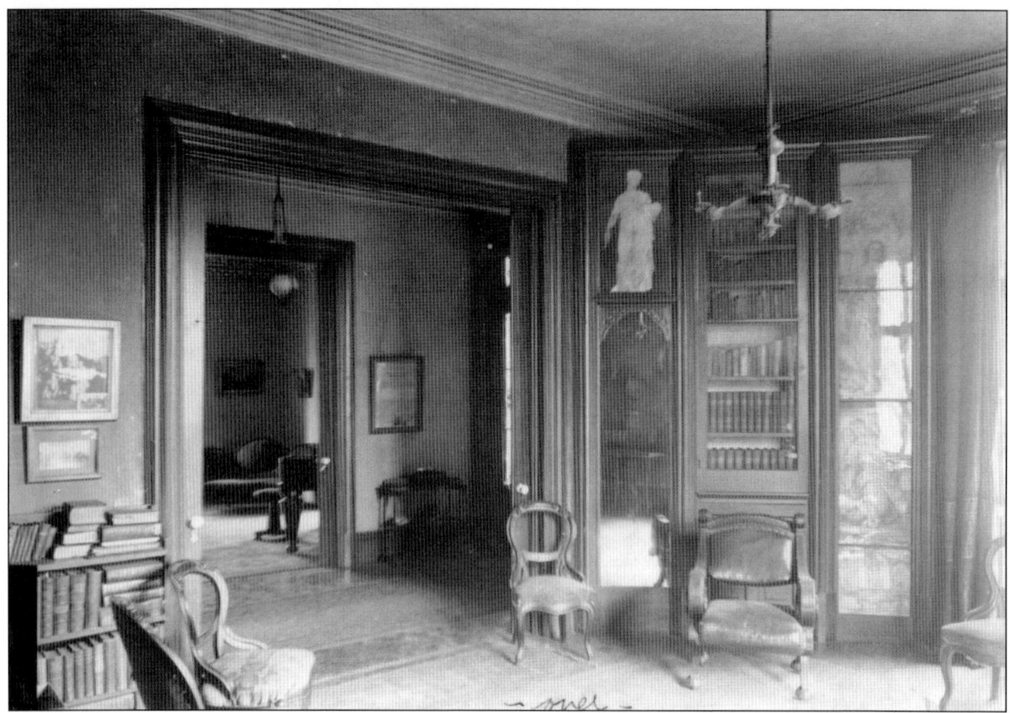

Wallace's leadership at the Hornets Nest at Shiloh held off Confederate assaults long enough to make a difference, but many historians have given Gen. Benjamin Prentiss the credit that really belongs to General Wallace, because Wallace died and Prentiss lived to tell the story. (Both, JR.)

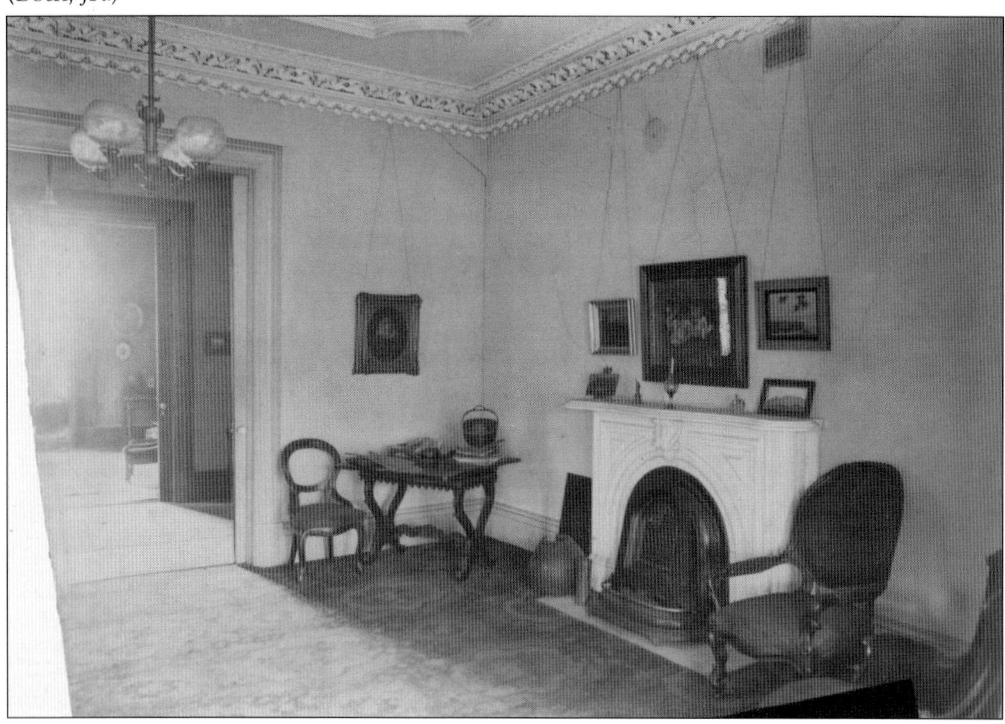

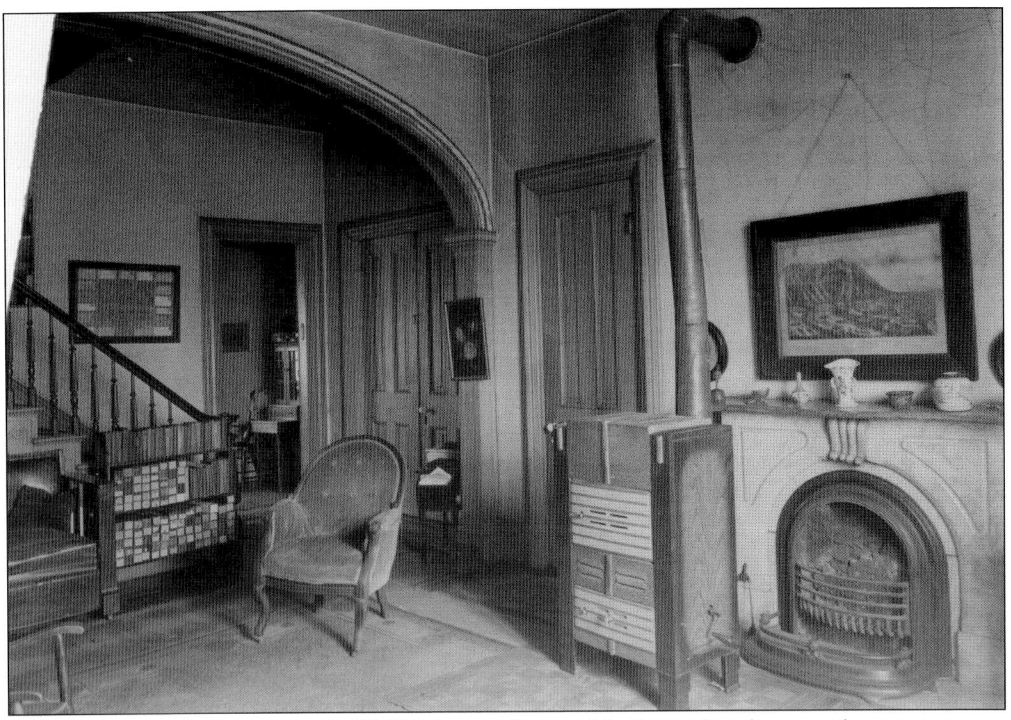

Modern historians now recognize Wallace's contribution. Not long after the war, a large monument to General Wallace was built at the Shiloh battlefield. (Both, JR.)

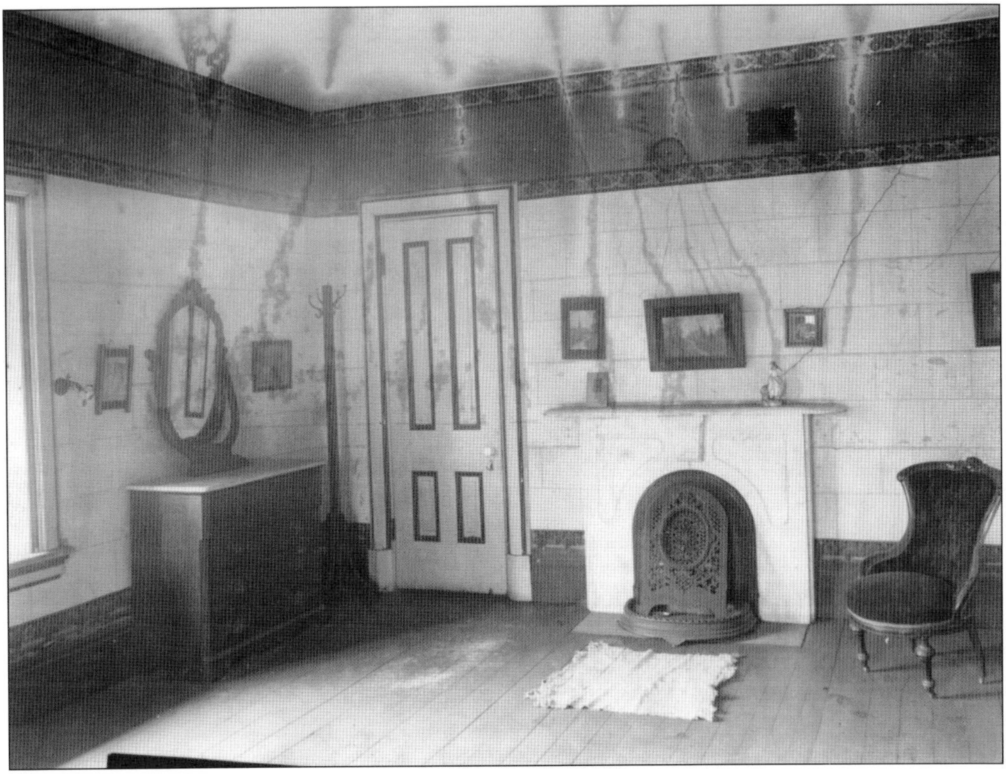

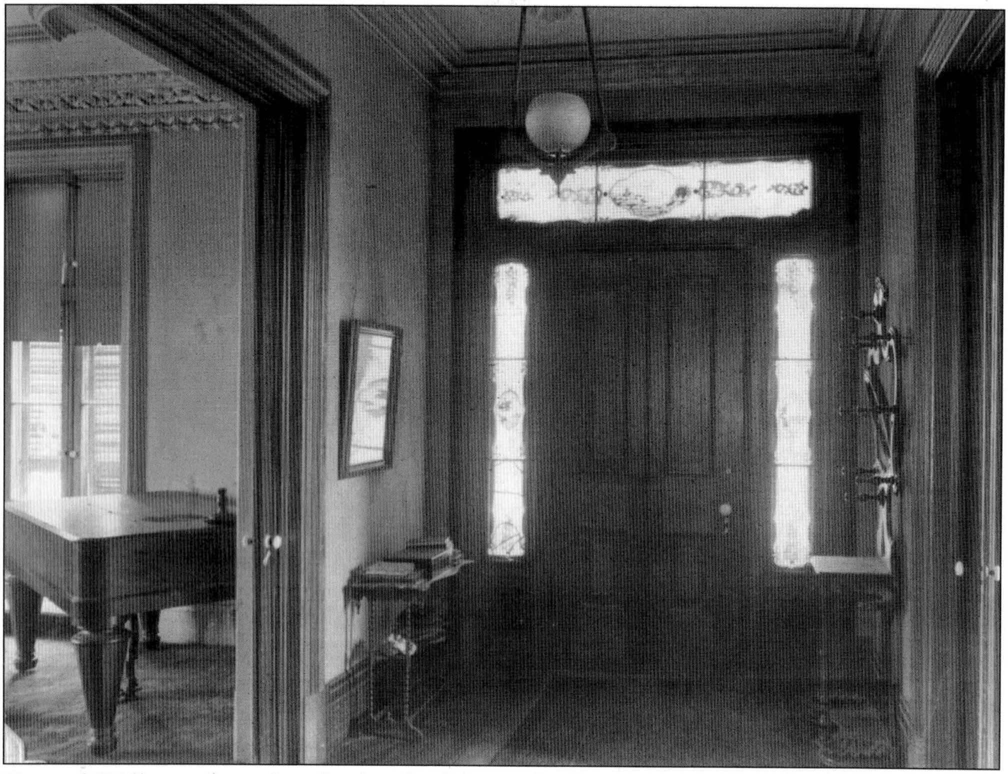

General Wallace is buried in the family plot near his home on the north bluff of Ottawa. His horse, Prince, is also buried on the property. The family graveyard, pictured below in 1939, has fallen into disrepair. It is on a steep ravine, and erosion and neglect are threatening to send the bodies down a hill. (Both, JR.)

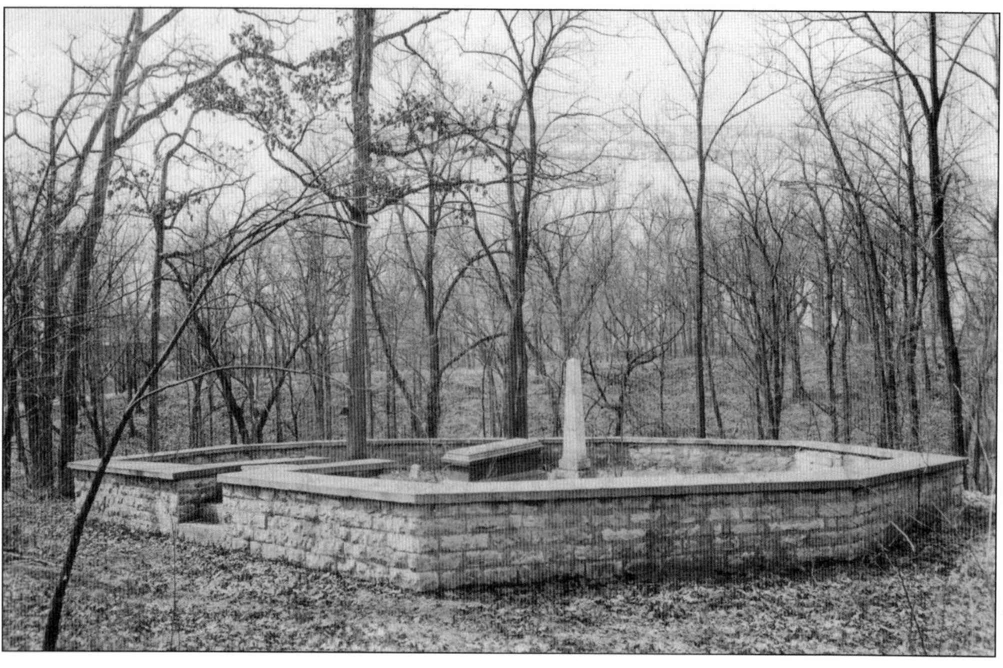

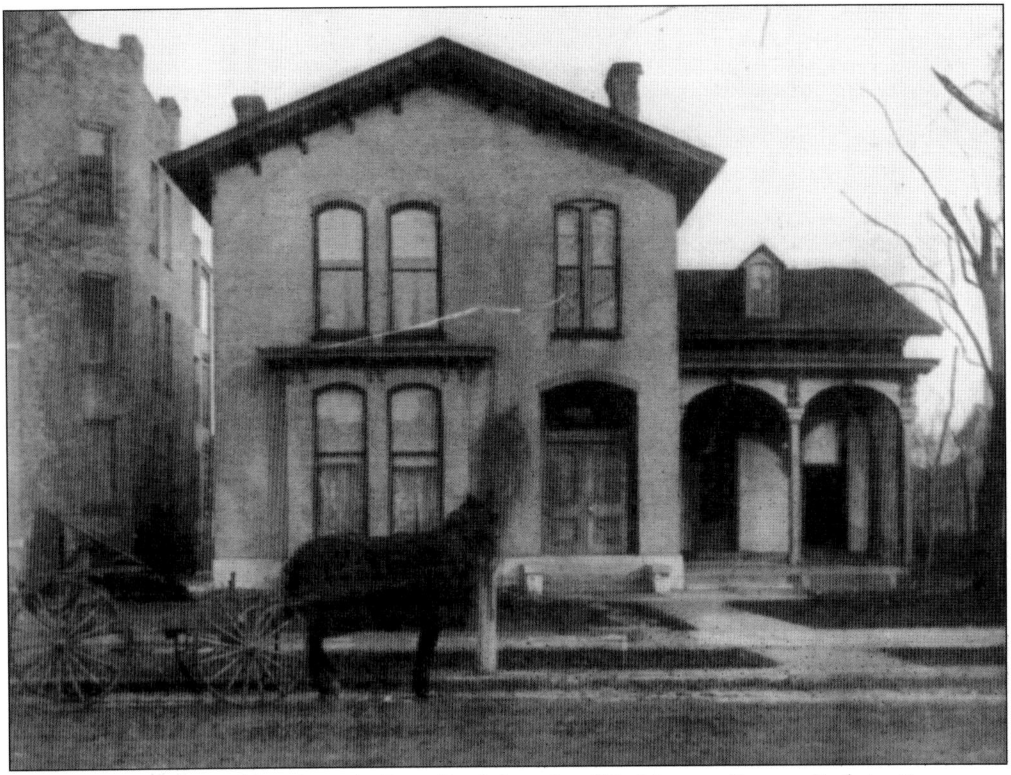

Abraham Lincoln and Stephen A. Douglas debated in Washington Square Park in Ottawa on Aug. 21, 1858. Approximately 12,000 people were there. Lincoln stayed at the home of Mayor Joseph O. Glover (pictured above), near the park on Columbus Street. The house was torn down in 1958, and a parking lot is now on the site. Pictured below is Ottawa's Colonnade on Ottawa Avenue, built in 1918 to commemorate the state's centennial. (Both, JR.)

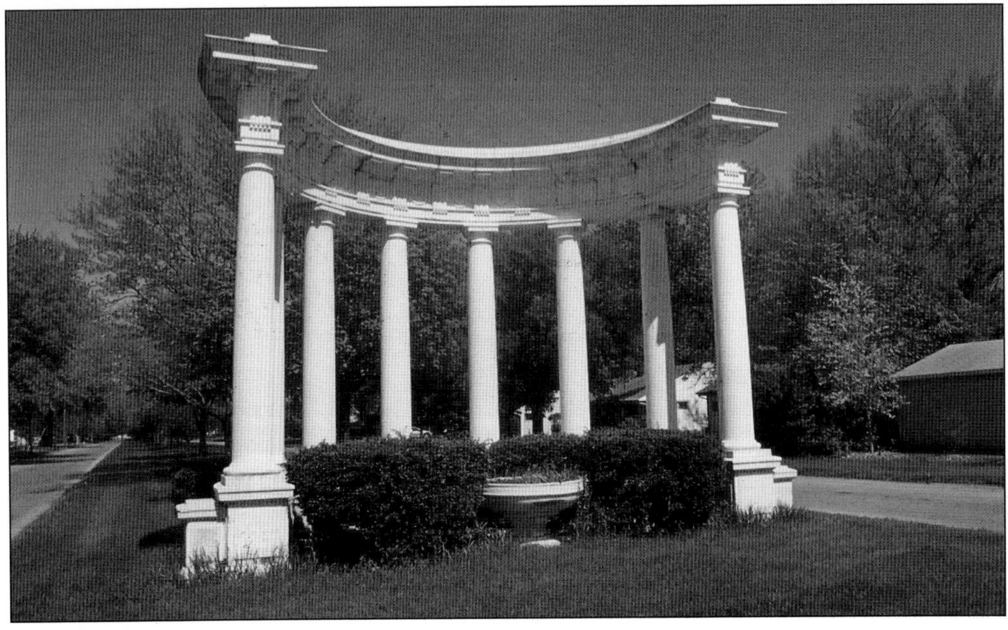

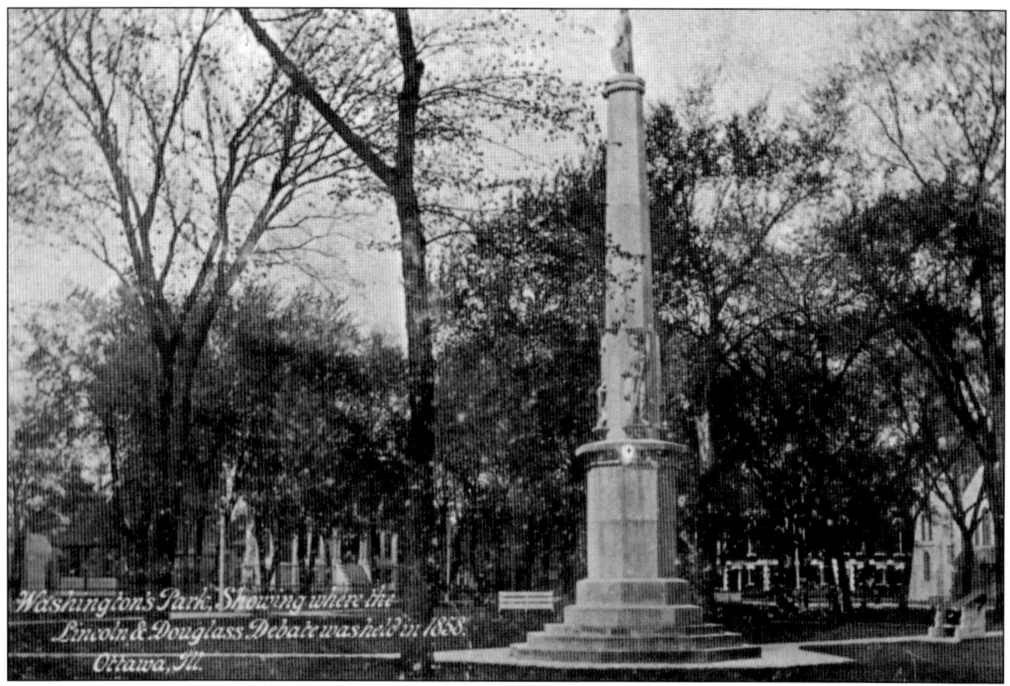

Many historians claim that Douglas was the better debater. Stephen A. Douglas won the election for an Illinois US Senate seat in 1858, but in a rematch two years later, with the presidency at stake, Lincoln was the winner. (JR.)

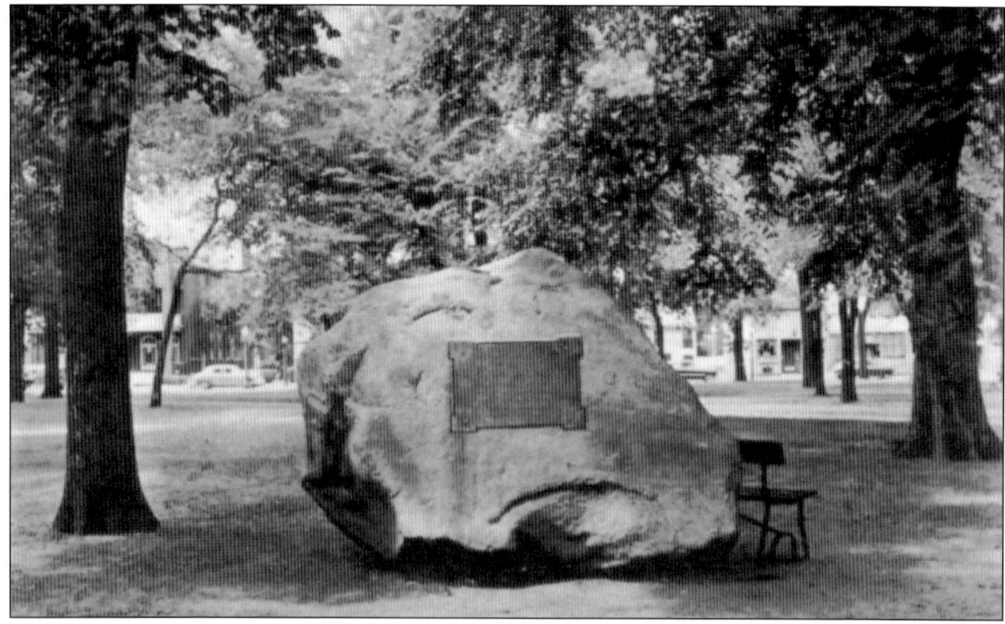

A huge boulder was dedicated with a plaque in 1908 to honor the 50th anniversary of the Lincoln-Douglas Debate. The sons of Lincoln and Douglas were invited to the dedication. Stephen A. Douglas Jr. came and made a fine speech, but Robert Todd Lincoln did not show up. (JR.)

Among the memorials that have been placed in Washington Square Park are a fountain (right), which was melted down for scrap iron during World War II, and an obelisk (below) with the names of men from the area who gave their lives during the Civil War. The obelisk and a six-foot "Goddess of Liberty" statue were created by Edward McInhill, an Irish immigrant and marble stonecutter. More than 6,000 people attended the dedication of the monument in 1873. However, McInhill was cheated out of money he was owed for his years of work. George Houghton raised pledges for the monument, swindled the city, and then fled. McInhill suffered financial hardship for the rest of his life. When he died, in 1907, McInhill's family could not afford a tombstone in St. Columba cemetery for the stonecutter who made so many of the existing tombstones in the cemetery. After laying in an unmarked grave for more than a century, Ottawa citizens raised funds for a proper headstone in 2009. (Both, JR.)

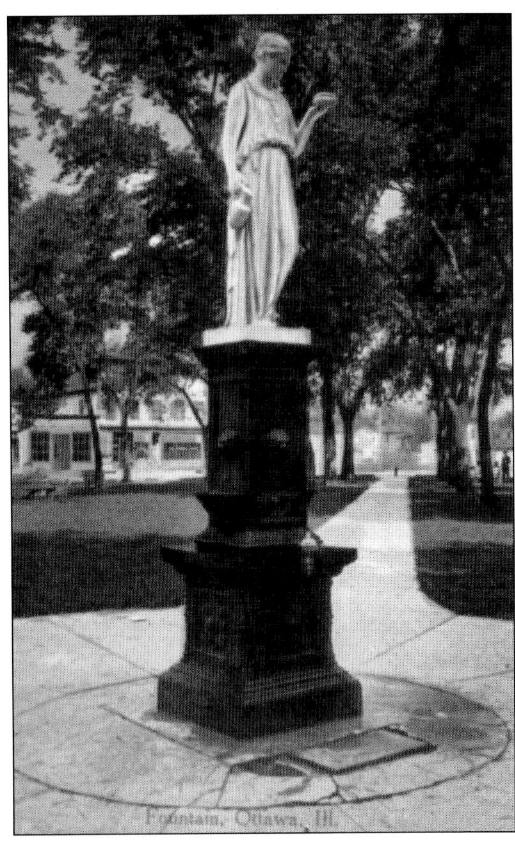

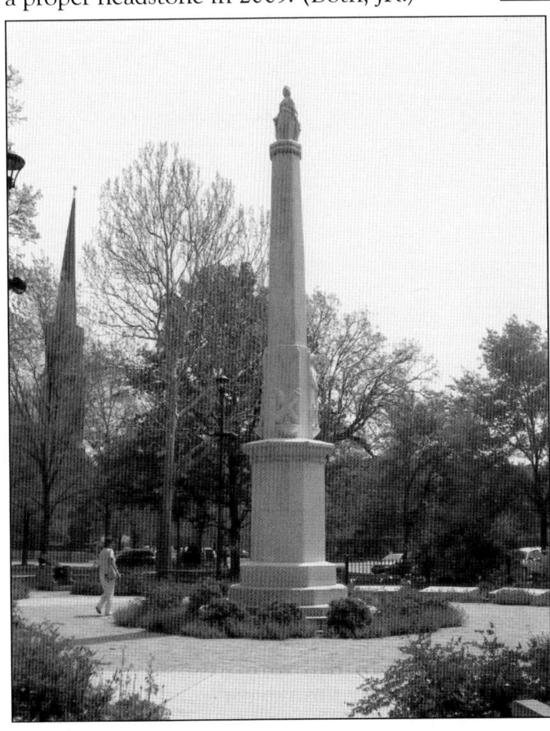

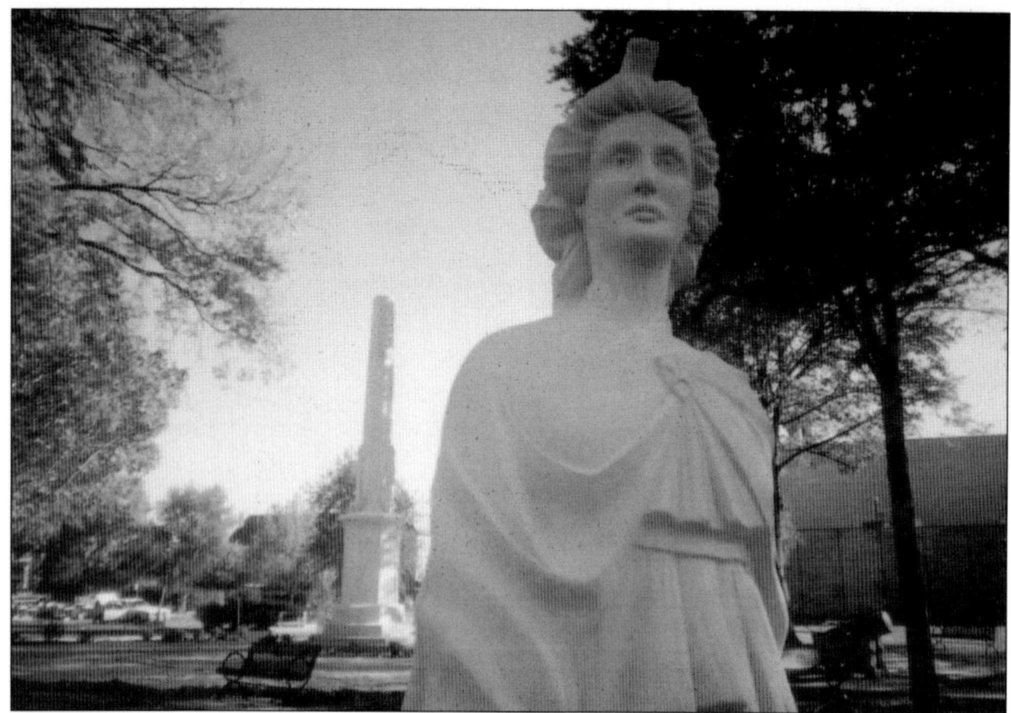

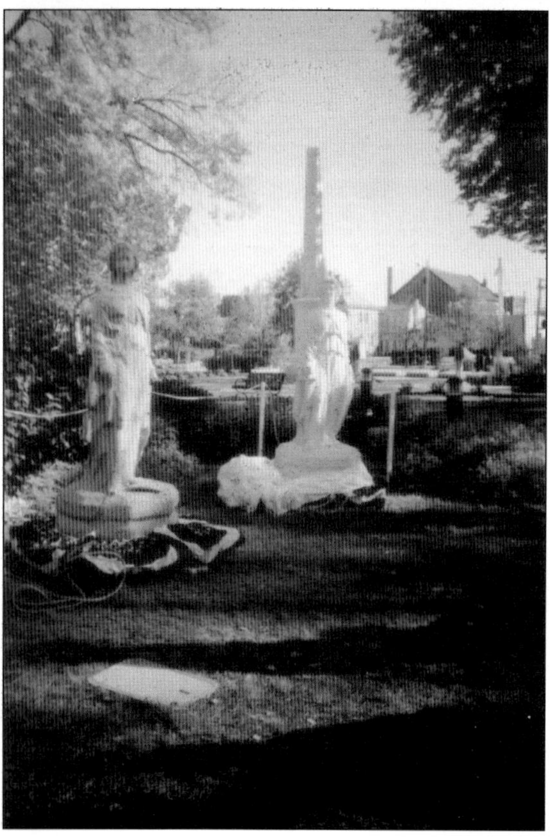

After 132 years of being exposed to harsh weather, McInhill's statue and the names on the monument were severely eroded. The statue was removed in 2005, but it was too damaged to be repaired. A new statue was made, and the names of the war dead were carved in new granite tablets. The new monument, in a Civil War memorial plaza, was dedicated on October 14, 2006. (Both, DC.)

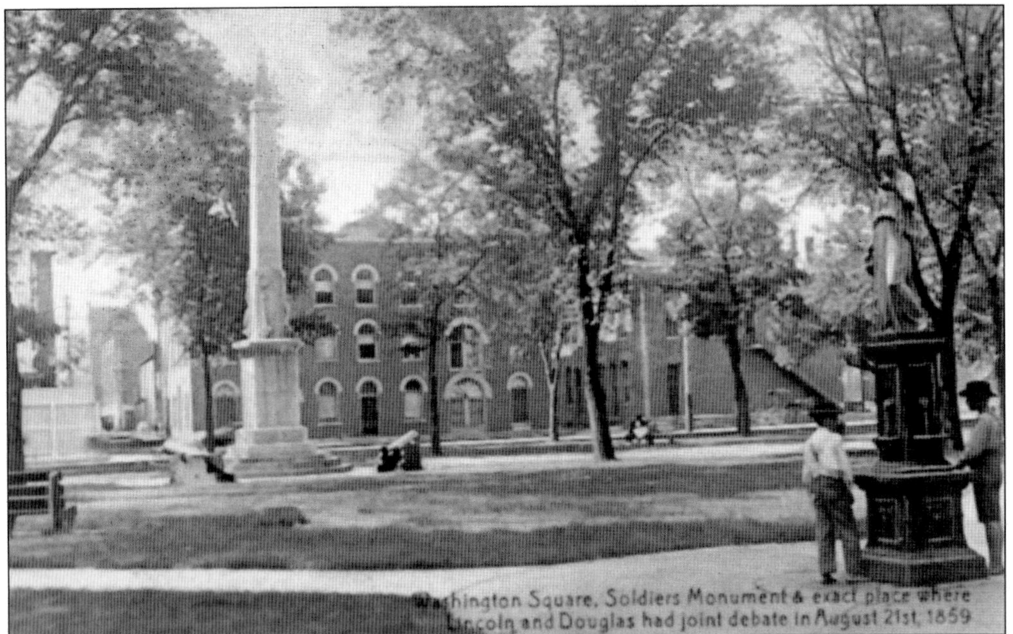

A number of memorials to those who served this country have been placed in Washington Square Park over the years. The Civil War monument includes the names of those who died in the Spanish-American War. There also is a dignified granite monument with the names of those who died in World War I, World War II, the Korean War, and Vietnam. (JR.)

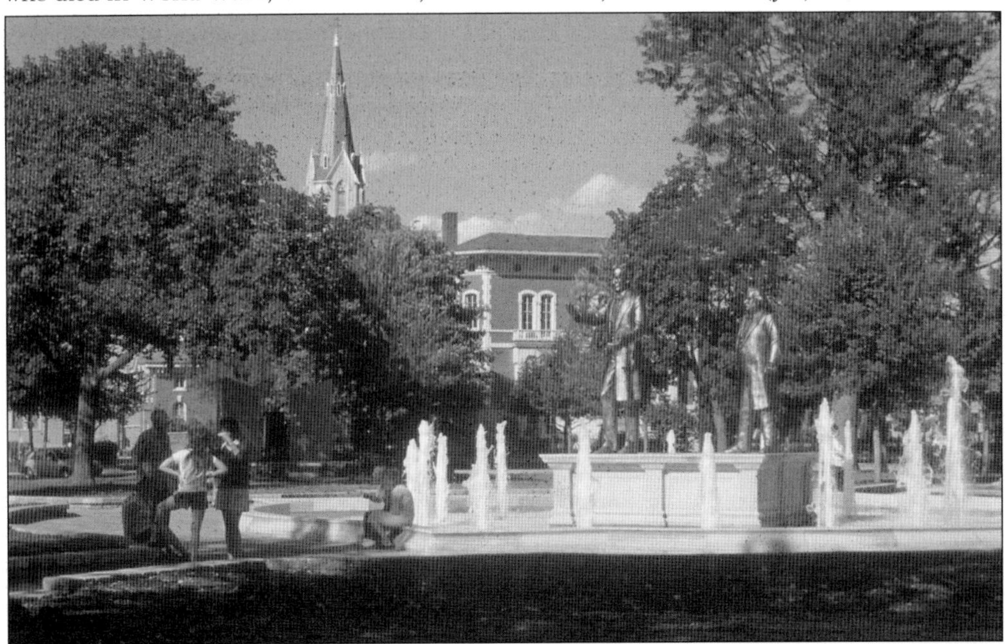

Life-size statues of Lincoln and Douglas, set in a large fountain arrangement, were erected in Washington Square Park in 2002, near the spot where the two men debated on August 21, 1858. The plaza was designed by Ottawan Margaret Martyn, who also designed the new *Goddess of Liberty* statue. Shown here in the background are Reddick Mansion and the steeple of St. Columba Catholic Church. (JR.)

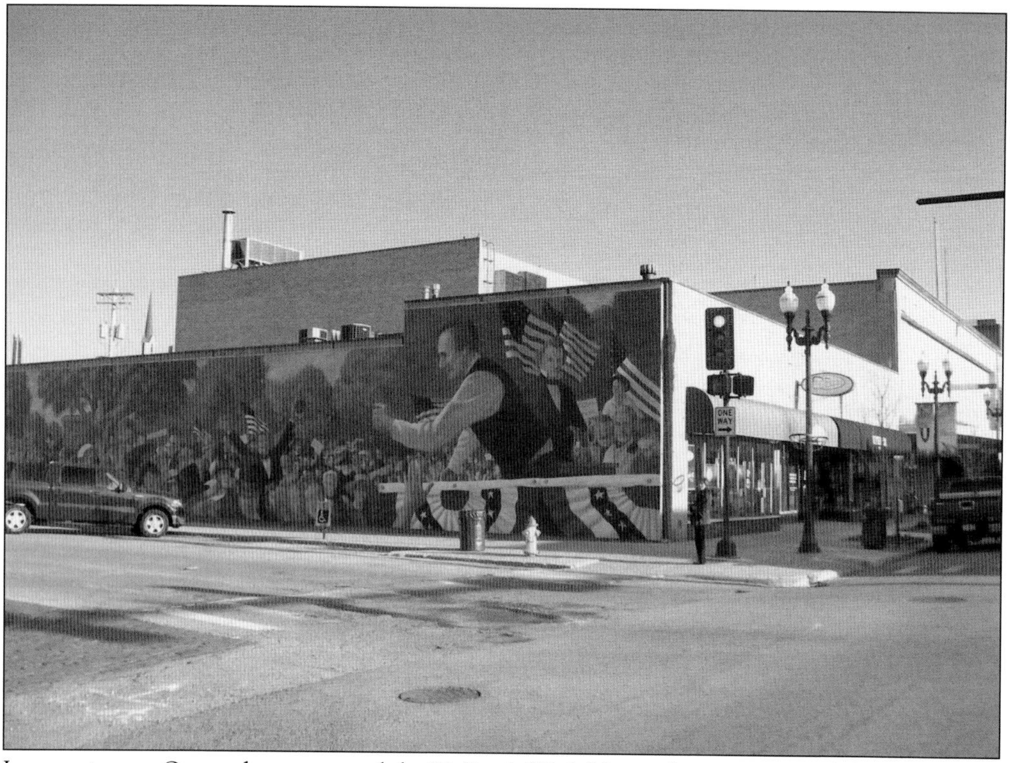

In recent years, Ottawa has sponsored the "A Brush With History" project—murals have appeared on several buildings in town. The Lincoln-Douglas debate is commemorated on the side of a building along Jackson Street at LaSalle Street. Farther up the block, on LaSalle Street, Gen. W.H.L. Wallace leads his troops in the mural shown below. (Both, JR.)

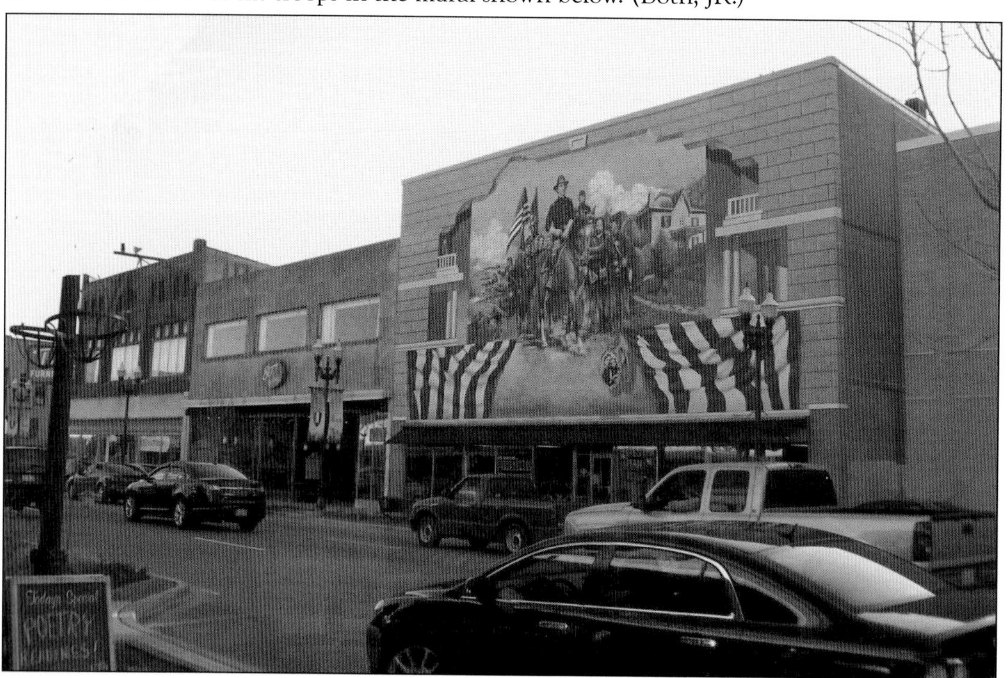

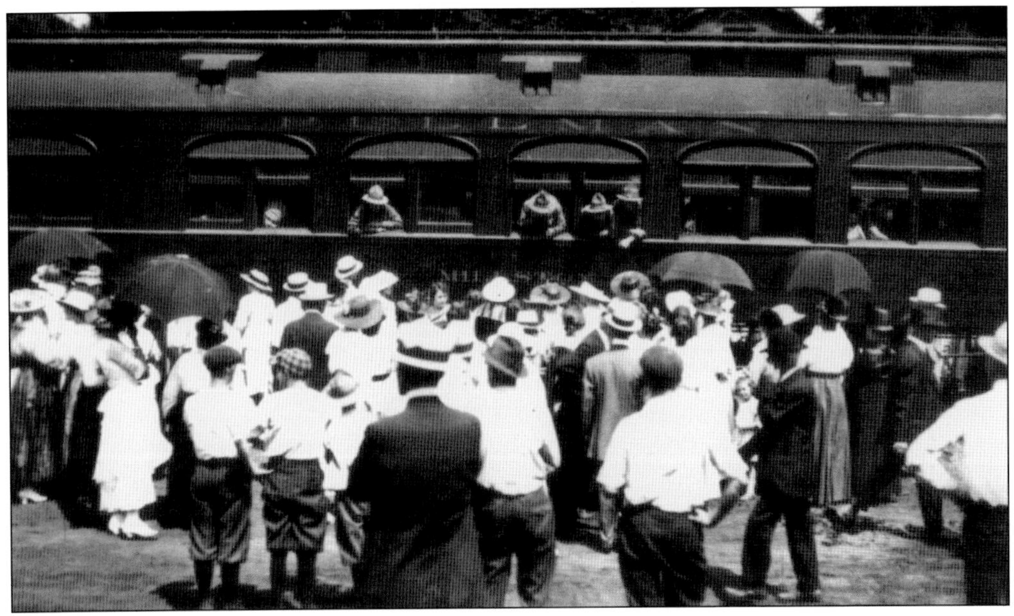

Soldiers returning from service in World War I are pictured above. The parade to welcome the veterans home to Ottawa is shown below, as one float passes the Hotel Ottawa on Columbus Street. (Both, Ottawa Scouting Museum.)

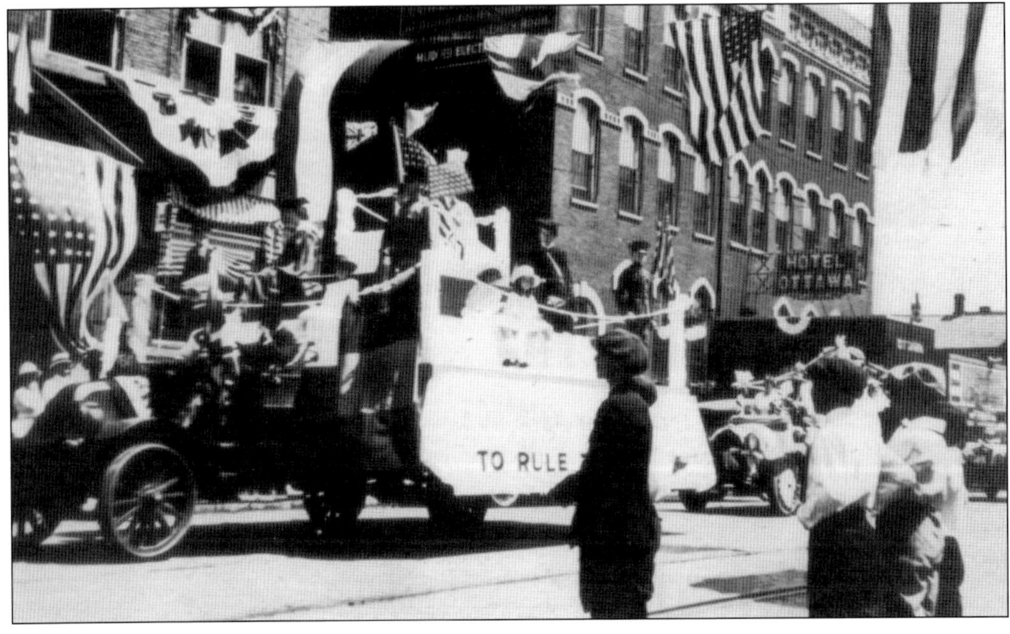

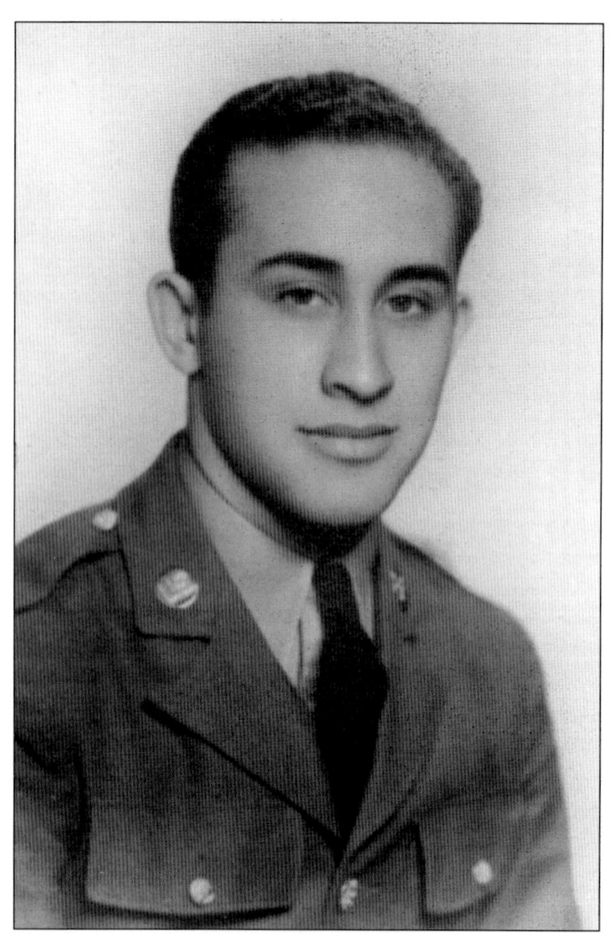

Robert Saleda was a star athlete at Ottawa Township High School and an intelligent young man with a bright future. He joined the Army Air Corps when World War II broke out and was awarded the Air Medal for his bravery in several battles in North Africa. T.Sgt. Robert Saleda was killed on April 9, 1944, when his plane was shot down by the Nazis over Poland. He was 20 years old and was one of 146 Ottawa men who gave their lives in the war. Below, Ottawa citizens gather in unity in December 1941 outside the local armory, around the time of America's entry into the war. (Left, Saleda family; below, JR.)

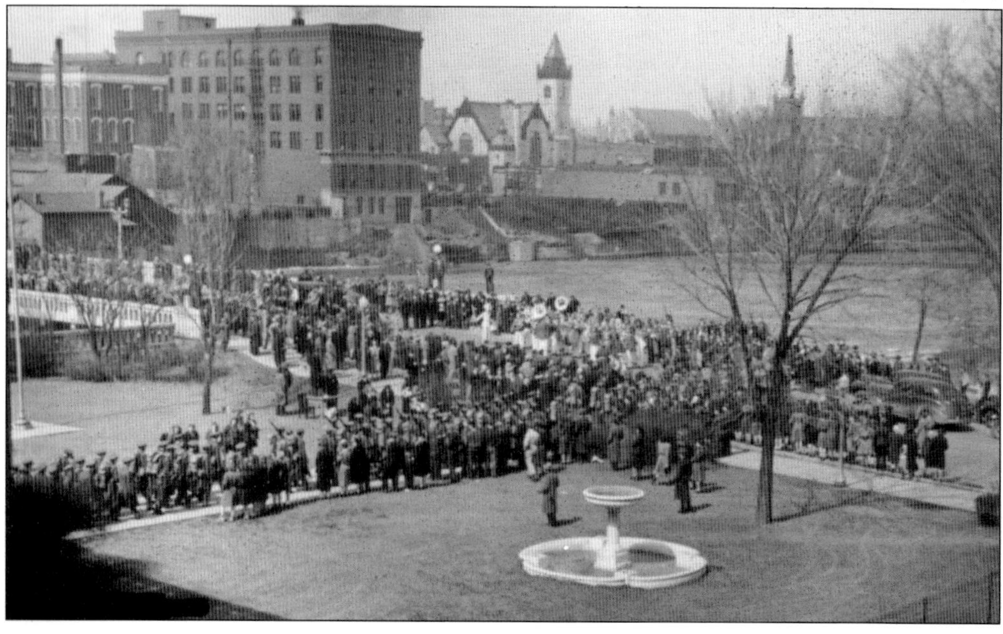

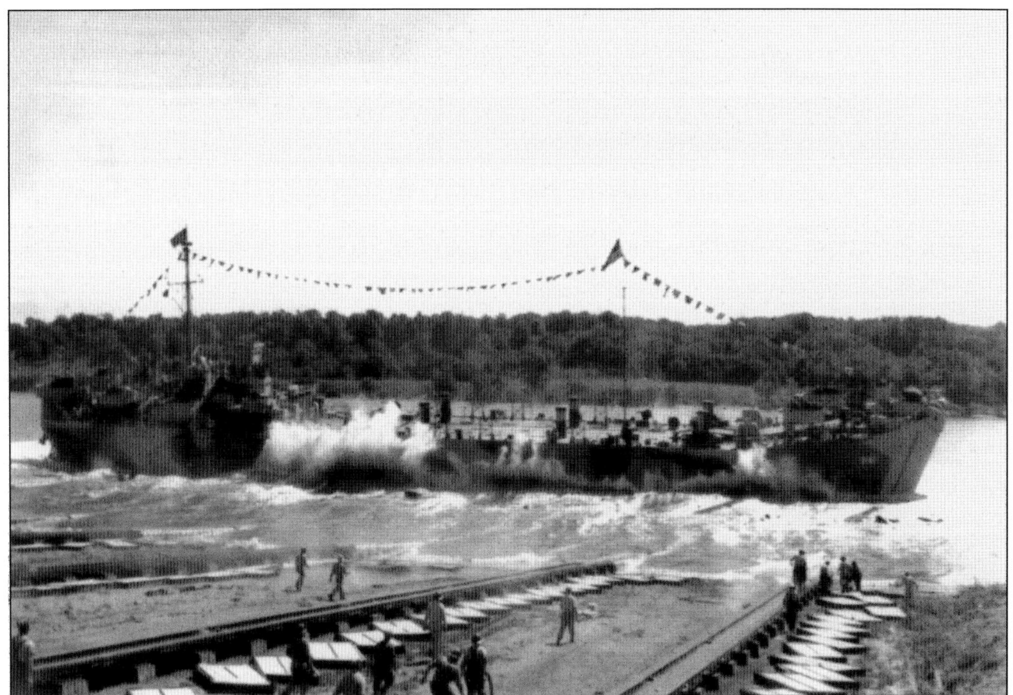

The Seneca shipyards built 157 landing ship tanks (LSTs) during World War II. As many as 11,000 people worked there. These pictures show the launching of LST 641 into the Illinois River on September 4, 1944. (Both, DC.)

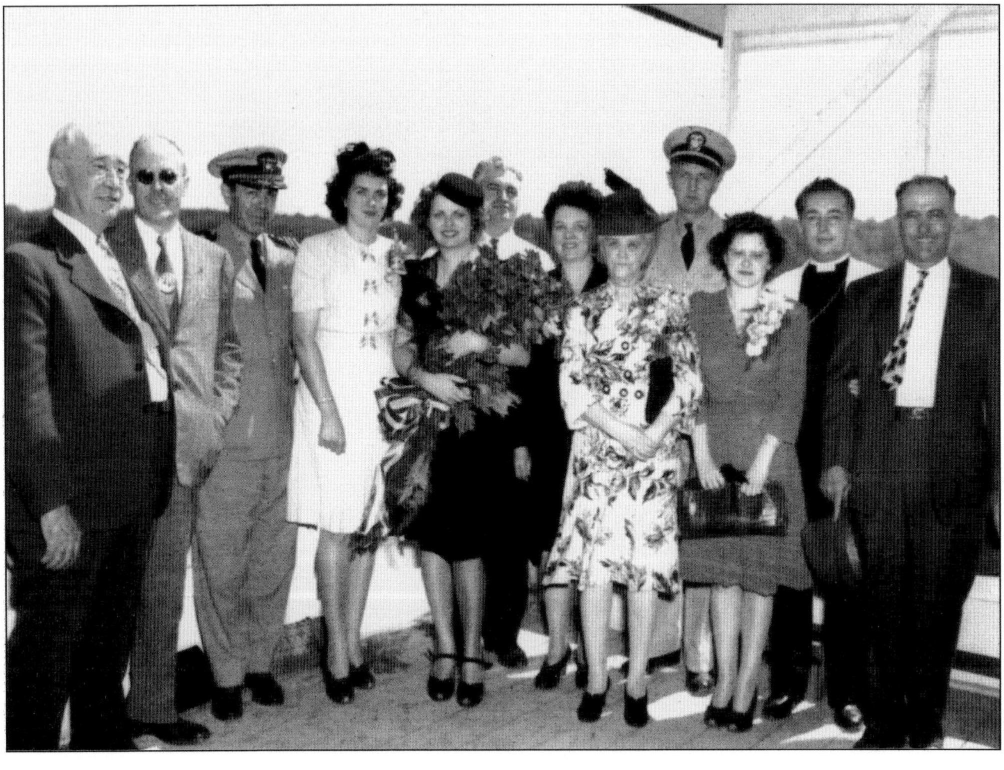

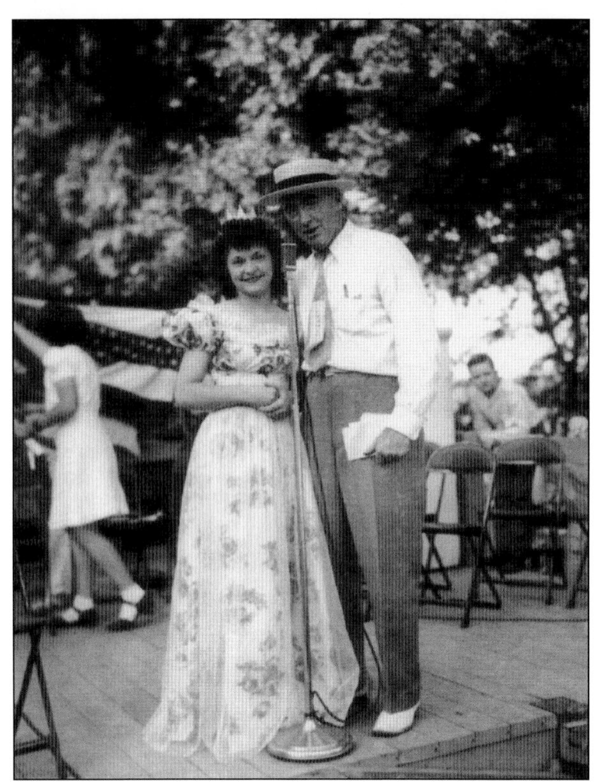

Lee Carroll introduces Helen Hagi, of nearby Ransom, as Seneca Shipyard Queen on July 30, 1944, at Starved Rock State Park. Naval dignitaries proudly stand with LST 325 as it prepares to go to war. The photograph was signed to Dorothy Clemens of Ottawa by Donald Lockas. (Left, Ottawa Scouting Museum; below, DC.)

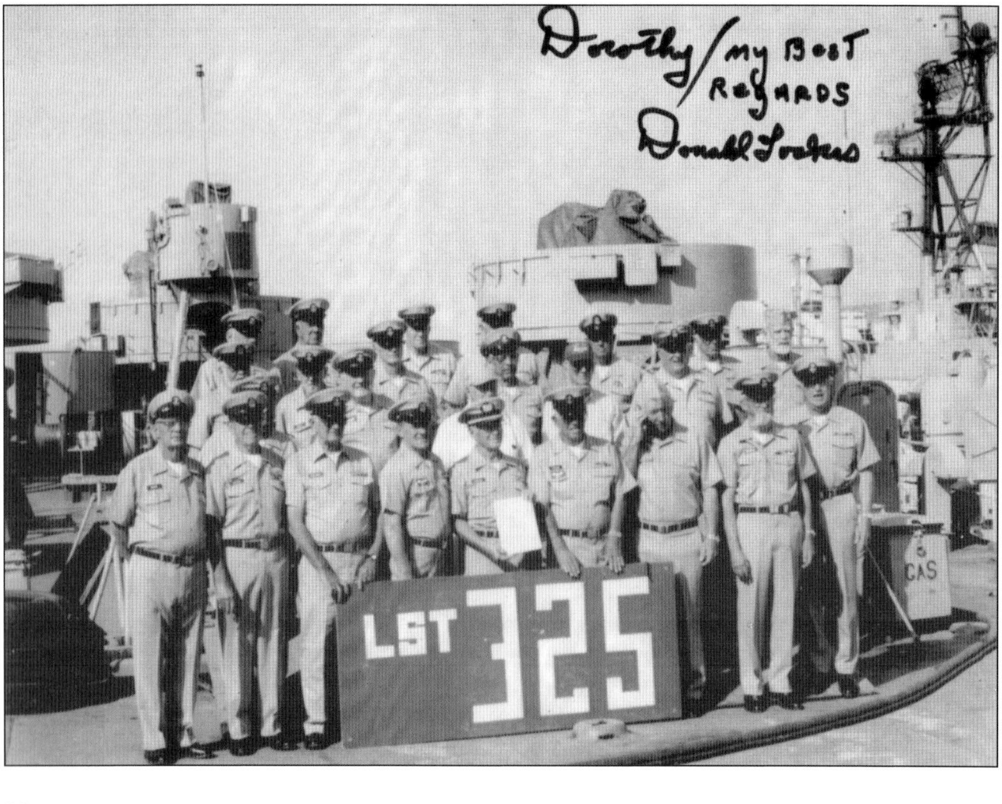

Six

Business and Industry

Ottawa has always been known as a factory town. Figures from 1940 showed 3,000 people worked at 34 factories. In 1950, the number was 4,000 people employed at 40 factories.

Ottawa was home to quite a few large factories. A few industries have survived these changing economic times, but most are gone. Some of the biggest factories have been Sanders Brothers Manufacturing, Gay & Sons wagon factory, United States Silica, Hill & Formhals Carriage & Wagon Manufacturers, King & Hamilton farm machinery factory, Victor Roller Mills, E.P. Johnson Piano Co., Western Cottage & Piano factory, Ottawa Brewing Co., Sanicula Mineral Springs, J.E. Porter Company, Knowles Foundry and Machine Shop, Ottawa Silver Company, LaChapelle Lamp Chimney Company, Peltier Novelty Glass Company, Pioneer Fire-Proof Construction Company, Standard Fire Brick Company (Brickton), Terra Cotta Tile Company, American Hoechst Company, and Borg-Warner Chemicals (Marbon).

At one time, National Plate Glass Company (later Libbey-Owens-Ford and still later Pilkington) in Ottawa was the largest plate glass factory in the world, and Ottawa Silica was one of the largest silica mining operations in the nation.

There have also been countless small businesses, which are the backbone of any community. Many of these businesses have lasted for decades. A few of the familiar names are J. Bell's Clothing, Stiefel and Sons Clothing, Bianchi's, The Cheese Shop, Bake-Rite Bakery, Clegg-Perkins Electric, Gladfelter Chapel, Illinois Office Supply Company, Jobst Memorials, Jordan Hardware, and Pitstick Dairy.

However, nothing is as certain as change. Some Ottawa businesses naturally had to go, including manufacturers of buggies and carriages, companies that sold coal and ice, cigar makers, the horse collar and fly net factory, and the garter and corset factory. And, while many businesses and industries, both large and small, have come and gone over the decades, Ottawa has remained strong and vital economically. The downtown area is thriving, which bucks the trend among older cities. Outlying areas, particularly the north side, are booming with new businesses. Tourism, both in Ottawa and the nearby state parks, increases every year.

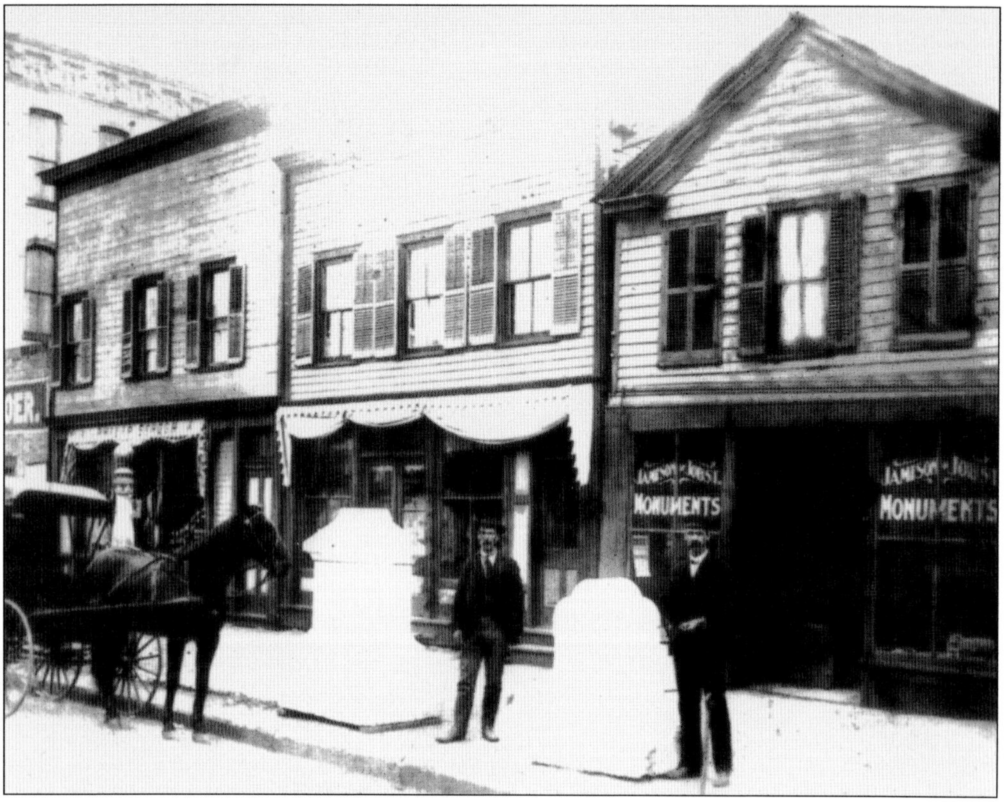

Jobst Monuments started in Ottawa in 1903 and is still in business. Gladfelter Chapel is a business that goes back about 150 years and is still around. Gladfelter was a furniture maker and undertaker, a common combination in those days. (Both, DC.)

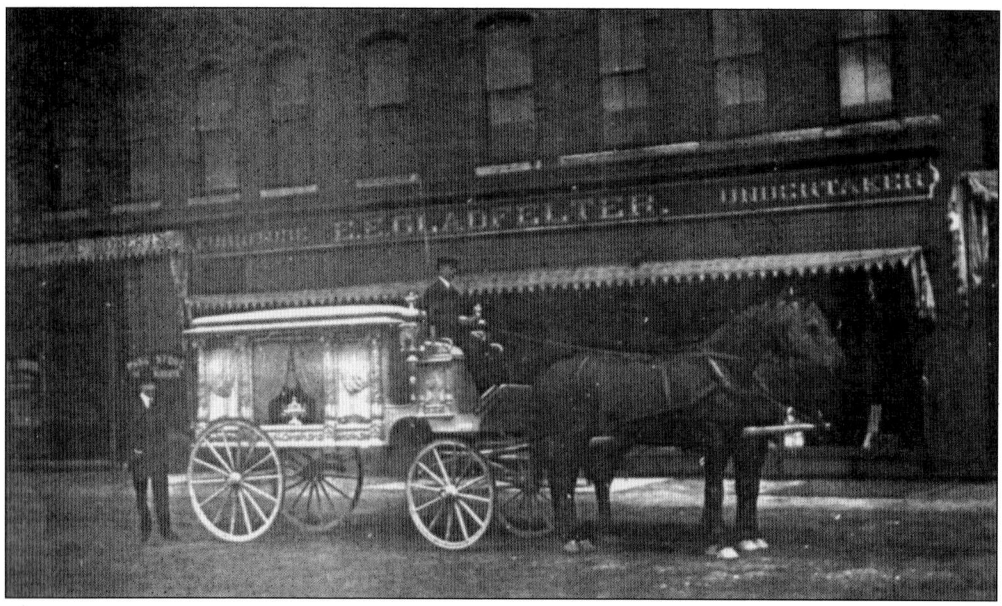

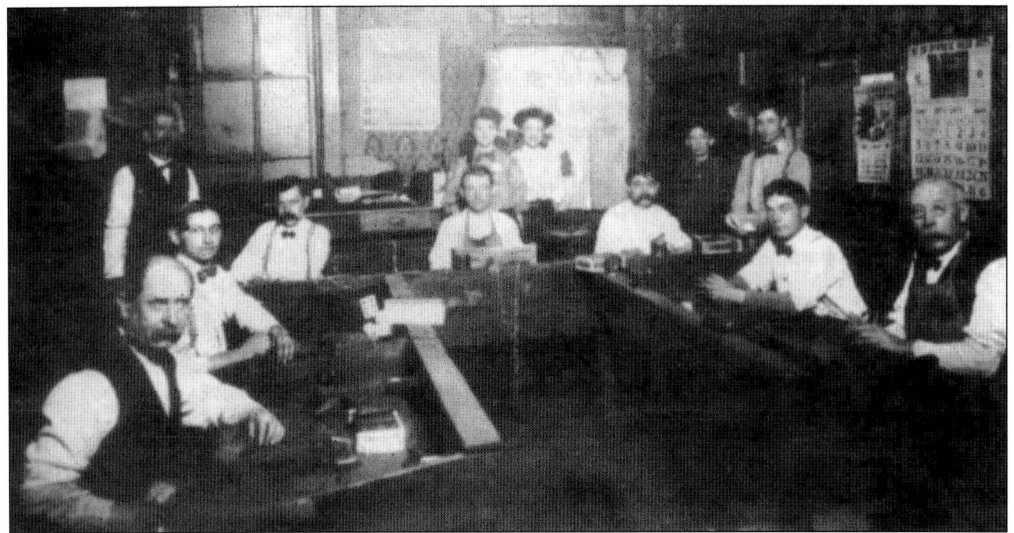

Cigar making was once a thriving American industry, and Ottawa had several cigar factories in the late 1800s and early 1900s. Pictured here are workers at William Fletcher's cigar-making shop at 214 West Madison Street. Harry Hess is third from the right. Fletcher is at far right. The 1884 directory listed cigar makers M.B. Mitchell at 7 Court Street, Amos Hess at 209–211 Main Street, H.W. Fowler at 718 LaSalle Street, and J.E. Kelly at 126 West Madison Street. A 1900 directory lists Mitchell, Fletcher, and Henry Waldecker at 112–114 Main Street. Later directories showed James Flynn at 1129 Columbus Street and R.M. Richardson, who took over Mitchell's shop in 1910. (DC.)

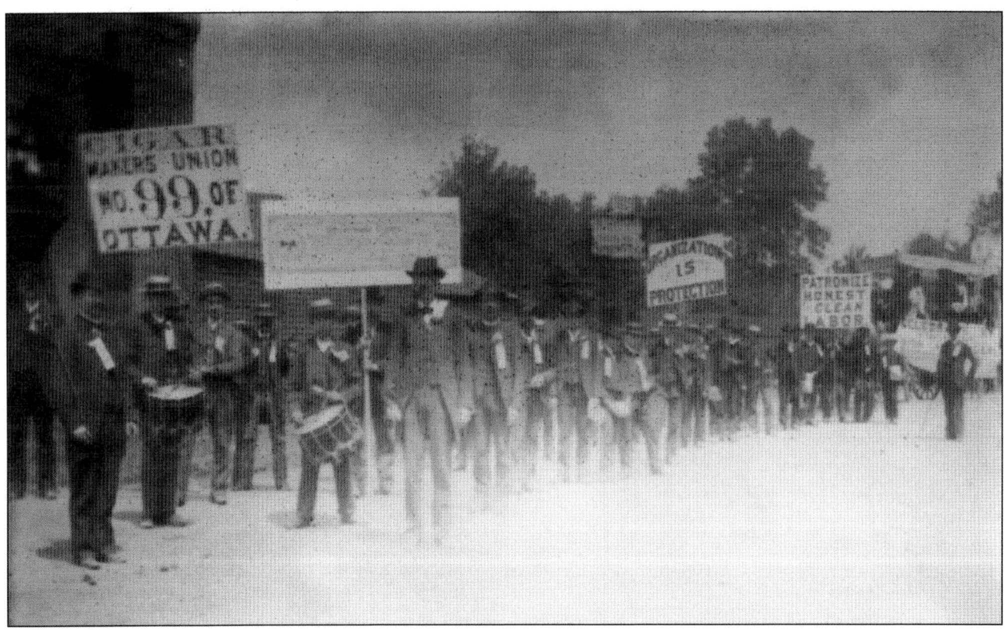

Some local accounts have described this picture from around 1900 as a strike by union cigar makers. More likely, it is a parade, as evidenced by the men with drums, the number of people, and the float at the rear. (DC.)

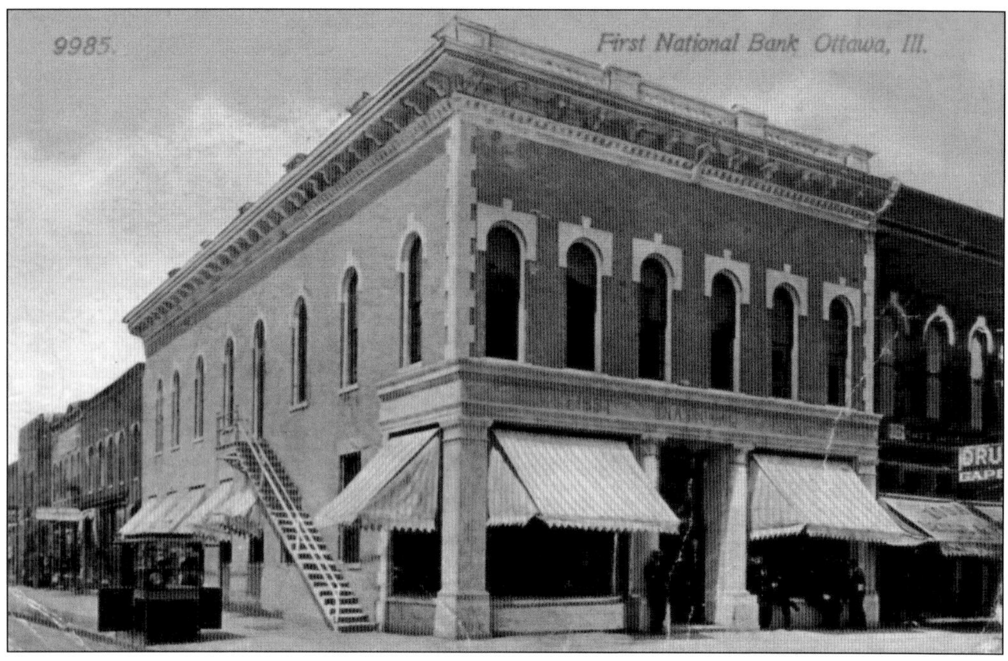

First National Bank of Ottawa started in 1865. It was located on the northwest corner of Main and LaSalle Streets until 1904, when it moved to the northwest corner of Madison and LaSalle Streets (above). It was the only Ottawa bank to survive the Great Depression. Ottawa Banking & Trust (below) opened in 1903 at LaSalle and Jefferson Streets. A few years later, it moved to LaSalle and Madison Streets. The bank failed in the early 1930s, during the Great Depression. (Both, JR.)

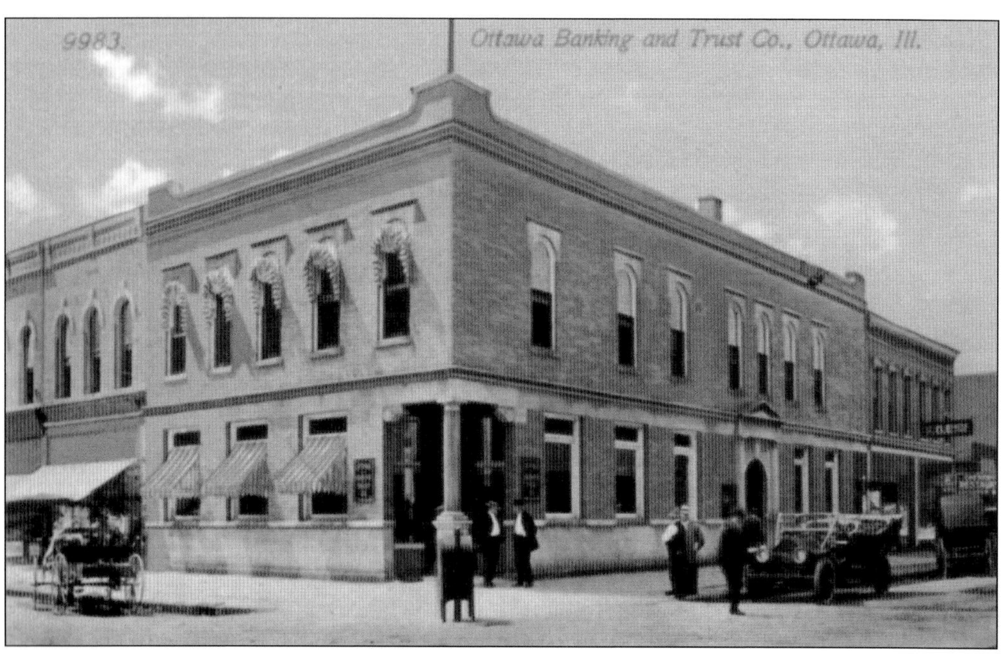

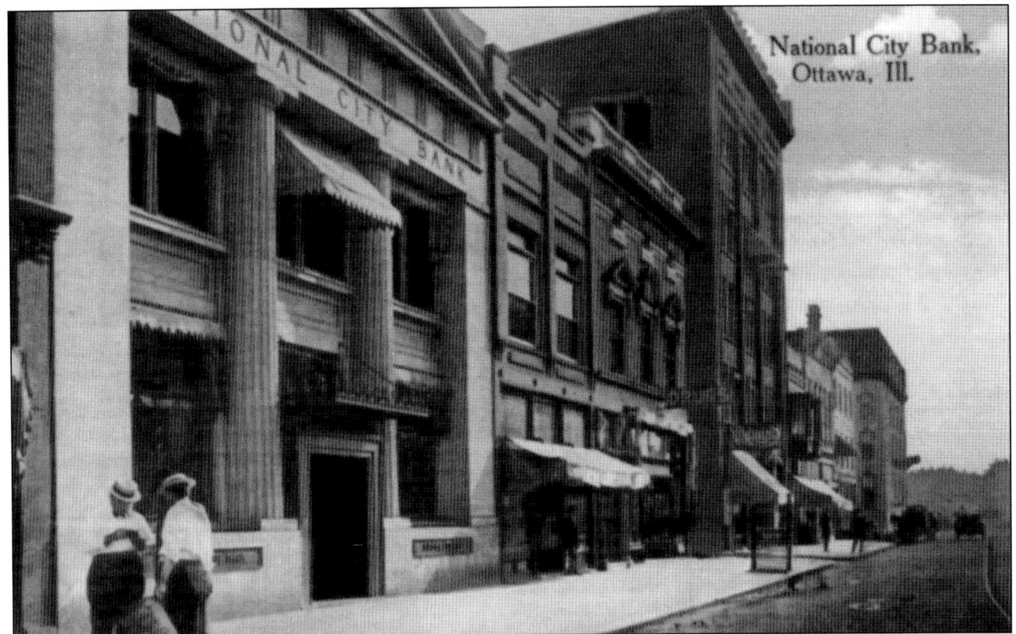

National City Bank was chartered in 1865 and was located on Madison Street. It failed during the Great Depression, but the building has been the home to several other banks since then. The tall structure down the block was the Maloney Building. On the right, across Columbus Street, is the Clifton Hotel. (JR.)

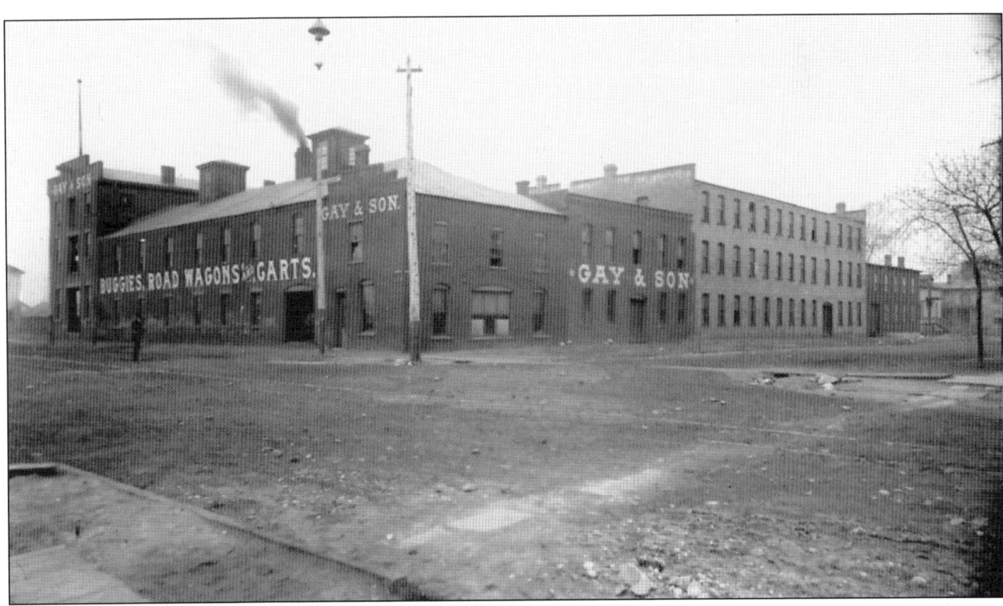

J.G. Gay opened a carriage factory in 1846. It employed up to 100 people. The factory pictured above was built in the 1890s at Clinton and Lafayette Streets and was torn down in 1927. (JR.)

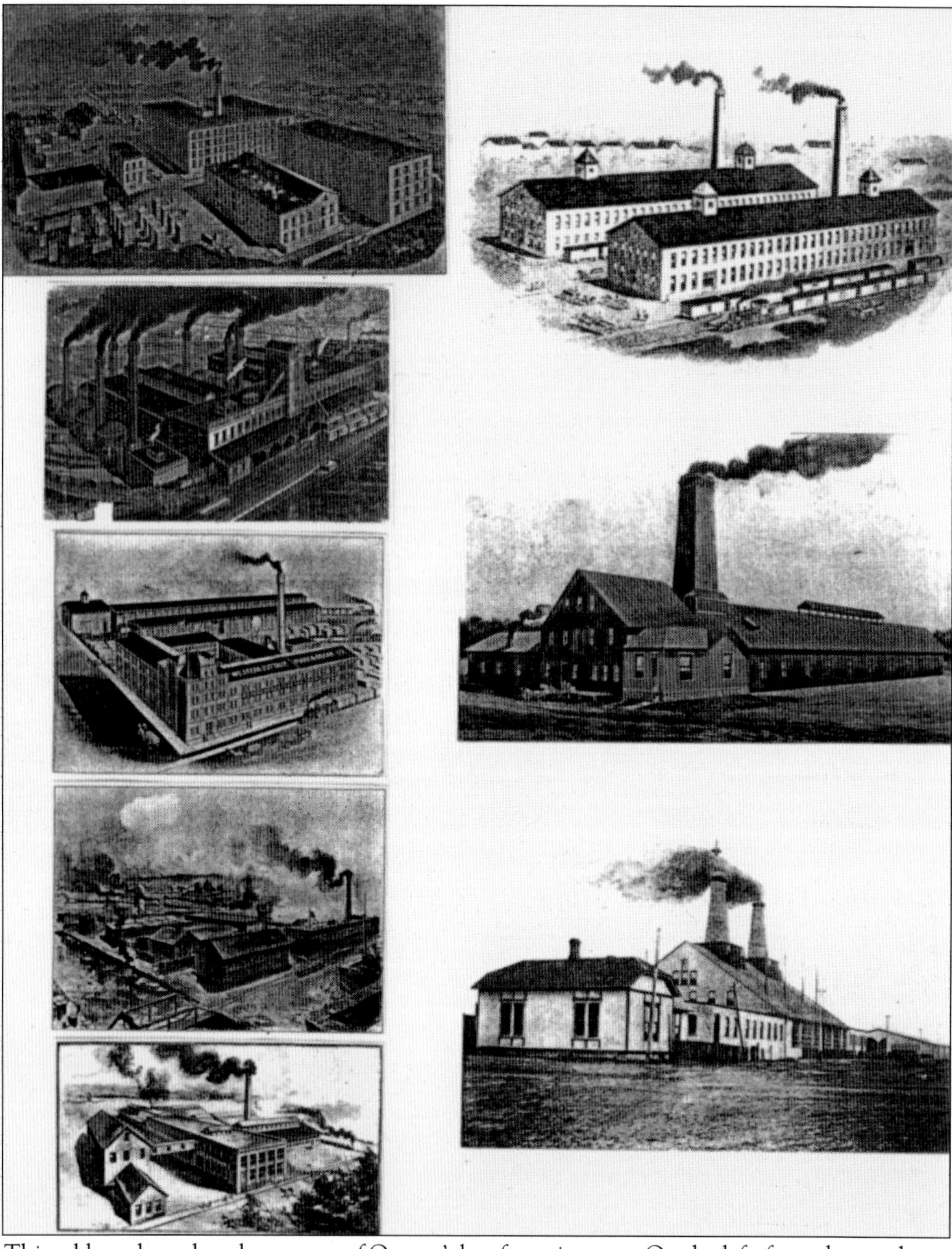

This tableau shows how large some of Ottawa's lost factories were. On the left, from the top down, were King & Hamilton farm equipment manufacturers, Pioneer Fire-Proof Construction Company, Western Cottage Piano & Organ Company, Sanders Brothers Manufacturing Company, and J.E. Porter Company (farm and hardware equipment). On the right column, from the top down, were Ottawa Silver Company, Peltier Novelty Glass Opalescent Glass Works, and Chapelle Lamp Chimney factory. (JR.)

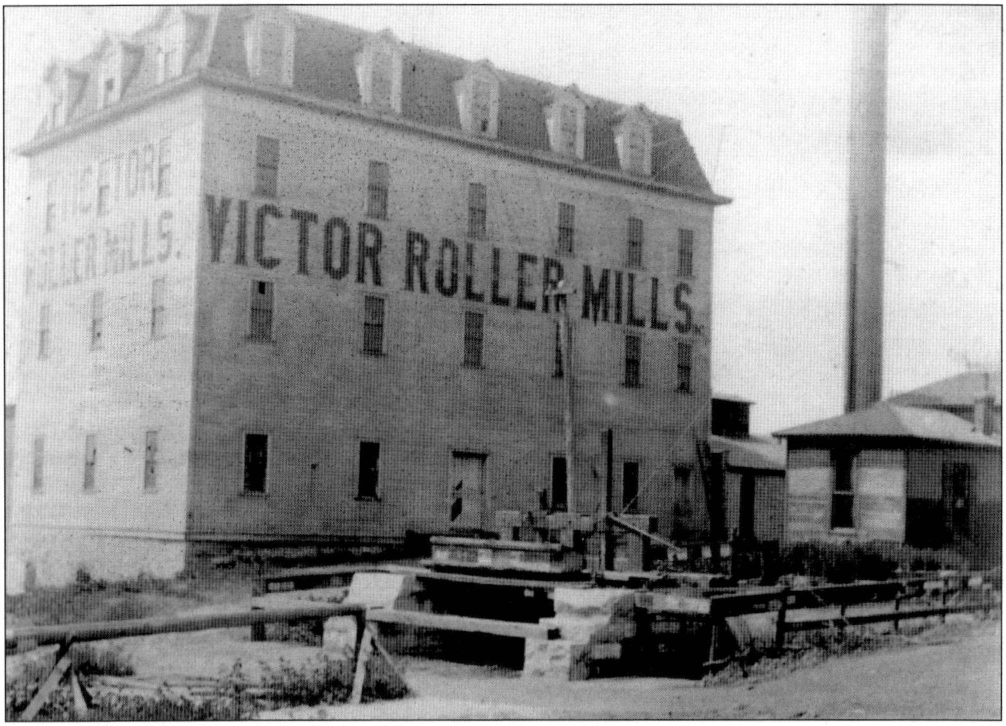

Victor Roller Mills was at the Fox River, at the south end of Columbus Street. It was built in 1882 and torn down in 1903. Western Cottage Piano & Organ Co. (below) was located at Joliet and Riale Streets. It built a large factory in Ottawa in 1887. It burned in 1895, but a bigger building replaced it. At its peak, the company employed 125 people and produced 5,000 organs and 1,500 pianos annually. It later became the Ottawa Pianophone Co.; a 1918 fire ended the company. The present-day site contains the AutoZone, a gas station, and the Walgreen's. Ottawa had another large piano factory, the E.P. Johnson Piano Factory, on Ottawa's north side. (Above, DC; below, JR.)

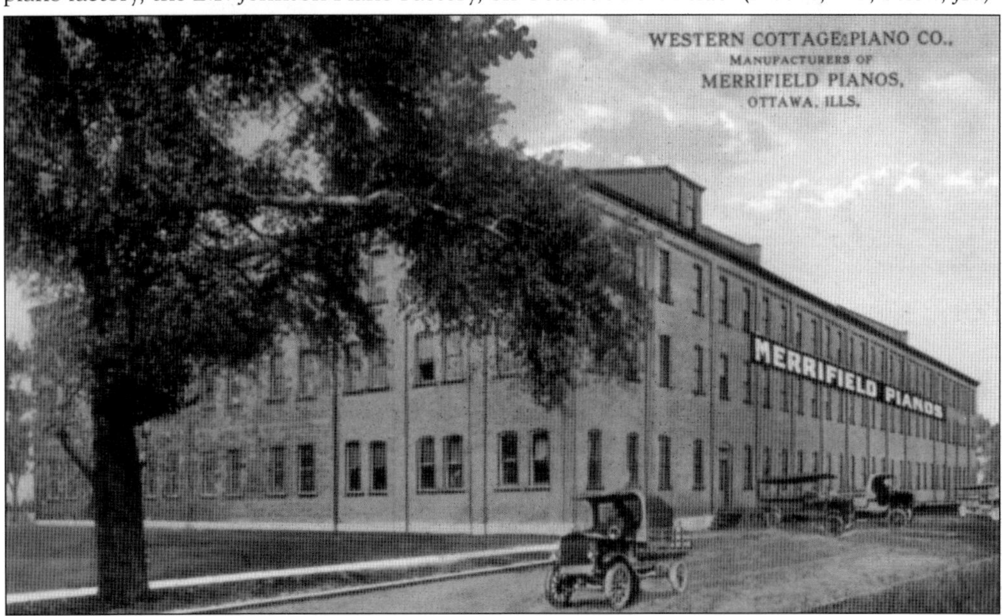

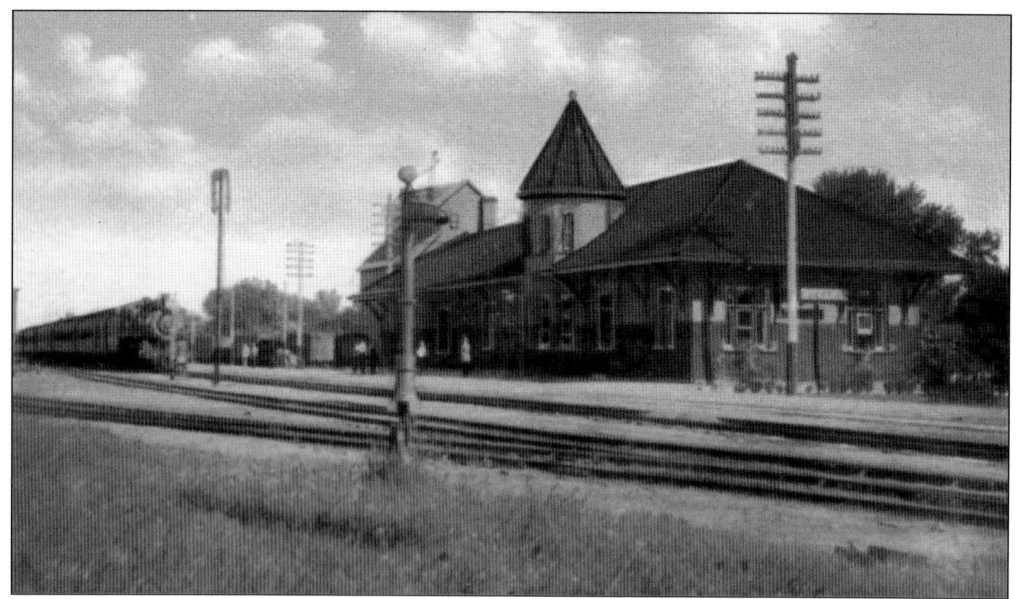

The railroads were very important in the development of Ottawa. This is the depot of the Chicago, Rock Island & Pacific Railroad, also known as just the Rock Island. The first passenger train service from Chicago arrived in 1853. Freight trains still cross through Ottawa several times a day, although the last passenger trains ran in 1979. (Both, JR.)

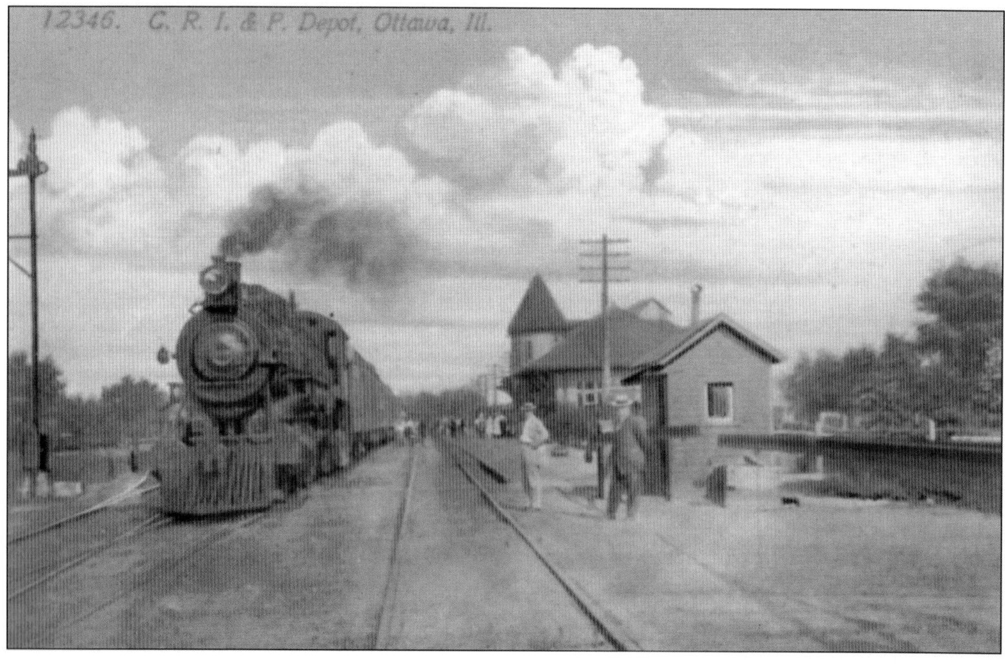

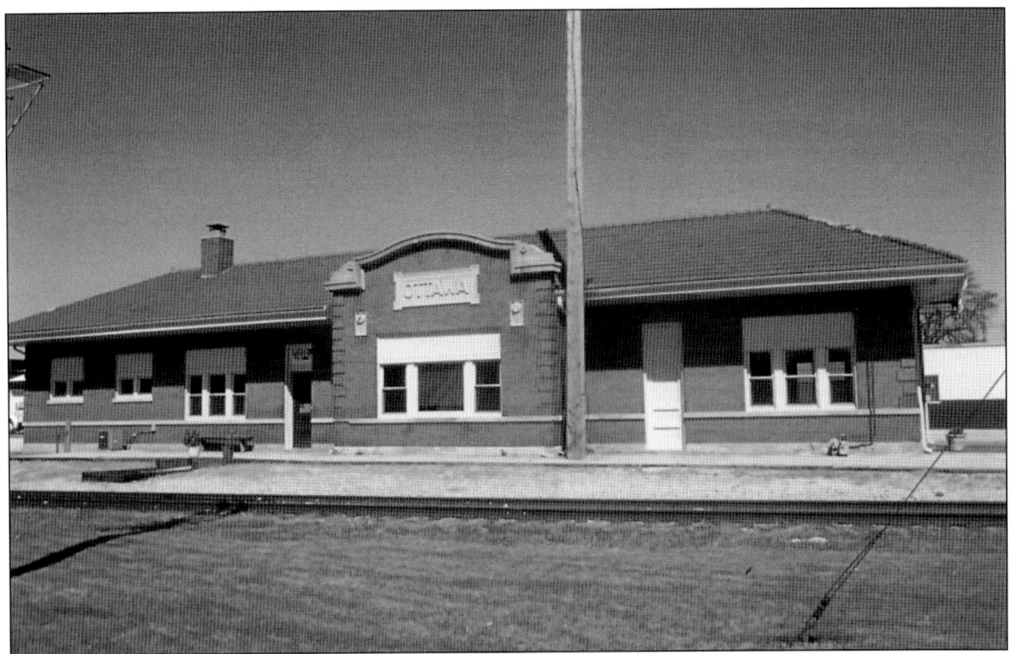

Ottawa's other rail depot was on the city's west side and belonged to the CB&Q (Chicago, Burlington & Quincy) Railroad. The "Q" railroad came through Ottawa in 1870. Passenger service ended in 1952. This depot was built at Walnut and Madison Streets in 1913. (JR.)

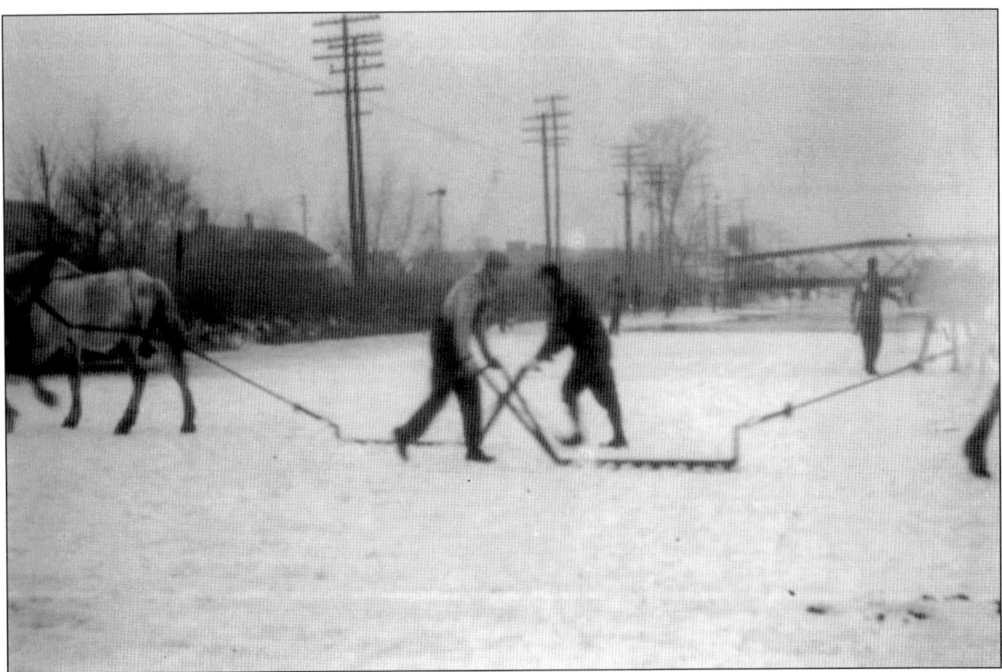

In the years before refrigeration, people cut ice from rivers in the winter and kept it all year long. Icehouses were a big business in every community, and Ottawa had its share. In this picture, men cut ice from the I&M Canal in 1926 for Glover's icehouse. (DC.)

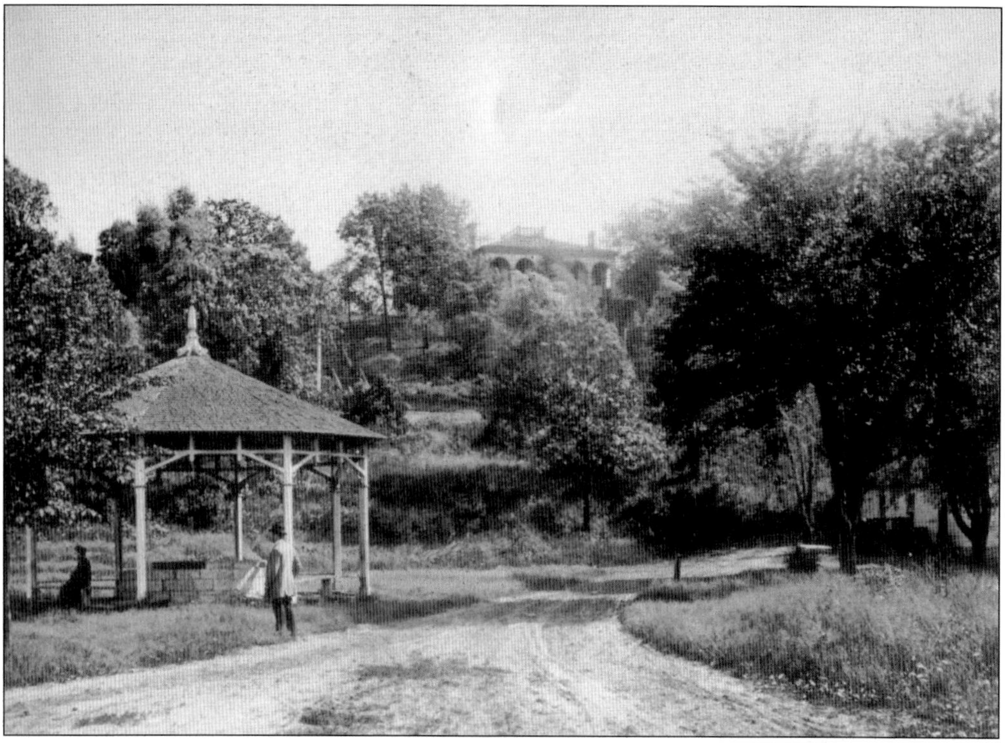

Ottawa Mineral Springs (seen above in 1893) started in 1877 and was on the south bank of the Illinois River. It later became Sanicula Mineral Springs Company. Drivers for the company are pictured below in the 1920s. The plant burned down in 1931. Two years after the fire, Fred Willet acquired the company and built a soda bottling plant at 1501 West Main Street, which stayed in business until the 1980s. (Both, JR.)

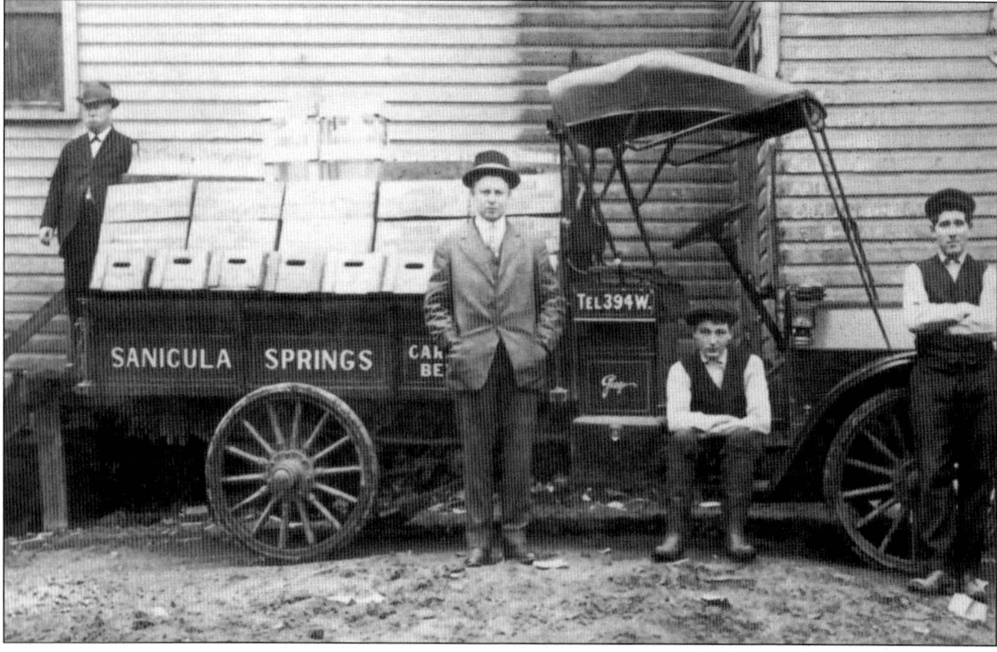

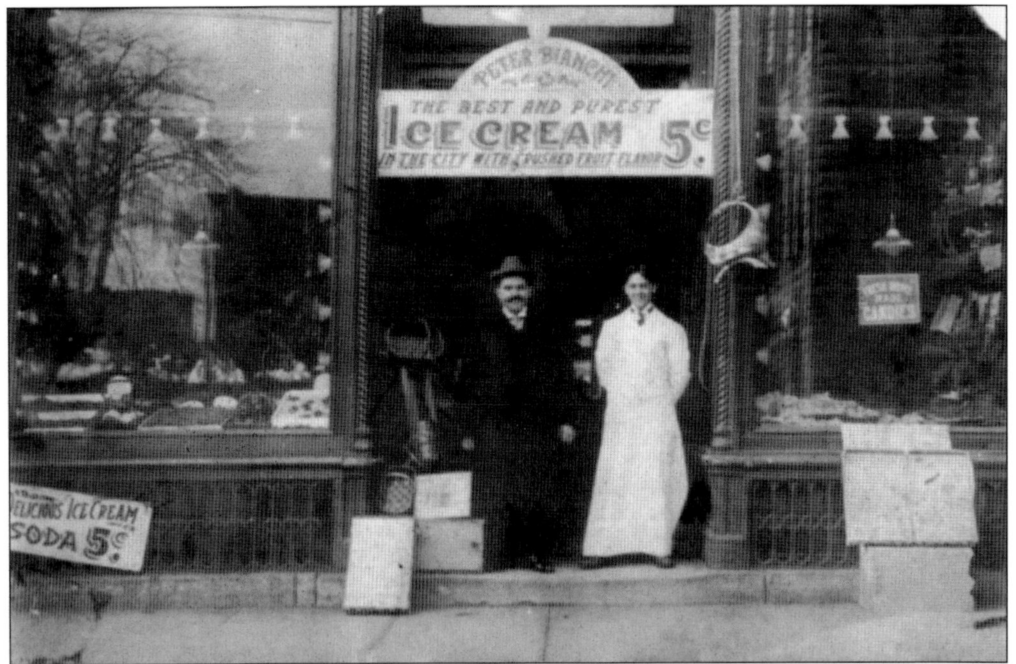

Peter Bianchi (left) and Billy Sartini stand in front of Bianchi's Marble Palace in 1909. John and Peter Bianchi came from Italy in the 1890s and opened an ice cream parlor on LaSalle Street in 1904. The business remained in the family until 1961. The new owners continued it as a soda fountain and confectionery until 1969, when it became a pizza parlor. Below is the inside of the Woolworth's store on LaSalle Street in 1923. Identified are Bertha Rossiter, 10th from the front behind the left counter, and Nellie Lawrence, third from the left in the aisle. (Both, DC.)

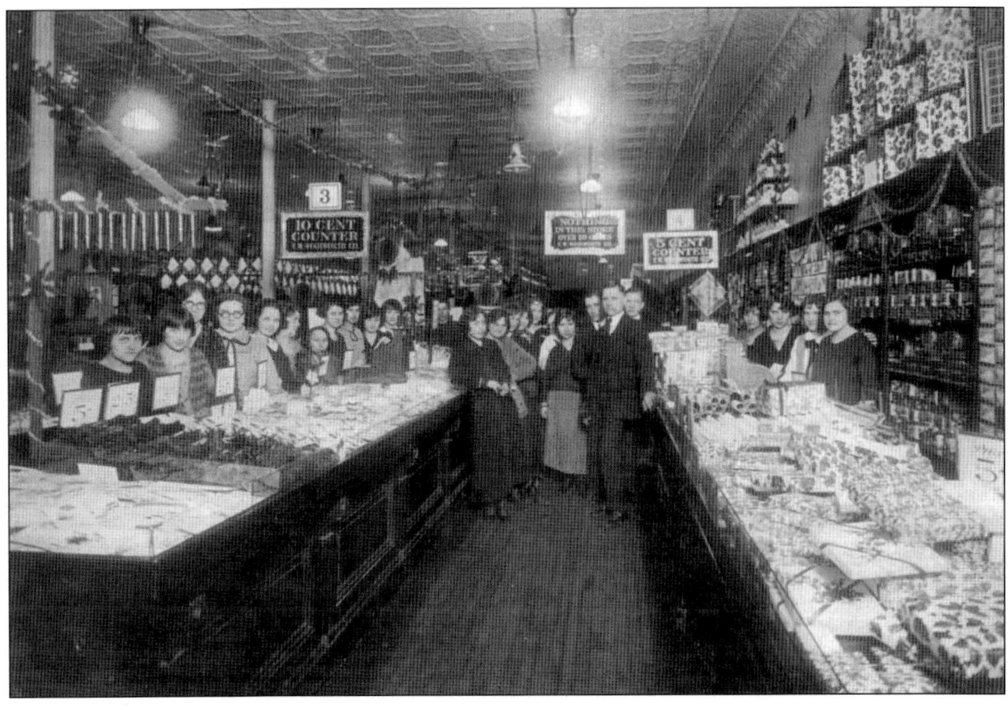

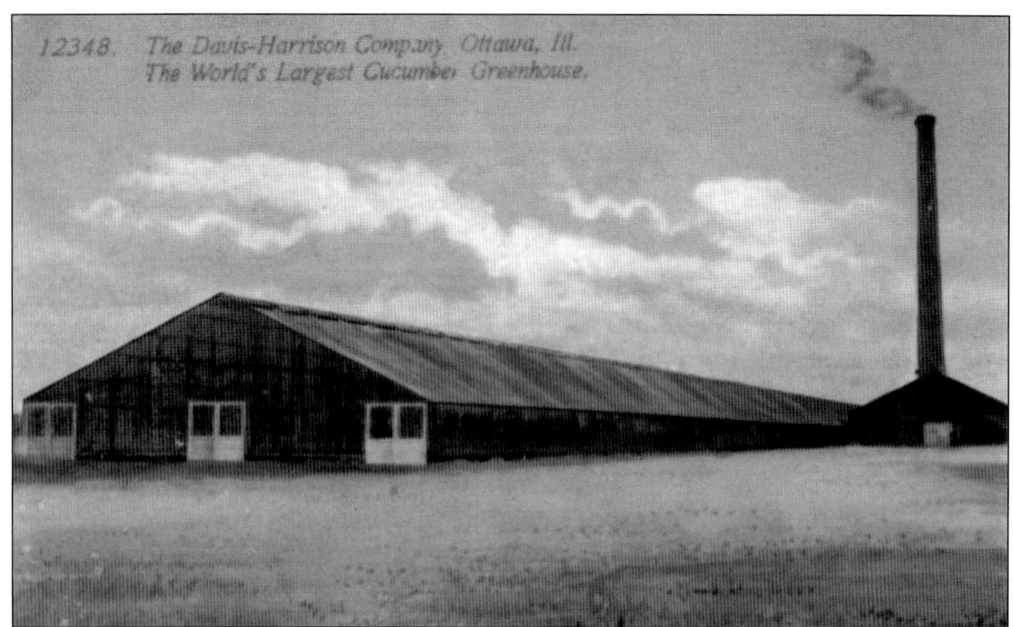

"The world's largest cucumber greenhouse" was built on 17 acres along West Superior Street in 1912. The main greenhouse was 60 by 800 feet. The factory had other greenhouses, a boiler room, and a packinghouse. The smokestack was 130 feet high. Five swarms of bees were kept in the greenhouse to pollinate the plants, since there was no breeze inside to spread the pollen. Within two years, 6,000 plants were producing 150 dozen cucumbers per day. (DC.)

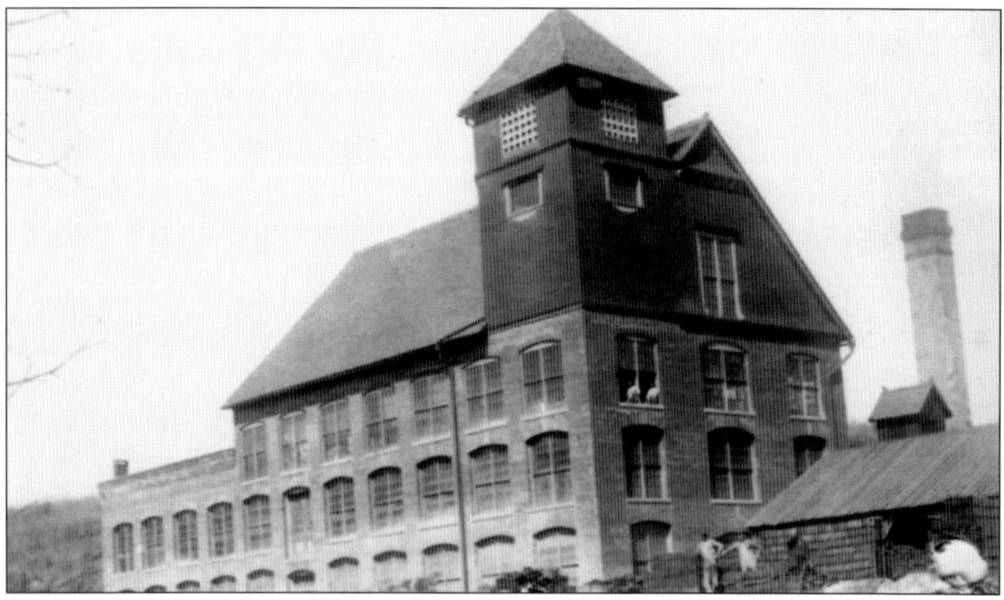

Just northwest of Ottawa was the Terra Cotta Company, a manufacturer of drain tile. It went through a series of owners and was rebuilt after a 1912 fire. (DC.)

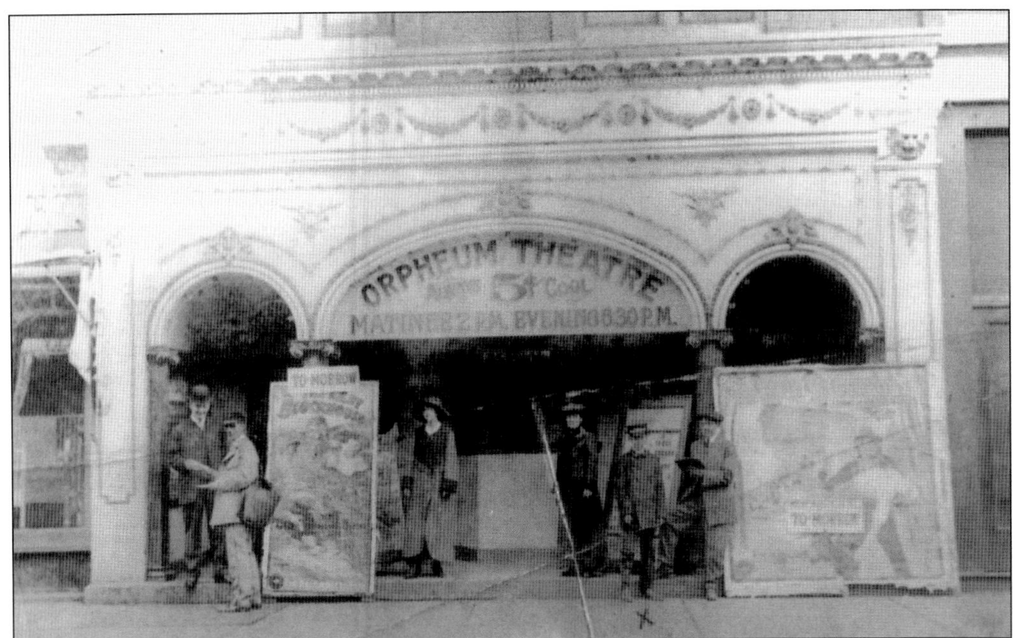

A fire on February 7, 1932, destroyed the Orpheum Theater (pictured above in 1913) at 107 West Jefferson Street. The fire also damaged the adjoining People's Trust & Savings Bank and several stores. Firefighters poured 350,000 gallons of water on the blaze. Pictured below is the rebuilt theater on its opening day in 1937. The Baptist church is on the left. The theater was razed in 1971 to make room for a drive-up bank facility. (Both, JR.)

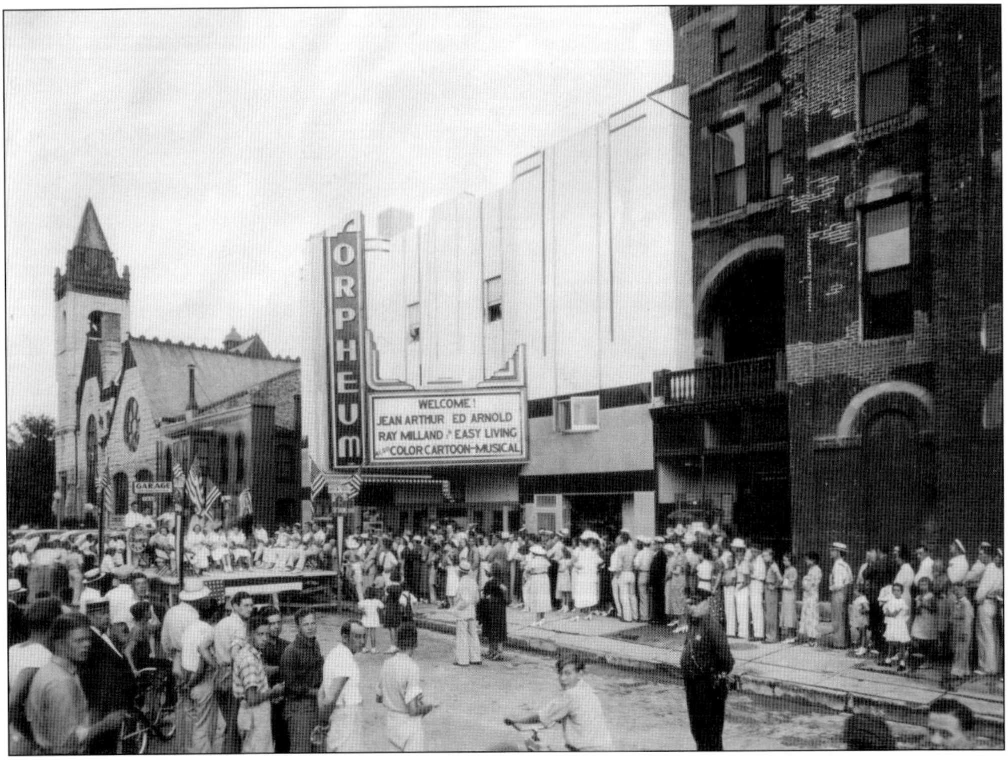

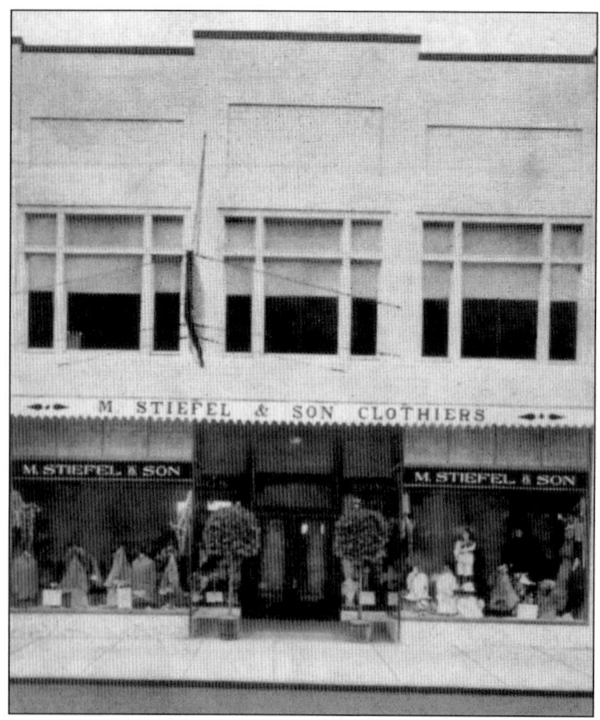

Stiefel's clothing store was typical of the small yet steady Ottawa businesses that lasted for decades. Moses Stiefel (1842–1927) was a German immigrant who opened a store in Ottawa in 1864. It was located at Main and LaSalle Streets, and it changed locations several times over the years. For awhile, Stiefel also ran an overalls manufacturing factory. Stiefel's store moved to 711 LaSalle Street in 1913. The store was run by several generations and closed in 1994. Motta's honey business, in nearby Utica, served a wide area of LaSalle County in the late 1800s and early 1900s. (Both, JR.)

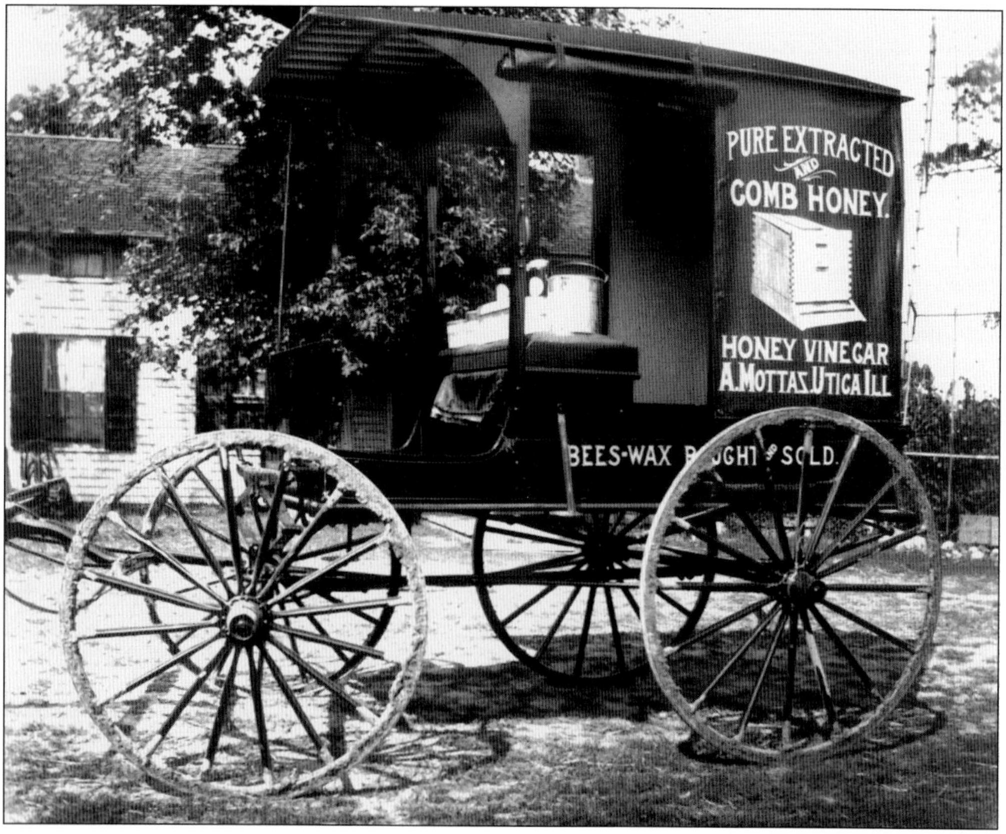

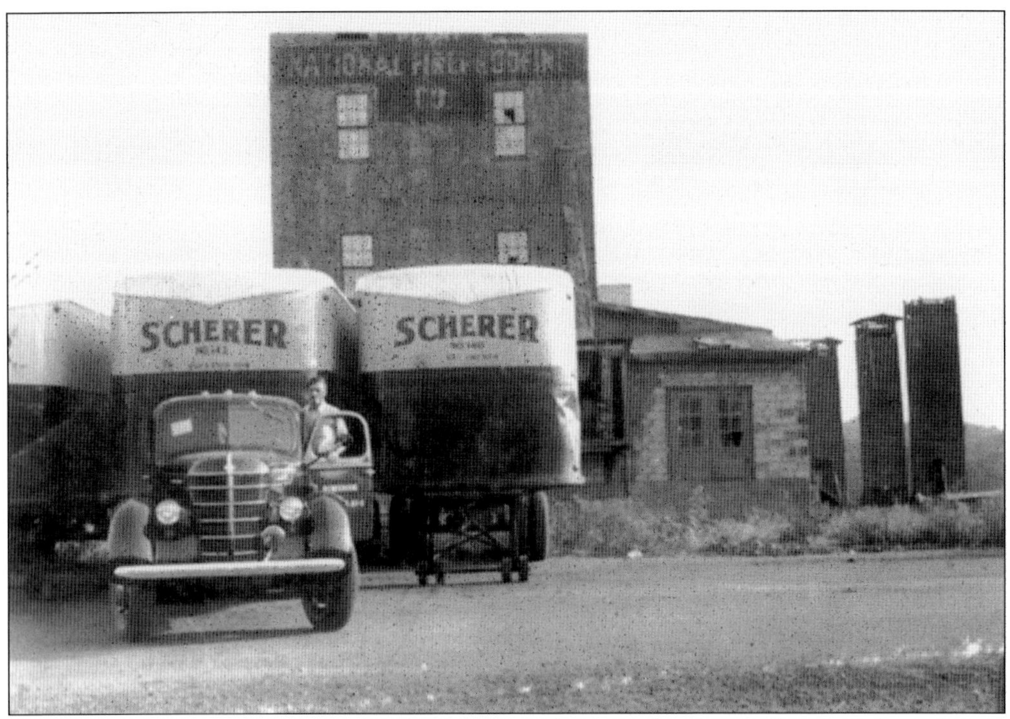

Fred Scherer is pictured here with a few of his trucks near the National Fireproofing plant at LaSalle and Mill Streets. Scherer Brothers Transfer & Storage was located on Madison Street at the Q Depot. The family cartage business began in 1863. (DC.)

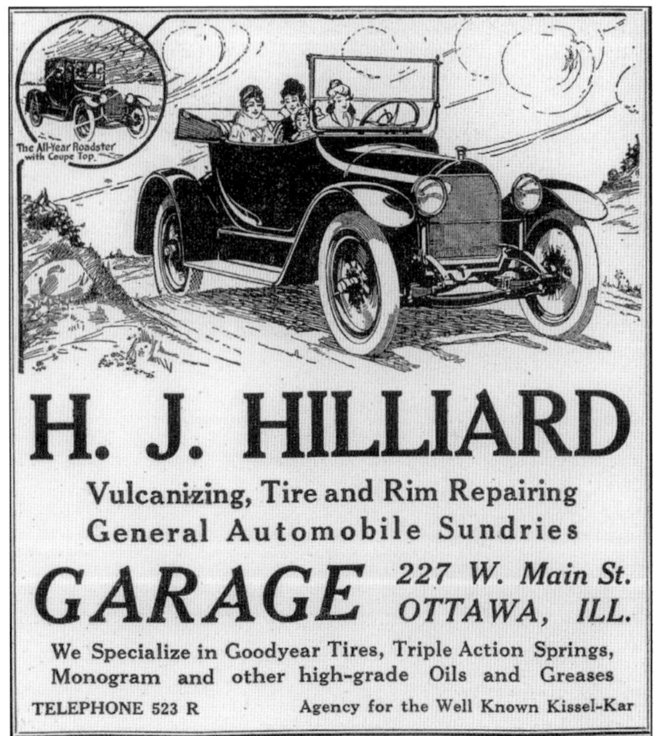

Hubert Hilliard built a garage in 1909 at 229 West Main Street. Hilliard was mayor of Ottawa from 1927 to 1935. The bridge over the Illinois River, completed in 1933, was named for him. Mayor Hilliard organized the local churches, civic groups, and businesses to form a combined charity to help the needy citizens of Ottawa. One of Hilliard's projects was filling in the hydraulic basin of the I&M lateral canal, which created a street between LaSalle and Clinton Streets. (JR.)

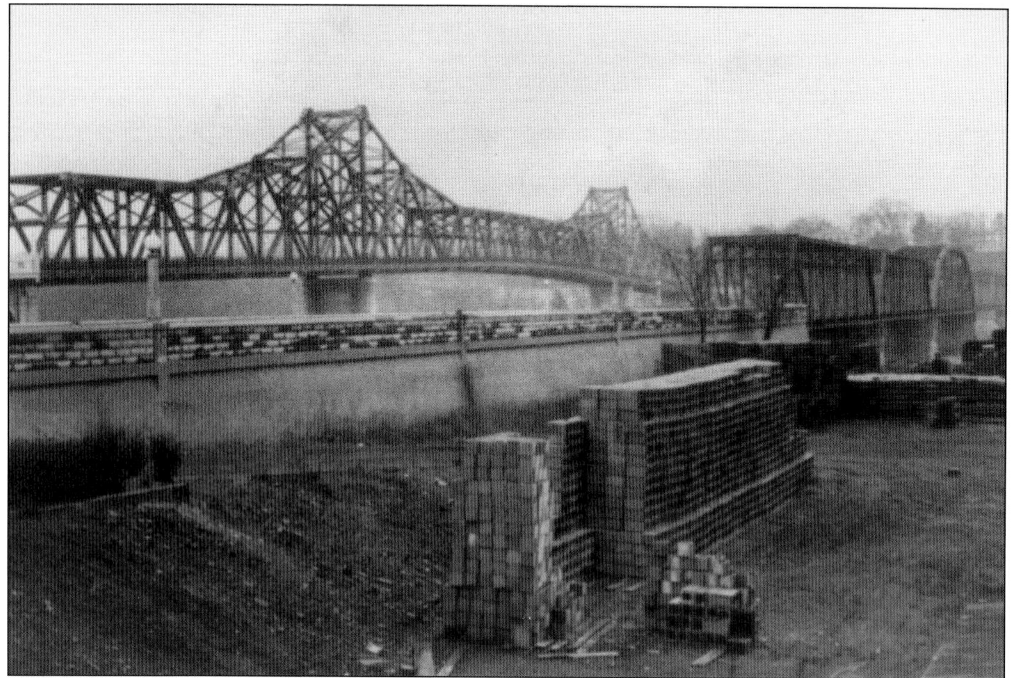

Ottawa is a river city, with the Fox and Illinois Rivers being an important part of Ottawa's economic and tourist life since the city's founding. The Hilliard Bridge, over the Illinois River, was built in 1933. The old iron bridge it replaced is at right, partially dismantled. Hilliard Bridge was replaced in 1982 with Veterans Memorial Bridge. (JR.)

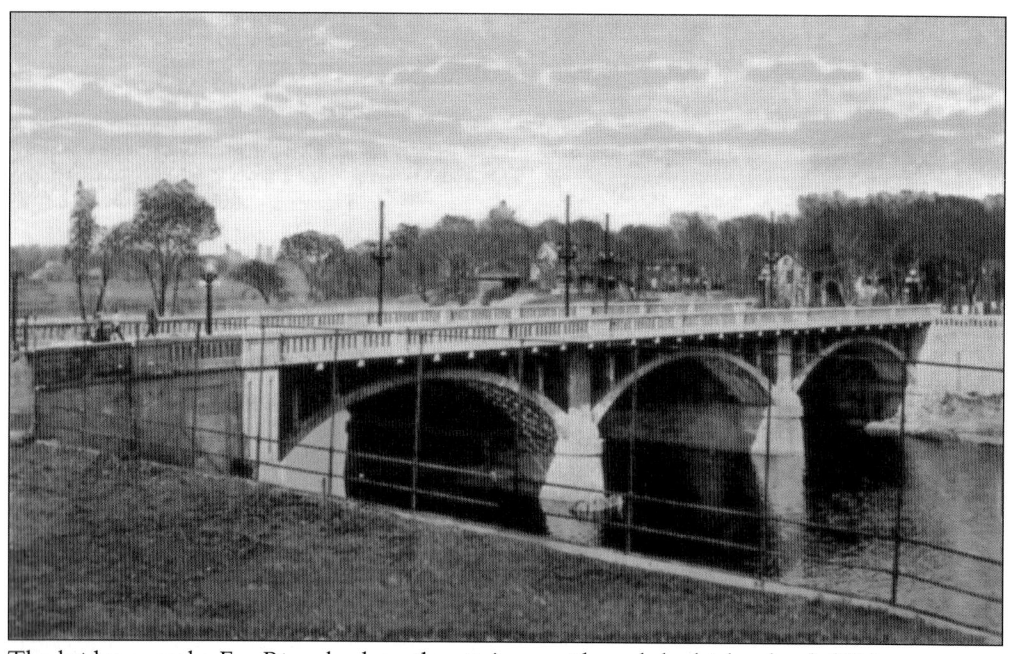

The bridge over the Fox River leads to the city's east side and the high school. (JR.)

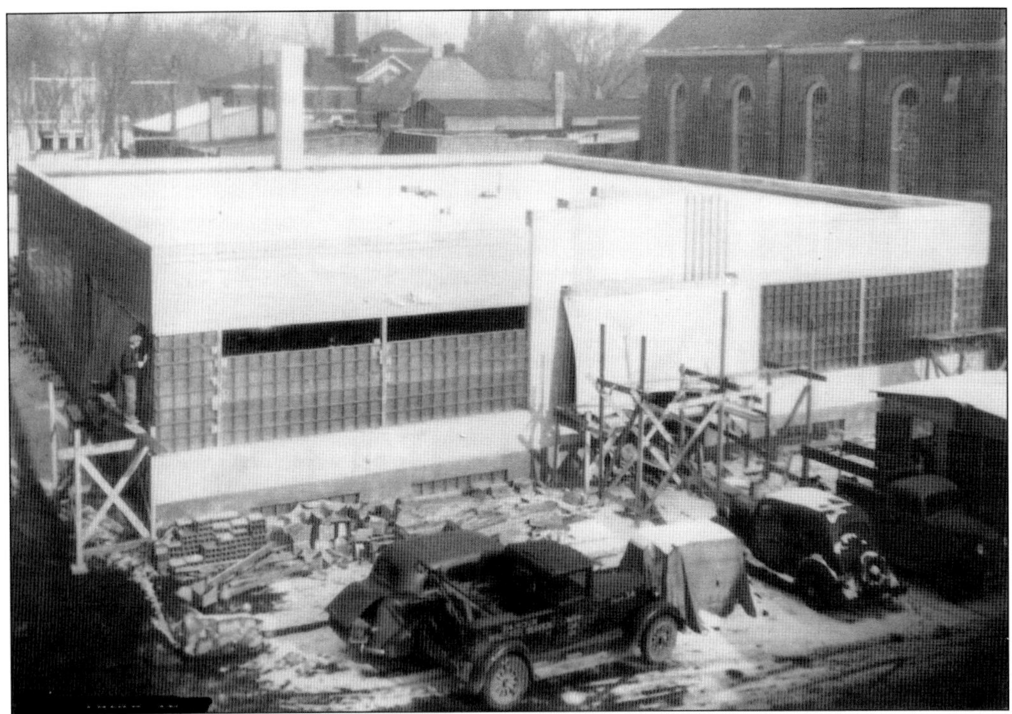

A new location for the *Daily Republican-Times* was built in 1939 on Jefferson Street, next to the First Methodist Church. With no windows—its only light came from glass blocks—it was an architectural innovation for the times, and is still an architectural gem. The newspaper later became the *Daily Times* and today is known as the *Times*. (Both, JR.)

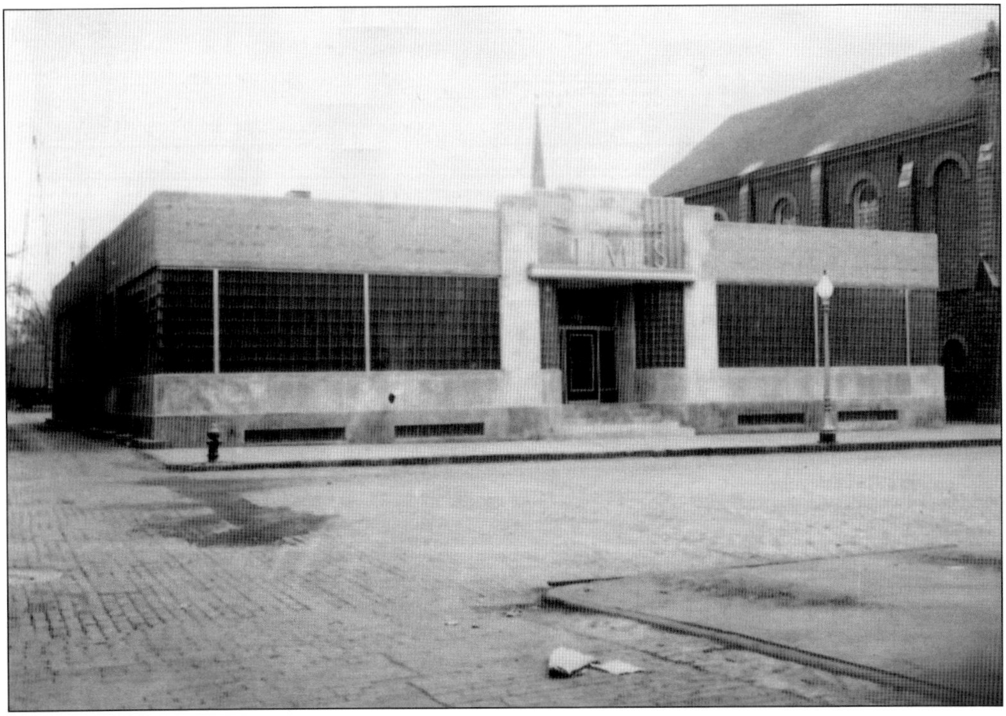

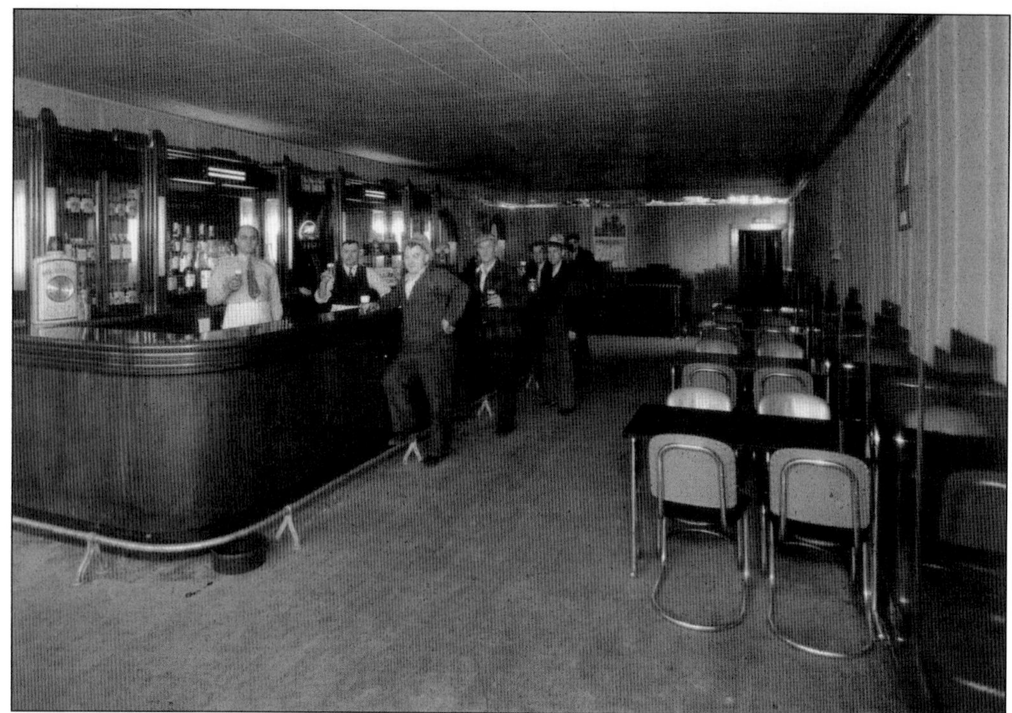

Taverns always are popular in a factory town. Above is Gene & Pasquale's tavern at 1409 LaSalle Street in the 1930s. Behind the bar are Gene Monterastelli (left) and Pasquale Vignochi. (JR.)

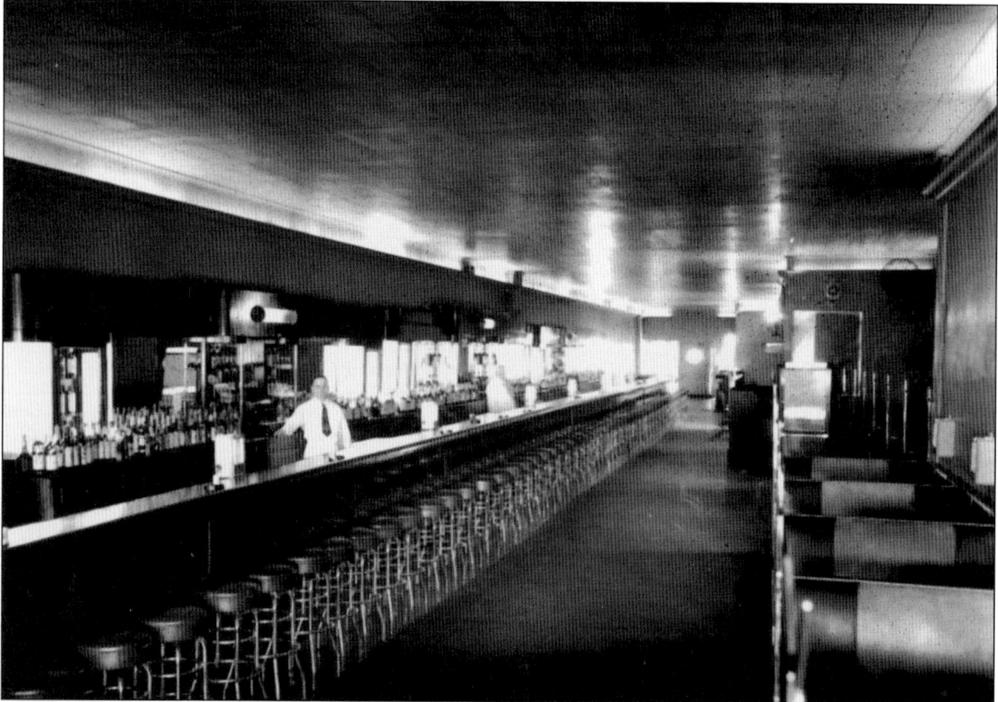

The Senate Tavern was at 606 East Court Street and was advertised in the 1940s as "the longest bar in the world." Tim O'Connor was the proprietor. (JR.)

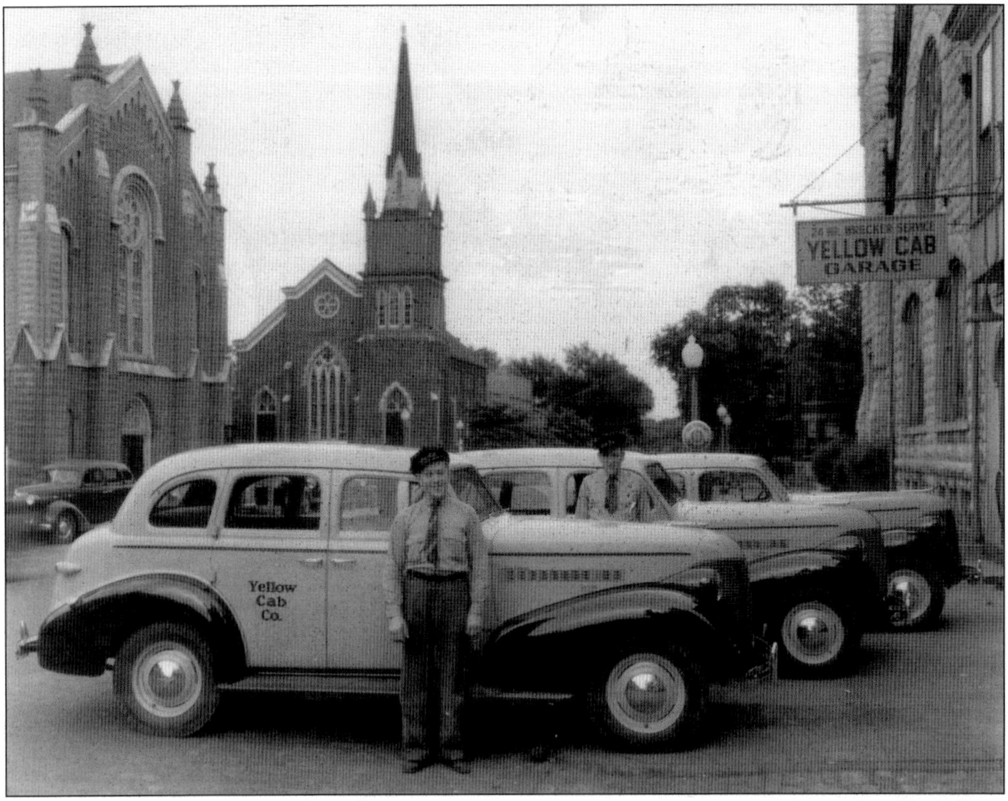

Yellow Cab Company was on Jefferson Street in 1940. In the background are the Methodist, Presbyterian, and Baptist churches. (JR.)

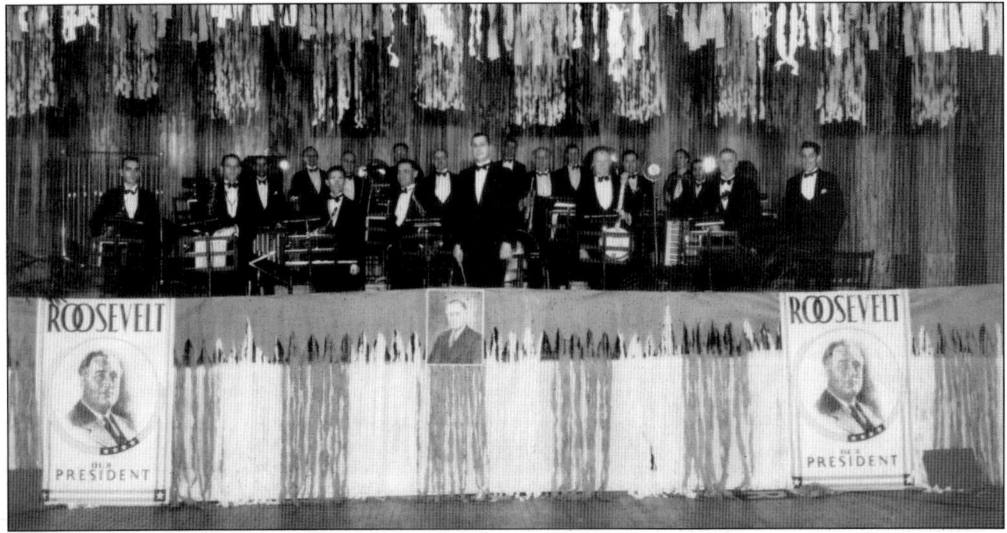

The American Federation of Musicians, Ottawa 391, played the President's Ball at the Armory on January 30, 1934, raising funds to fight polio. Pictured are, from left to right, Al LaVelle, Al Bailey, Andy Leix, Clarence Wentz, A. Wilson, Ray Johnson, Elmer Long, Clay Carr, Harry Jehly, Art Hentrich, Leo Jennings, Al Schwartzbach, Sam Raymond, Chuck Jehly, Sis Karr, Carlos Santucci, Fred Chalot, and Gordon Bellrose. (DC.)

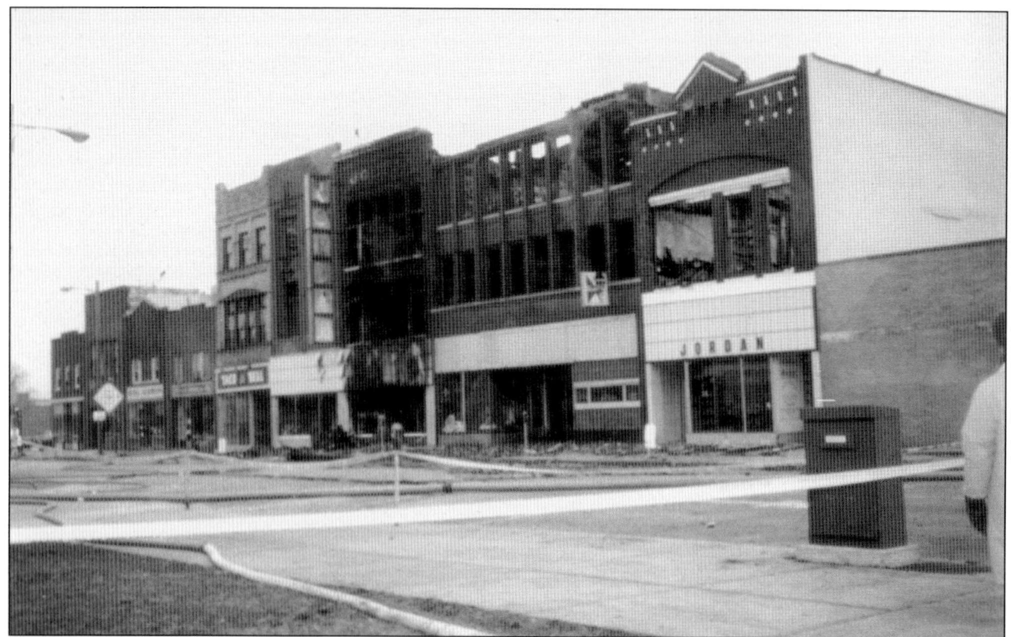

Jordan Hardware was recognized by the state of Illinois as being the state's oldest business run by the same family at the same location. John Manley started the store in 1840 on Main Street. His son-in-law Richard Jordan followed, and the fourth generation operated the store until the family sold it in 1983. Jordan Hardware and several adjoining buildings burned down on March 18, 1998. The ruins were cleared in December 2006, and today, the block is a city park. (DC.)

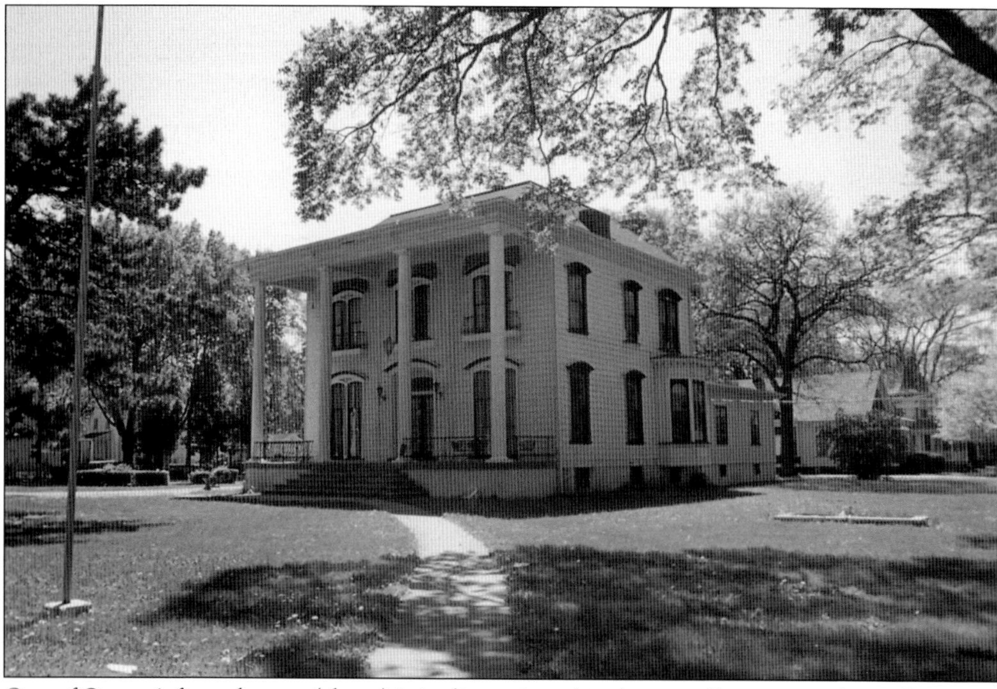

One of Ottawa's finest houses (above) is in disrepair and in danger of being torn down. For many years, it was the Hulse Funeral Home on West Madison Street. (JR.)

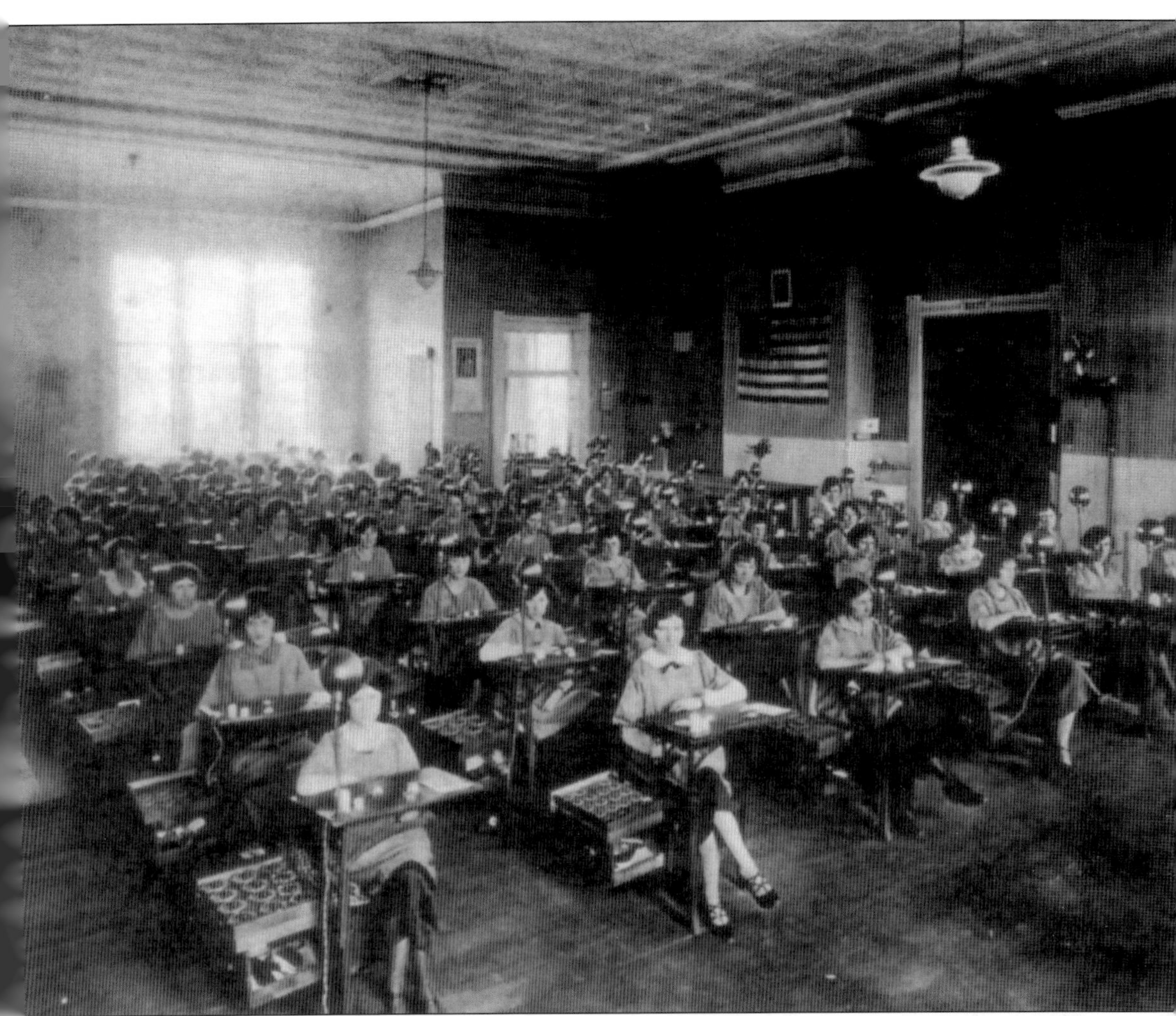

Radium Dial Company moved into the old high school building on Columbus Street in 1922. Young women painted radium on clock dials to make them luminous. The women were taught to put the tip of the paintbrush on their tongue to get a better point on it. Some women painted their teeth, eyelashes, and fingernails to make them glow in the dark. Their bosses told them radium was good for them and "will put a glow in your cheeks." Instead, young women by the dozen died agonizing deaths of cancer from radium poisoning. Limbs were amputated and jawbones disintegrated. When workers became sick, they were fired, so that their presence would not cause alarm. Newspapers called the women the "Ottawa Society of the Living Dead." The company insisted radium was not the cause of cancers and deaths, and it fought every lawsuit and worker's compensation claim. The scandal inspired new laws concerning worker safety. And yet, even though three dozen workers died of radium poisoning by the mid-1930s, women continued working at Radium Dial because it was the Great Depression. (JR.)

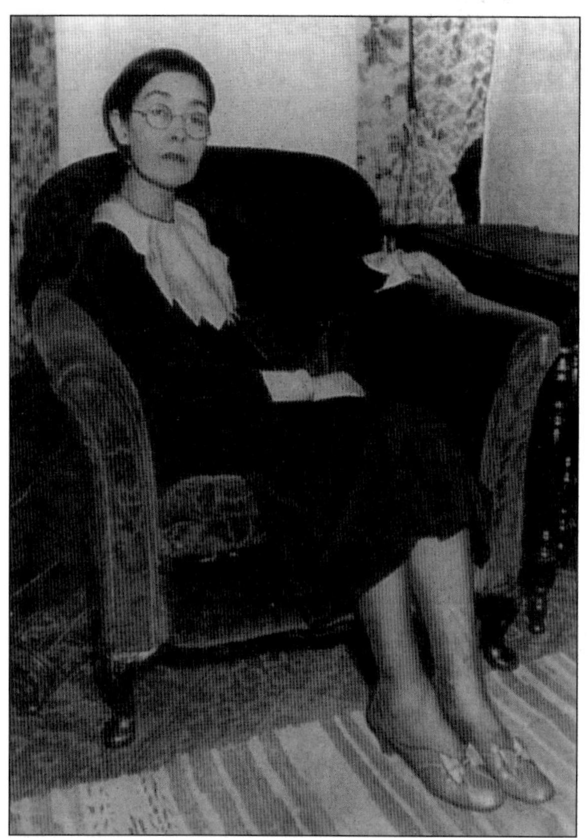

Court hearings were held in March 1938 in the home of Catherine Donahue (left), at 820 East Superior Street, because she was too weak to get off her couch. She died in July. Radium Dial closed in 1937, after the panic and the lawsuits became too great. However, the company reopened later that year as Luminous Processes on Clinton Street. It continued operating for another 40 years. In 1978, *Daily Times* reporter Jim Ridings wrote a series about the large number of Luminous Processes workers with cancer and about the plant's safety violations and it became a national news story. The factory shut down and never reopened.

In the following years, the Luminous Processes building (below) was razed; its rubble along with material from other sites in Ottawa was hauled to toxic waste dumps. (Both, JR.)

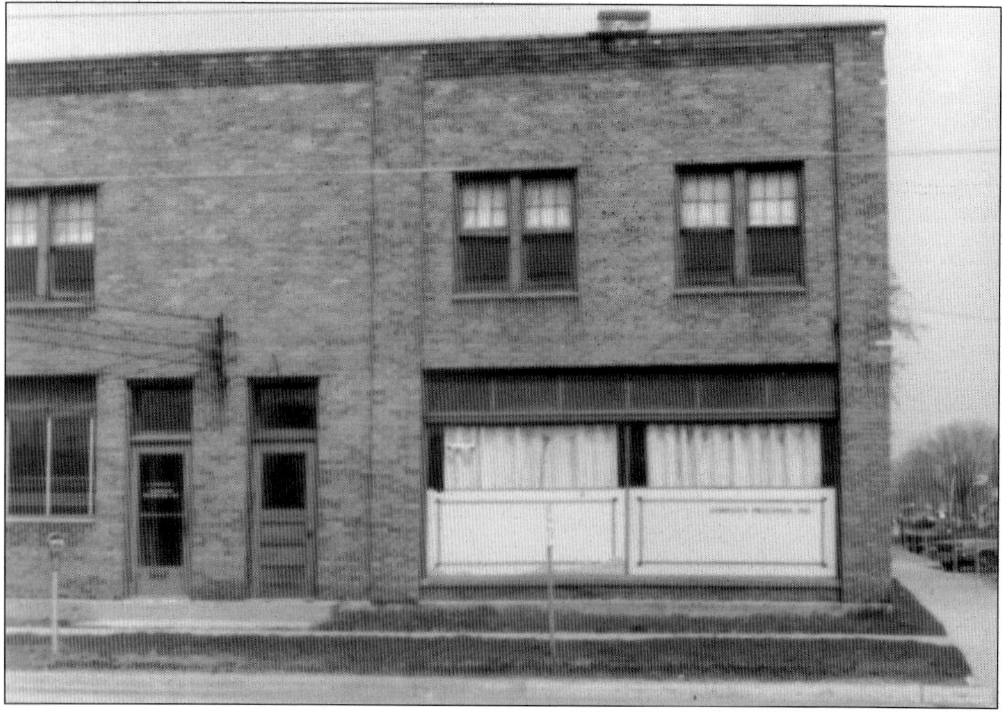

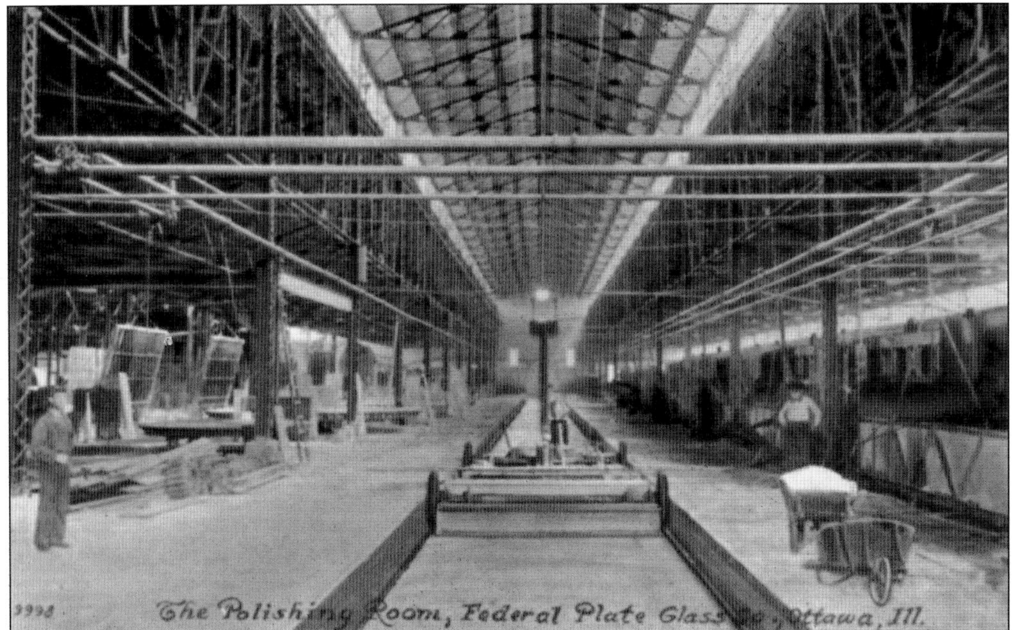

Federal Plate Glass factory opened in 1907, and it became National Plate Glass in 1921. Libbey-Owens-Ford bought it in 1931. At its peak in the 1950s, LOF was Ottawa's biggest employer, with 3,500 people on the payroll. Pictured below are a few LOF employees celebrating a milestone in 1970. (Above, JR; below, Saleda family.)

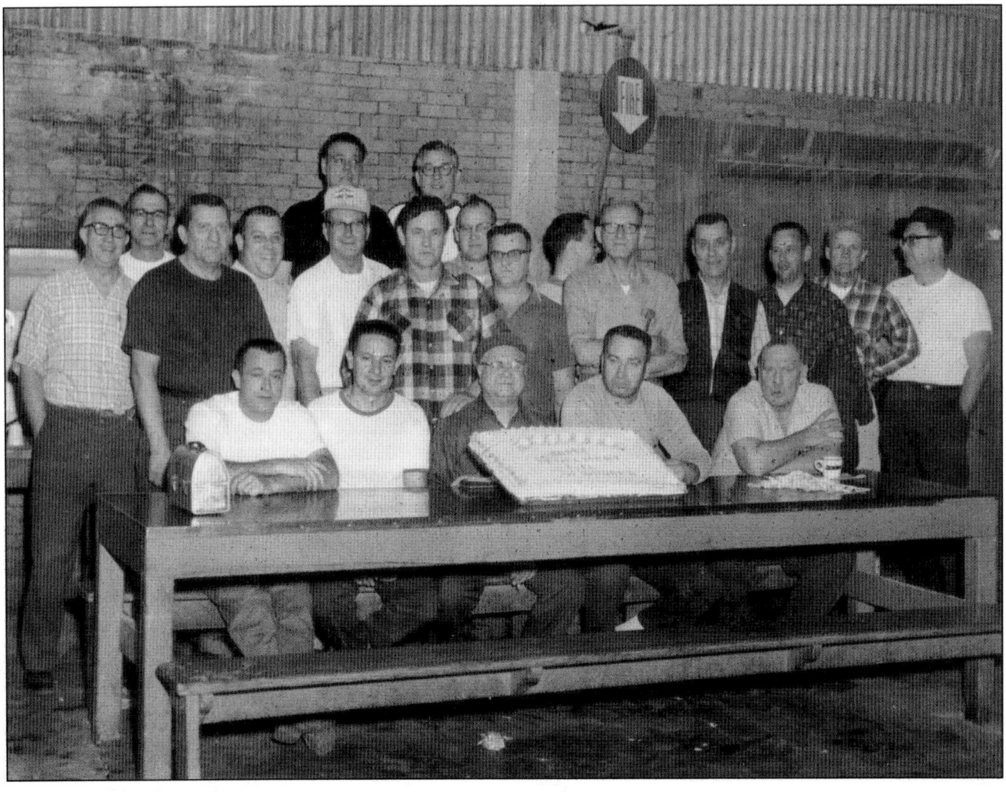

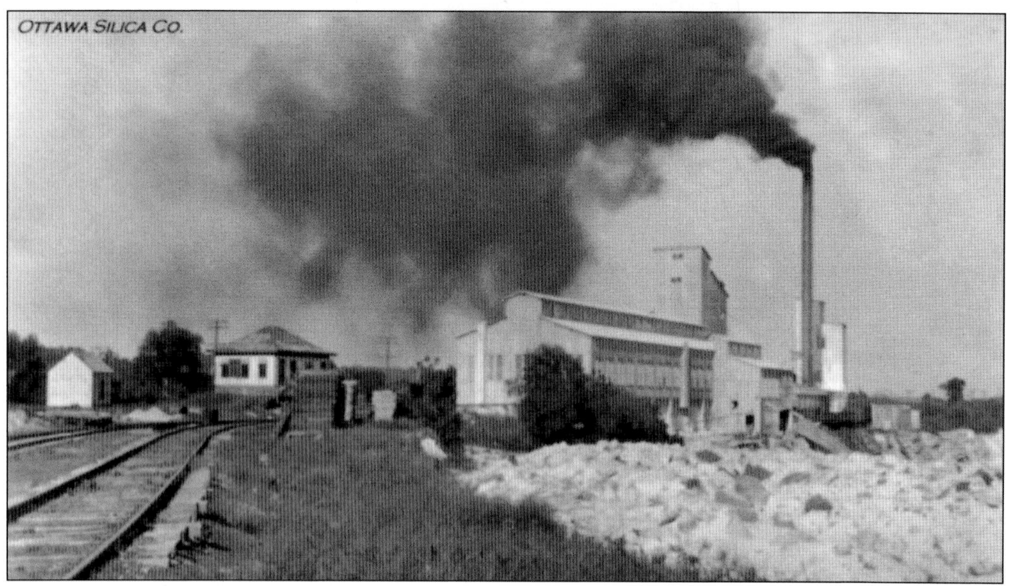

Along with the glass plants, silica mining has been one of Ottawa's chief industries. Mining began in the 1890s and continues today. Silica sand is used in manufacturing glass, abrasives, and more. (Both, JR.)

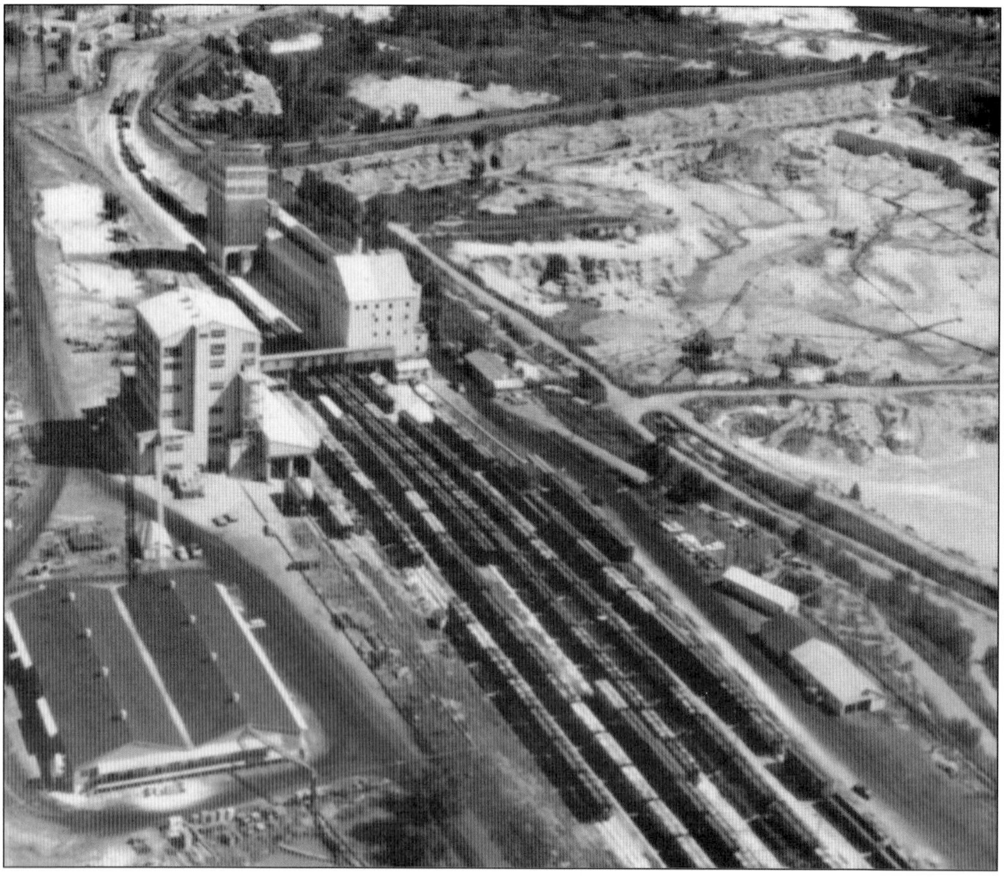

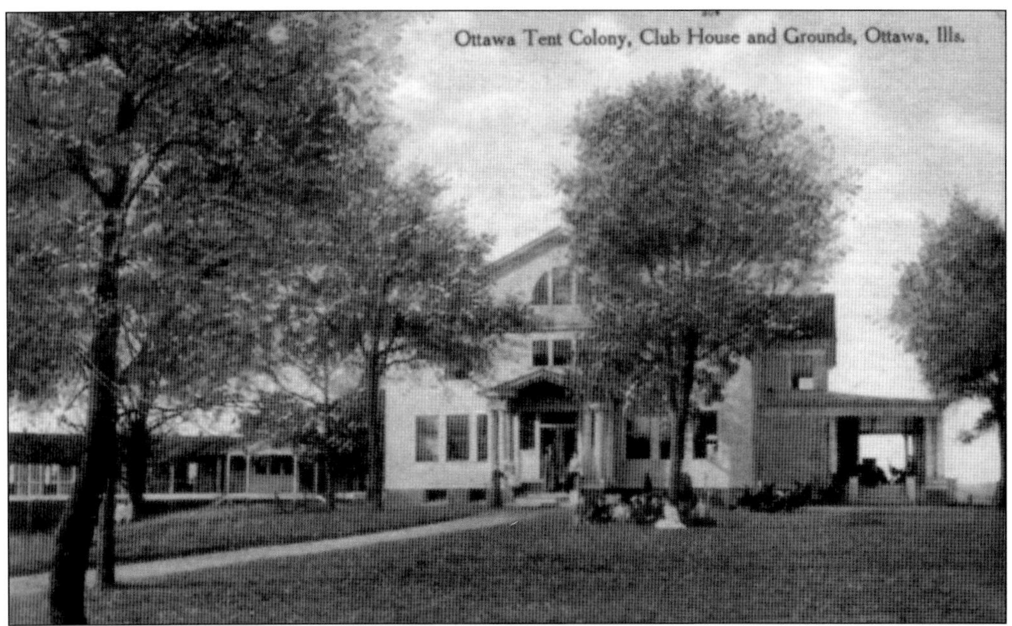

Dr. J.W. Pettit founded a facility in Ottawa in 1904 for the cure of tuberculosis. Dr. Pettit was a nationally respected physician who was elected president of the Illinois State Medical Society. Patients from across America came to Ottawa for treatment. His facility, known as Ottawa Tent Colony, started as a row of canvas tents. Wood-frame cottages later replaced the tents. More complete buildings for offices, nurses' quarters, and a dining hall were constructed in 1918. (Both, JR.)

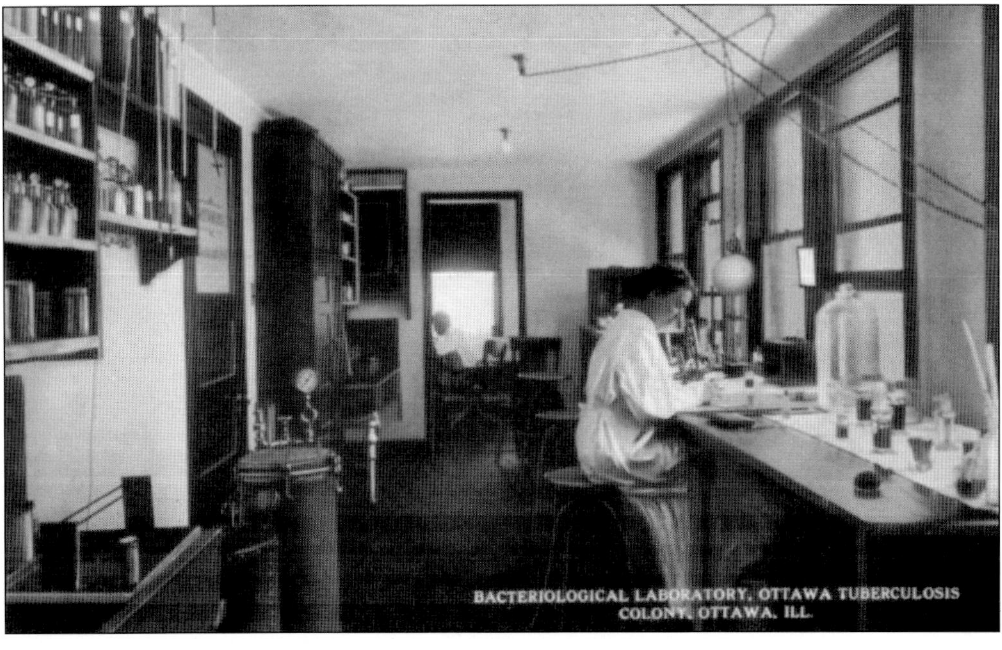

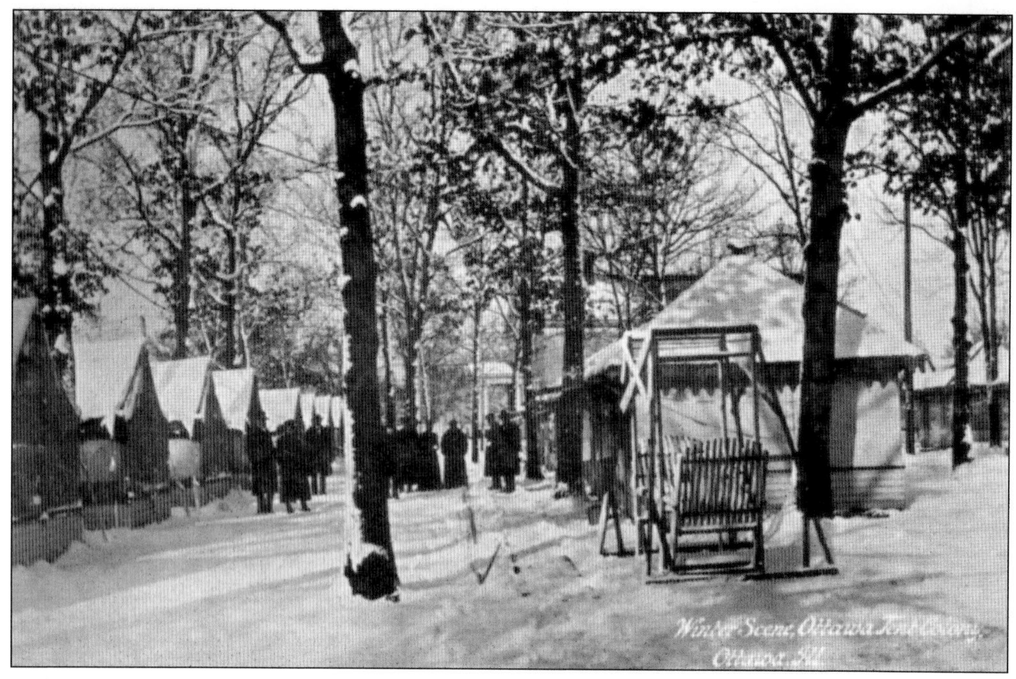

It was Dr. Pettit's theory that fresh air could cure tuberculosis. Rows of tents went up, and patients stayed outside there, even in the freezing Ottawa winters. The Ottawa Tent Colony was located on Center Street. In later years, the facility became the Ottawa Tuberculosis Sanitarium, then the Ottawa Arthritis Sanatorium, and after that, it became Ottawa General Hospital. It is now gone. (Both, JR.)

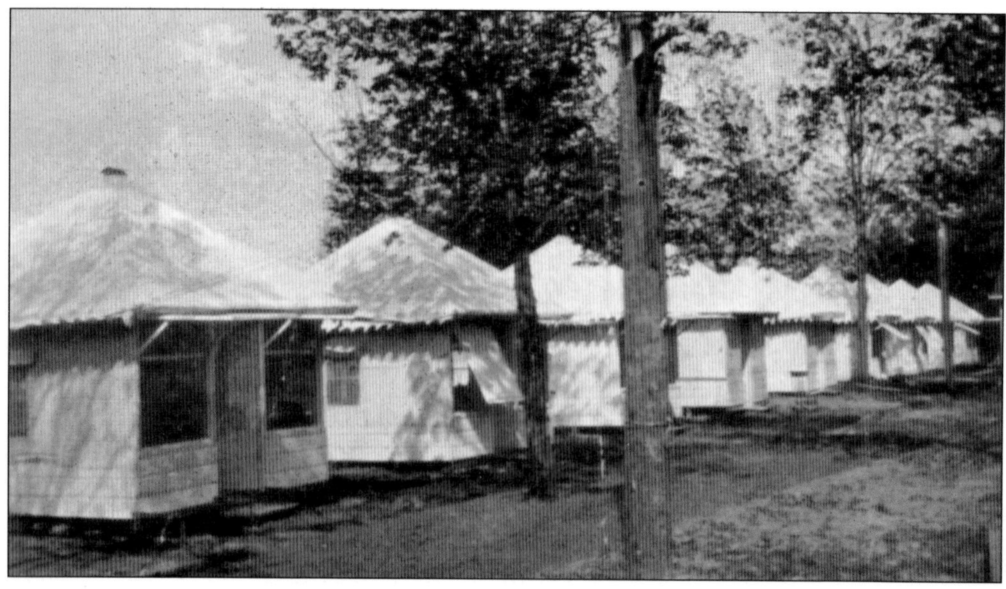

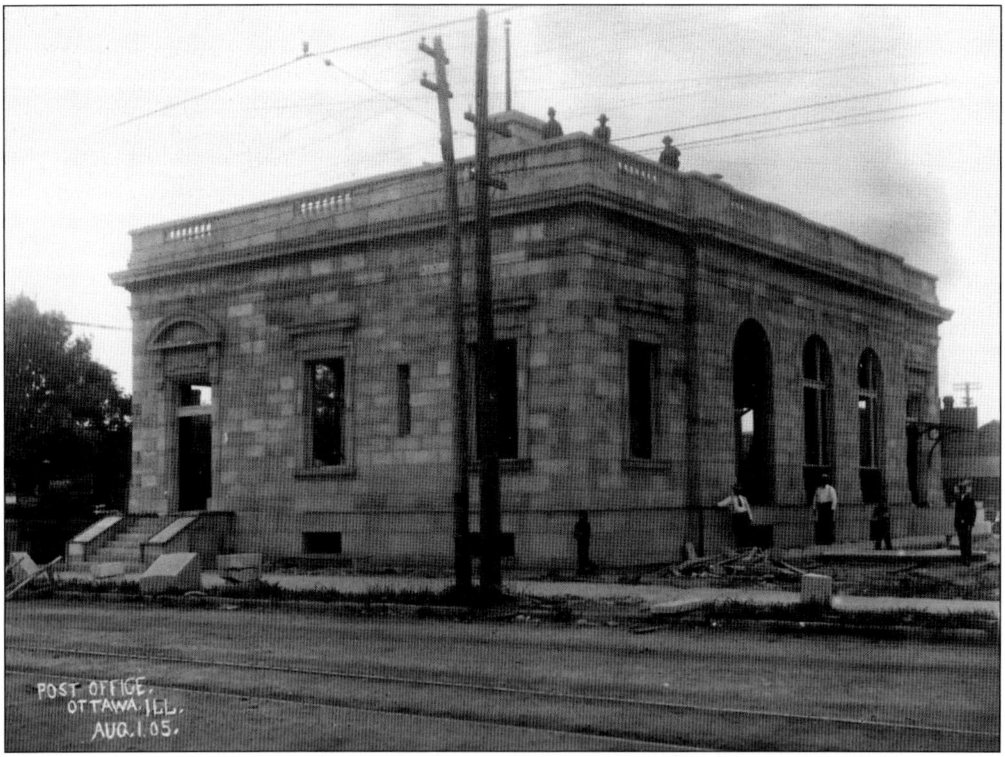

A new post office building (above) was constructed at Madison and Clinton Streets in 1905. It served its purpose until 1962, when a new post office was built on Main Street. The post office again moved, after a new facility was built on Etna Road in 1996. The 1905 building became city hall in 1963. (JR.)

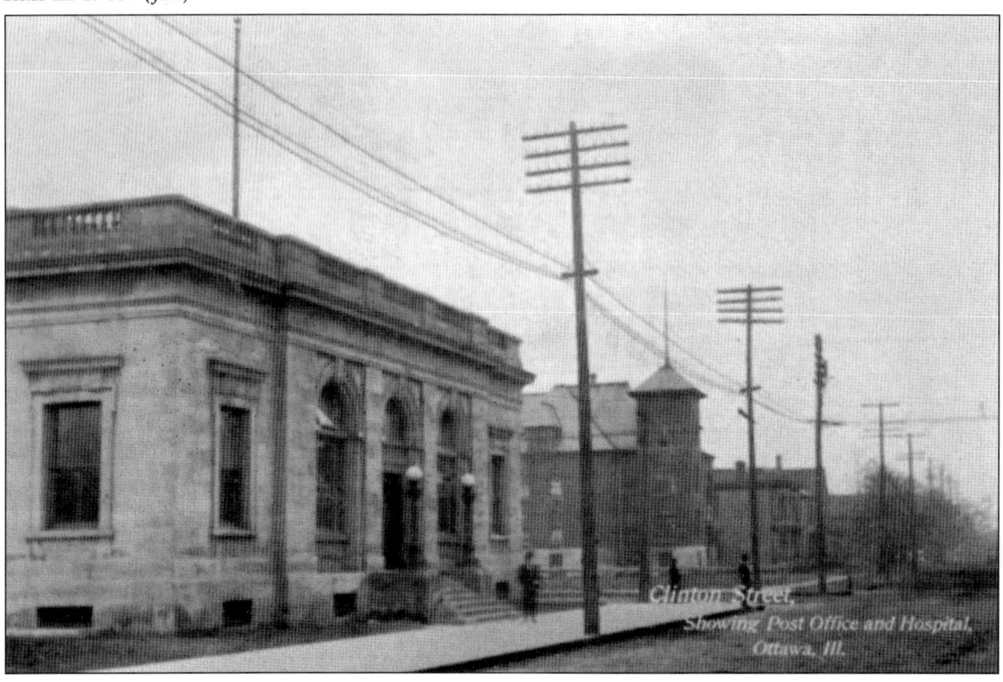

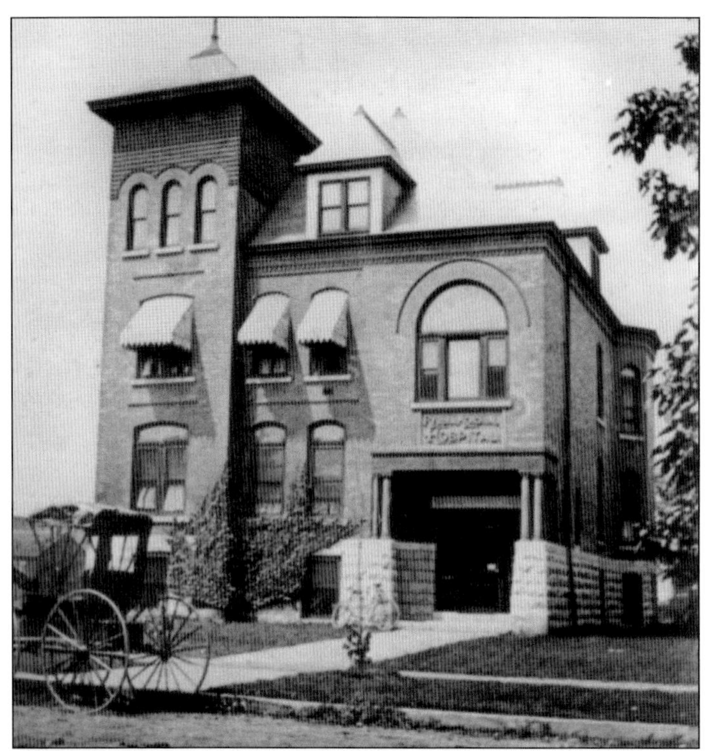

Dr. John Stuart Ryburn came to Ottawa in 1875. Ryburn led an effort to build a hospital in Ottawa. He died in 1892, and his widow Cecelia donated money for a hospital in his name. Ryburn Memorial Hospital opened in 1895. In 1909, local businessman Solomon King gave $40,000 for an annex, and it became known as Ryburn-King Hospital. More additions were built in 1939 and 1944. The hospital started a nursing school, which continued until 1953. On the left is an early view of the hospital, before the annex was built. Pictured below is a view from 1953. (Both, JR.)

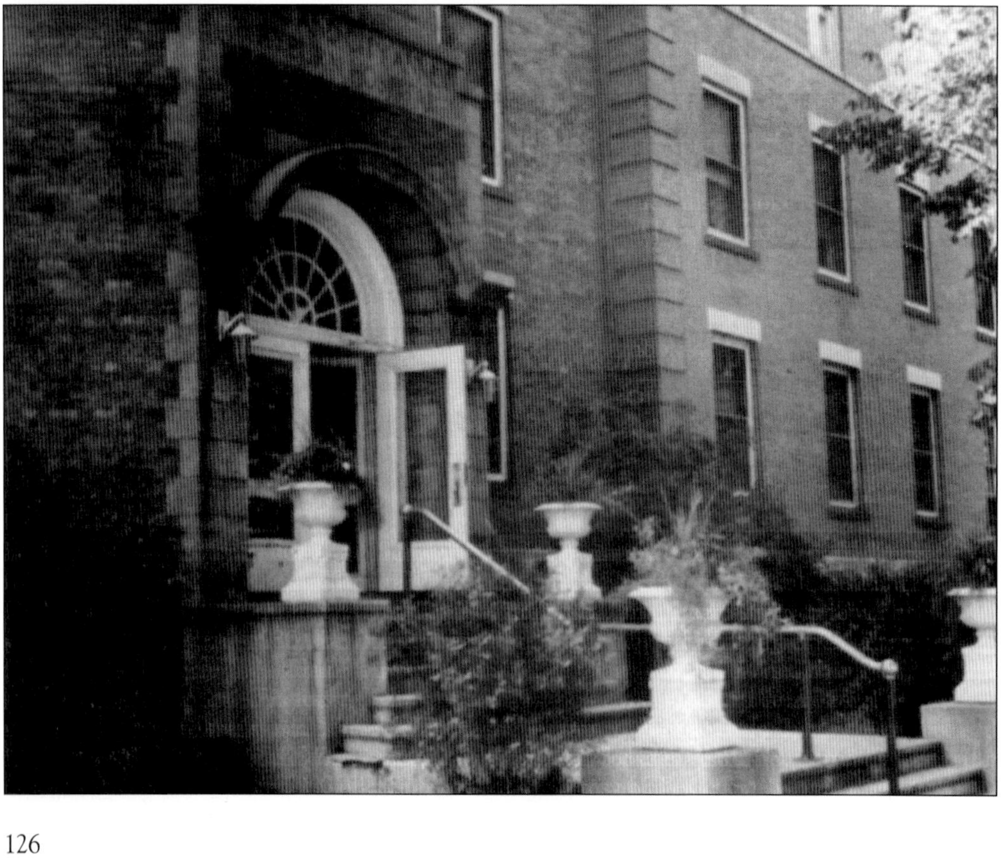

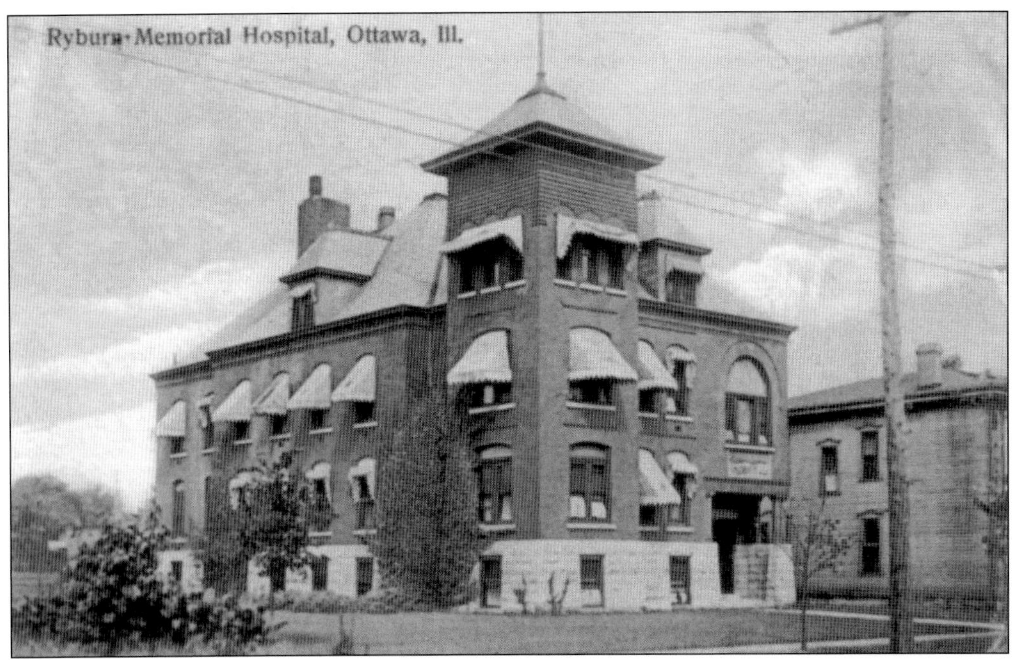

The hospital went through hard times in the 1940s and 1950s. It was owned by the city, which ruled it on a political basis. Mismanagement caused such discord that it was the subject of a *Time* magazine story in 1958, after the city council pressured the entire hospital board to resign. A committee of Ottawa businessmen formed a nonprofit corporation to take over the hospital. Fundraising began, and a 30-acre site on East Norris Drive was donated in 1969 by Ottawa Silica Company. A new building was completed in 1974 and was called Community Hospital of Ottawa. Ryburn-King was demolished in 1978, and a bank drive-up facility is now on the spot. These pictures show the original hospital and its annex. (Both, JR.)

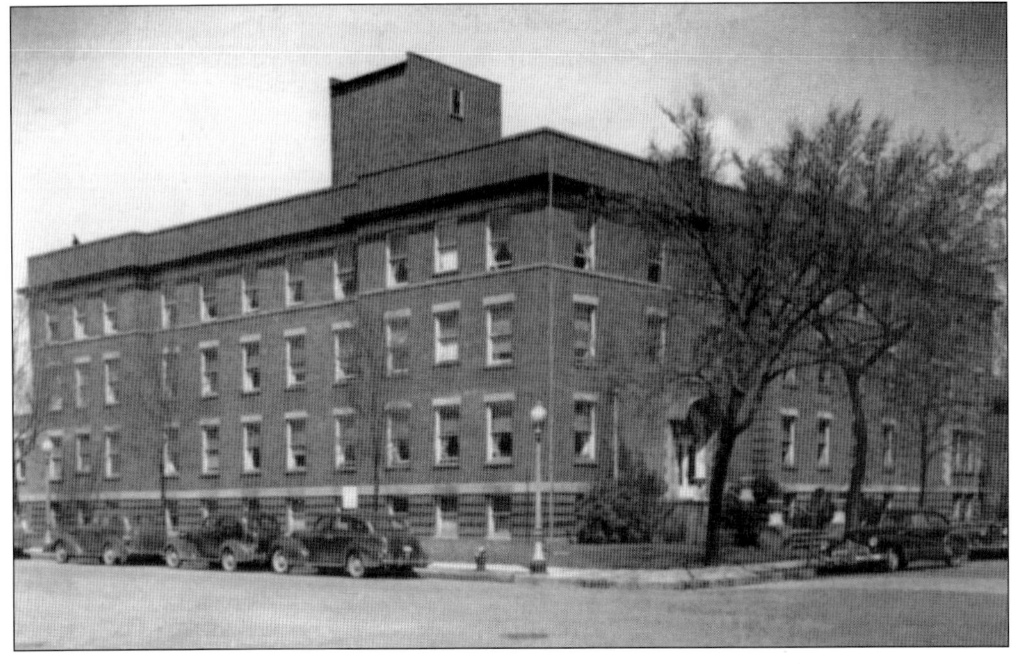